IT ALL STARTED IN NAZARETH: A MEMOIR

MAURICE N. KHOURY

Copyright © 2023 Maurice N. Khoury.

All rights reserved. No part of this book may be used or reproduced by any means, graphic, electronic, or mechanical, including photocopying, recording, taping or by any information storage retrieval system without the written permission of the author except in the case of brief quotations embodied in critical articles and reviews.

This book is a work of non-fiction. Unless otherwise noted, the author and the publisher make no explicit guarantees as to the accuracy of the information contained in this book and in some cases, names of people and places have been altered to protect their privacy.

Archway Publishing books may be ordered through booksellers or by contacting:

Archway Publishing
1663 Liberty Drive
Bloomington, IN 47403
www.archwaypublishing.com
844-669-3957

Because of the dynamic nature of the Internet, any web addresses or links contained in this book may have changed since publication and may no longer be valid. The views expressed in this work are solely those of the author and do not necessarily reflect the views of the publisher, and the publisher hereby disclaims any responsibility for them.

Cover painting by Adel K. Afifi

ISBN: 978-1-6657-4517-8 (sc)
ISBN: 978-1-6657-4516-1 (hc)
ISBN: 978-1-6657-4518-5 (e)

Library of Congress Control Number: 2023910823

Print information available on the last page.

Archway Publishing rev. date: 06/12/2023

I dedicate this work to Grace—my wife, my partner, and my love—and to Lulu, who prodded me, lovingly, to write.

Cape May, New Jersey
2022

A Project of the Arab Cultural Trust

"I'll tell you how I came to think of it," said the Knight. "You see, I said to myself, "The only difficulty is with the feet: the head is high enough already. Now, first I put my head on the top of the gate—then I stand on my head—then the feet are high enough, you see—then I'm over, you see."

"Yes, I suppose you'd be over when that was done," Alice said thoughtfully: "but don't you think it would be rather hard?"

"I haven't tried it yet," the Knight said, gravely: "so I can't tell for certain—but I'm afraid it would be a little hard."

Lewis Carroll, *Through the Looking Glass*

Contents

PART ONE

Preamble xvii
    March 8, 1946

Introduction xxiii

Life in Haifa 1
    My Formative Years / My Immediate Family and Surroundings / Haifa, Port City and Center of Business / Our Life and Family and My Father's Work / Our Family Origins

The British Mandate 18
    Deceptions

Wadi el-Nisnas 24
    Experiment with My Brother Yusuf / We Attended Parochial School

Nazareth 33
    Our Life in Nazareth / Churches / The Land / Our House and Home / Childhood Games / Other Nazarene Families / We Attended Government School / Clerical Interventions / Summer Jobs / The Boy Scouts / A Crazy Act that I Regret / Changing Times / Leaving Nazareth

History: The Sykes-Picot Agreement 54

Beirut 58
> *Early Life in a New City / Adjusting to Property and Financial Losses*

Academic and Other Education 65
> *I Joined the International College / Challenges and Early Jobs / I Joined the American University of Beirut / Dean Harvey Baty / Dr. Stephen Penrose and Me / Aub: Incubator of Ideas and Ideals / Aub Students' Cooperative / Other Jobs and Continuing to a Master's Degree*

Jordan 81
> *Beginnings in Amman / Grace, Home, and Friendships / Anecdotes from Jordan / The Dead Sea Scrolls / Sir John Bagot Glubb, Arab Legion General / Reflections on My Early Years / Life and Work in Jordan*

The Jordan Phosphate Mines Company 90
> *A Short History of the Company / Consulting for JPMC, 1954–1955 / Termination of Services of the Financial Officer of JPMC / Appointment as General Manager at JPMC, 1956–1958 / Candidates for Major Positions at JPMC / King Hussein's Special Visit to Rusaifa Mines / The Monarchy in Jordan*

The Road to Aqaba 107
> *The International Bank for Reconstruction and Development*

The Muslim Brotherhood 112
> *Ideological Islamic Groups*

Back to Amman 121
> *My Last Offcial Trip to Europe / Return to Amman by Official Invitation / Emperor Haile Selassie / Thoughts on Jordan*

A Summary of My Consulting Jobs in Jordan 130
> *The Liquidation of the Copper Mining Company / The Marble Mining Company (MMC) / Water Distribution in Amman / The Municipality of Amman, 1956–1957 / The Jordan Electricity Company*

PART TWO

Preamble 141

Management Consulting... 143
    Associated Management Consultants, SAL (AMC) / Associated Business Consultants, SAL (ABC)

Kuwait: Jobs in the 1960s.. 146
    Adviser to General Motors and Al Ghanem, 1960–1964 / The Conclusion of Gm Work in Kuwait / The Chrysler Corporation / The Consolidated Contractors Company (CCC) / Kuwait Transition and Development / The Al Ghanem Family / New Kuwaiti Currency Replaces the Rupee

Al-Ra'ed al-Arabi... 162

Iraq-Kuwait Political Turmoil, 1961 164
    A Kuwaiti Delegation to South America

Interlude... 170
    Thoughts and Miscellaneous / Jordan National Bank Looking for Investments / Iran, 1969 / Algeria, 1976

Saba & Company..174

Saudi Arabia, 1965–1970 177
    General Motors / A Digression / Saudi Arabian Airlines, 1960s

Jordan Radio and Television.. 182
    Early 1960s and On

ABC East Africa, 1967 186
    Kenya / Sights and Safaris

About Beirut in the 1960s 188
    Amazing Dr. Dahesh / A Tale by Visitors to Dr. Dahesh / The Beautiful Young Girl / Dr. Dahesh, Art Collector / Beirut Optimism

The June War of 1967 and After 195

Lebanon, 1965–1970s... 198
   Market Research / Image Studies / Partner Consulting Companies / Traffic Study, 1968 / Hotel Management / The Oberoi Family

The Bahrain Franchise, 1972–1975... 205

The Years 1973–1976 212
   Rania / The Market Collapse, 1973–1974

Beirut, 1975 218
   The Intercontinental Hotel, Jordan, 1976

Lebanon: The Civil War, 1975 221
   I Was Shot by a Sniper / The Lebanese Forces

Dubai Municipality, 1978 227

The 1980s 231
   Leila, 1982 / Al-Hakawati / Nicosia, Cyprus, 1985–1989 / Intelligence Agencies

The Last Decade of the Twentieth Century and After.................... 236

Lebanese Personalities 238
   Kamel Al-Assad / Sheikh Maurice Gemayel / President of Lebanon / Salim El-Hoss

Beirut: Two Major Projects Entrusted to Me 243
   The Public Corporation for Housing / The Investment Development Authority of Lebanon (IDAL)

The Young Men's Club 245

APPENDICES

Appendix 1 Hussein–McMahon Correspondence: 1915–1916 249
Appendix 2 The Sykes–Picot Agreement, 16 May 1916 271
Appendix 3 The Balfour Declaration, November 2, 1917 277
Appendix 4 The British Mandate for Palestine, 1920 279
Appendix 5 Israeli Absentee Property Law, 5710-1950 289
Appendix 6 Some Twentieth-Century Wars and Coups in the
            Middle East 317

PART ONE

Preamble

This is the story of a Palestinian in diaspora whose life, times, tales, and tribulations were many and diverse, some difficult and many verging on the bizarre. I record a sequence of events that changed my life and the lives of my parents, siblings, and aunts, following a terrible incident; it became the turning point in generations of my family's roots and home. The Greek Orthodox Church and the Melkite Greek Catholic Church records in Nazareth, supported by the Ottoman Nufus Registers, have the family's ancestry living in Nazareth for three hundred years.

This Palestinian, in his diaspora but with roots and history in a parallel universe, tells his story.

MARCH 8, 1946

On the eve of a cold Friday, March 8, 1946, at about 7:30 p.m., armed men carrying handguns and wearing Arab garb attacked my family's home in the old section of the town of Nazareth. All the members of our household—brothers, sister, aunts, and parents—were at home. I was in the liwan, which is the principal room closest to the side door, and in answer to a knock, I opened the door. I was startled by the sight of men carrying guns, who, without words, began shooting at me, the only target in the room. And so it happened that I bore the brunt of an attack, the purpose of which was and still is a mystery.

Without even thinking of the enormity of the task, I fought back, attacking the men, seven of them, with my bare hands. At least for the minutes that the fight went on, my young arms did not fail me. I continued fighting. Finally, I tried to force shut the door outside of which they were still standing and firing.

The door was heavy and try as I might I was unable to push it shut. For just a moment, I nearly succeeded. Shortly, I started feeling dizzy, less sure, and less in control of my legs; my steps faltered. I was struck by five bullets: three through my face, two in my chest. I was exhausted from fighting, trying to keep the men at bay. The loss of blood from the wounds made these men more aggressive and, with a renewed attempt, they pushed me inside the house and into the dining room. I fell back under the table, unable to move, and that is where I got the second bullet in my chest.

I heard my Aunt Alice calling for help out of the window. She and my other aunts were screaming in fear and confusion throughout the gun fire and calling for the neighborly help one expects. My mother had to prevent my father, a sick person at the time, from leaving his bed and going for his handgun. Shots continued to be fired. The interior glass doors between the entrance and the liwan were shattered. I suspect the attackers expected a tough encounter and were unsure how the fight would end; obviously, they were not professionals. I owe my life to their limited capabilities and highly inefficient attack and the neighbors' help.

I did succeed in preventing these men from entering beyond the threshold. Fortunately, the neighbors came to our defense and fired shots at the men. A bullet hit one of them in the knee, and so the incursion into our home and life ended and saved me from more agony and certain death.

I suffered three serious bullet wounds to my face, all coming from the right side, exiting from the left, taking with them whatever teeth I had, cutting into my tongue, and splitting my lips on the right side. The last bullet entered the front of the left chest, passed through my body, and exited from my back, going through the lung, and cutting about one-third of its mass. It also broke some ribs. Another minor shot injured my back (and, for a long time, was painful).

The total number of shots retrieved by the police on the scene was forty-nine. My sister Thérèse, who was ten years old, witnessed all the action from a corner of the liwan, where she happened to be at the time of the attack, and later confirmed to me what I reported.

They were seven men armed with handguns; to me, at age fifteen, they looked as big as life and tall as devils. The attack lasted for only a few minutes but felt like an eternity, and with the tenacity of one fighting for his life, I held the men at bay until neighbors intervened. If I repeat myself in my telling about the fight and my role in it, it is because this incident was the preamble to a long story. It was an incident that marred my life and changed it from a happy, carefree one to one filled with strife that continued as an undercurrent all through my and my family's lives.

Once the shooting ended, my parents, aunts, and the rest of the household surrounded me in disbelief, hopelessly helpless and lost in what to do. My father, who himself needed help to move and walk around, was devastated. They couldn't tell how many bullets I had taken, but I was clearly badly injured. Blood poured from my chest and face.

I cannot say that I was alert when the attack was over. It must have taken some time for the shock to pass, and finally, Dr. Leo Less, our Jewish neighbor, a medical doctor and friend, came and saved the day. He climbed the long, exterior stone staircase to our house in time to see what was happening and to help. Once Dr. Less saw me, I heard him tell my father that I needed to be taken to the hospital immediately. He cleaned and bandaged the injuries as best he could with what was available in his clinic. He saved my life.

In 1946 there were no ambulances in Nazareth, so I was bundled up and carried to a pickup truck to transport me to the hospital. The pickup was waiting for us at the edge of town at a distance.

of fewer than 200 meters. Streets in the old city where we lived were not wide enough to allow cars through, so I was carried on a wooden plank down the staircase to the truck. Unfortunately, when deposited in the back of the pickup, the cargo bed was too short to accommodate all my length. My head was half dangling over the end of the vehicle, but it was the best that could be done. Speed was of the essence, so the car started on its way to the hospital situated on a hill far away in the south of the city.

The trip was painful. With every turn the pickup took I was jolted and bounced—a surrealistic trip par excellence; another doctor friend took over on our arrival at the hospital. They took me directly to an operating room, where the doctor cleaned my wounds and stopped the bleeding. It took a long time, and the cleaning was painful, but in the end, all proved to be a step in the right direction.

I recovered from the foggy and confused state of mind and started noticing things around me. I saw Dr. Less, whose face was familiar, and the nuns who helped treat my wounds. They spoke words of encouragement and assurance, giving me confidence that I was in good hands.

I had two primary operations: the first and the most urgent one was to repair the chest wound. The bullet had entered from the left side, passed through the lung, very close to the heart, and exited through my back. Wounds were a common injury, and doctors were always prepared to deal with bullet wounds, but the tools at the time were rudimentary at best. The doctor's tool was a rolled-up piece of gauze about the thickness of a finger; he inserted it into the wound and pushed it through until it came out the other side, where the bullet had exited. Once the gauze appeared on both sides of the wound, it was pulled up and down, again and again, until it became too bloody, and then a fresh strip of gauze replaced it.

This process was employed to absorb blood and debris, bone fragments, and broken parts of the lung membrane. On the following days this painful ordeal was repeated, and the wound was dressed again, but it did not do the job well; my body continued to expel debris for many decades to come. Antibiotics had not made their way to Palestine in time to help me recover at this small hospital at a nunnery in Nazareth, so it was a miracle that I didn't have any complications.

The operation to my face was even worse. My upper teeth were no longer where they should be, and my upper right jaw was shattered, with some pieces of broken bone lodged deeply in my tongue, my palate, my cheeks. The aftermath covering the sixty years that followed was an uphill survival kit. Not until I was over eighty years old was it possible for me to have teeth implants, especially in my case, because the bone on the right side of the upper jaw was thin and required advanced procedures.

The second facial injury was minor; it cut my lip on the right side, so the doctor just sewed it up, and I must say, not very well.

As the nuns cleaned my wound, sewing my lips and cheeks, extracting loose teeth, and removing pieces of jawbone from my tongue, I heard them praying for my young and shattered body.

To conclude, the doctor and the nuns employed all they knew to save my life. I am indebted to every one of them, not only for their professionalism but also for their dedication, support, encouragement, and love. I was a lucky person to have the attention of these caring people.

One surprise was in waiting. The attacker at our house who had been shot in the knee by a neighbor was brought to the same hospital, his admittance to the ward surrounded by great secrecy. He asked to see me, and a nun brought him to my room. He was in a wheelchair; his knee was shattered, and he would never be able to walk again. He began to apologize, saying what the attackers did was wrong and that our family were not the intended targets. I forget his name, at least the name he said was his. I did not say much to him. The police did not charge him with attempted murder or anything else; I think he left the hospital and was allowed to go free. I did not feel angry or vengeful or unforgiving toward him; I saw him this once and forgot all about him. He was just a hired hand.

News of the event was reported in the media of those times. My father received a letter from an associate in Jerusalem, dated March 13, 1946, sending good wishes for my quick recovery. He received an updated and similar letter from حزب المجاهدين الاحرار (approximately translated as "Old Militants Party"); apparently, someone had been spreading unfounded rumors that Ne'hme el-Khoury was buying land in Nazareth on behalf of the Zionists. In the letter, this group said they now knew there was no truth to the rumor. I wonder if this letter was an admission of their role in the attack.

This event had a permanent effect on my life. I have had constant dental problems. For decades, my teeth and mouth suffered many invasive procedures and repeated operations. I have had a dozen or more dentures fitted over the years because the wound changes slightly in shape and dentures needed to be refitted.

Introduction

The idea of writing this story emanated from continued and determined requests by my daughter. Though Leila's suggestions were not insistent, they stayed alive in my mind and heart. So, one day I started writing a detailed chronology of the highlights and exciting situations in which I was involved during my life at home, at school, and later, in the world.

This effort is a commission I accepted to undertake to tell my daughter, her children and grandchildren the story of her father and their grandfather. I wrote it to tell them where I came from, the effects of regional political uncertainties on my future, and what I did with my life. I hope it makes my times and life clearer to them, and I hope I have completed the mission so lovingly assigned to me.

This story is simply true. It has been an effort to remember and write down many of the details. I did not intend to relay a historically valid sequence of events; I wanted to relate experiences as I lived them. One would expect that some fantasies may creep into the script when the story is based solely on memory.

I feel comfortable and sure about the sequence and facts remembered. On a few occasions, I checked with old friends with whom I shared some everyday experiences. They verified my memories, and nobody remembered anything that cast doubt on my stories.

Life in Haifa

MY FORMATIVE YEARS

For a few years before the event of March 8, at home in Nazareth, there had been noticeable indications that something was not right, that something needed attention, but we all tried to go on as usual. A few weeks before the shooting, a farm supervisor on land my father owned in Dabburieh came to us with the news that some farms were being attacked, agricultural machinery had been destroyed, and sheep had been stolen or killed.

Dabburieh is a village in Marj Ibn 'Amer, south of Nazareth, also called the Jezreel Valley. The plain extends from the Mediterranean Sea to the River Jordan. With such reports making the rounds, some of our farm laborers were too afraid to go back to the fields. My father, who traveled around the area on horseback, did not seem to realize that what was happening was a precursor to more serious events.

With the tensions between the Jews and Arabs taking root, he would soon be unable to defend his lands. The times were troubled and what we experienced was way beyond the ordinary, yet all this escaped him, and he wrote off the recurring agricultural losses to troubled times. Explanations always found their way to my father to make him less anxious and cautious, mainly because other farmers had reported similar troubling activities. That was at a time when partitioning Palestine between the Palestinian Arabs and the Jews was becoming more and more a reality.

In hindsight, my father knew that he should have exercised caution and was unprepared to deal with what was happening and what was in store for us, including the attack on March 8. Unfortunately, he refused to understand that the usual measures he and all landowners had been taking, like having watchmen keep an eye on things, were not sufficient to protect his lands and family from the powerful changes that had come to north of Palestine and especially in the Galilee, where his time and interest were focused. Indigenous Arabs, Jewish immigrants and British soldiers were all fighting each other to hold onto or to gain land.

The police in Nazareth did not appear at our house until the following morning. The scene of the crime had been left untouched, and the police surveyed it, asked questions. They came to the hospital and wanted to hear the story from my perspective. I could not answer their questions because I did not know the answers, and the bandage covering my mouth made it impossible for me to speak anyway. The following day, the assistant district commissioner came to see me. He was a colonel in the British Army, neatly dressed, tall, and amiable. He sat beside me on the bed and assured me that he would find the culprits and bring them to justice. I remember he was addressed as "Lord Oxford." After he visited several times, I too began calling him Lord Oxford. I recently looked him up online: he was Julian Edward George Asquith, 2nd Earl of Oxford and Asquith, Knight Commander of the Order of St. Michael and St. George, a British colonial administrator and a hereditary peer. He served in Palestine as assistant district commissioner from 1942 to 1948. He said he would recommend to his government to confer on me the Medal of Courage. Less than a year after this promise, the country of Palestine was no more, and the promised medal, our land, home, and everything we owned or hoped to hold, had disappeared.

A few weeks later I surprised everybody when I walked the streets of Nazareth, limping but alive. When I first walked through the souk, people greeted me like a hero, and I made good use of it. Parents, aunts, uncles, siblings, other family members, friends, and neighbors pampered me. It helped me regain my confidence and helped my healing process. Everybody in town was supportive and showed a lot of interest in my state of health. Our home—and our kitchen—became busier, as visitors from Nazareth and from out of town dropped by to wish us well.

The memory of the shooting haunted me for a long time, and occasionally I have nightmares in which I relive that March experience. Grace, my patient and very understanding wife, told me she often woke me up at night when she heard me crying out, shouting, or being disturbed, as I relived in my dreams the events of March 8.

Bad news about restlessness on my father's land kept coming. One day, a farm worker came galloping to Nazareth on Khadra, my young mare, to deliver a message to my father about more disturbances on the land. As in previous springs, Khadra had been grazing in the vicinity of Mount Tabor. The farm worker's trip was too long and tiring for her, and she died of exhaustion a day or two later. I was brokenhearted. Khadra had been my companion for three years, and I loved her deeply. She was loyal and loving to me, and we had been happy in each other's company.

Many changes were taking place, and our lives were about to change too. The restlessness and uncertainties, hard to pinpoint, yet evident; the rumors; the monthly losses my father and many other landowners incurred. In hindsight, we were not prepared to deal with what was in store for us. The attack and the shooting on the threshold of our home and my father's ill health led to the family's decision to leave Nazareth. We had two options as a household with many children: we could either go to Jerusalem, which had good schools with a curriculum leading to what was called the British Certificate of Matriculation, equivalent to the freshman class in American universities, or to Beirut, which had good schools as well as good universities. My father decided, under the pressures of the moment, to go to Beirut. His long business relationship with Lebanese landowners and merchants added to his reasons to favor the move to Beirut. As it turned out, my father was ill-prepared for what was to follow.

MY IMMEDIATE FAMILY AND SURROUNDINGS

I was born at home in Haifa, Palestine, on Sunday, February 22, 1931. I was the second son of Ne'hme Yusuf el-Khoury of Nazareth and

Farida Atallah of Haifa. They were married in September of 1927. At that time, our family lived in Haifa, with frequent visits to the family's hometown of Nazareth. Haifa was the big port city and center of economic and industrial activities, while Nazareth was a rural town whose residents were involved in agriculture and related businesses. History tells us that Jesus lived most of his life in Nazareth, and so its religious and historical importance supported a flourishing tourism industry. It stands at an elevation of 1,138 feet above sea level, among the hills of the Galilee region.

The trades gave the streets their names: blacksmith's alley, carpenter's street, cobbler's corner, and tailor's lane are located inside the old city. Nazareth was known for handicrafts and similar skills. Needlework, knitting, embroidery, and the like were both a pastime and a business. The tourists always demanded the traditional handmade needlepoint sold in small shops along the streets leading to churches and sacred sites. Nazarene embroidery was considered the finest in Palestine.

My Aunt Amini was very skilled at needlework, and a buyer of such items came by our house regularly to see what she had made and was willing to part with. She was very proud of her work and set the prices accordingly. All through her life, she continued making extraordinarily beautiful baptism dresses, complete with a cap with satin ribbon, coasters and table runners, cuffs, and collars for dresses. She used a regular needle to do the work of a crochet hook.

Baptismal Dress

My three unmarried aunts who lived with us, Marie, Amini and Alice, occasionally needed a small supply of cash to bail out their brother, my Uncle Eliyah, from some financial worry or concern or worse, without telling their older brother, my father. My father was indeed "allergic" to my Uncle Eliyah's unorthodox way of conducting business. What's more, some of my uncle's financial dealings were embarrassing to my father. Aunt Amini occasionally mediated between the two men but preferred to resolve problems before calling them to my father's attention.

Uncle Eliyah was usually traveling, sometimes for months at a time, and when he came home, he was welcomed by my aunts and all the children because he had a lot of stories to tell and was very generous with us. He distributed a shilling (about fifty cents) to each of us kids. His travels took him to faraway destinations. My siblings and I were happy when he visited after his mysterious trips outside Palestine. We were never sure of the truth of his stories, but they were colorful and exciting.

One story he told us, after a long absence, was that he had gone to Iran for lack of good-paying jobs near home, and there he decided to pass himself off as a bishop. He donned the appropriate robes of a bishop and he said he enjoyed the attention and generosity of his "parish" very much, especially because he told them he had been sent from Nazareth. I am not sure any of his stories were true, but they gave me a lot to enjoy and dream about.

He loved cars. During the First World War, he was a truck driver for the Ottoman Army. At the end of the war, he applied to the local British officials for employment as a car driver. And he got the job based on his previous experience.

He told us that vehicles at the time did not have enough braking power to park safely on an incline. So, as our house was sited at the top of a hill, when he visited us, he tied his vehicle to a tree, just as you would tie up a horse or donkey so it would not stray.

Another unique family tale comes from Aunt Fairouz's husband, Raji Lahham, who traveled by ship from the port of Haifa to the Dominican Republic just before the First World War. He had extended family members who had settled on the island many years before. He told us stories about his voyages to the Dominican Republic via Marseille. One such story was of his first sea voyage, when the ship docked outside the Port of Marseille, awaiting her turn to enter.

He was walking on the ship's deck one night and noticed a small island nearby. He called his friends, and they all left the ship to visit what they thought was an island, taking with them food and drink and cooking pots to pass the time until their vessel sailed. While they were cooking and talking and enjoying themselves, they noticed that the island was moving and soon discovered that the island was but a giant whale. They were frightened by this discovery and ran to their ship and up the ladder—just in time. When they looked back and saw that the island was no longer in the place they had visited, they felt relieved to have survived the adventure.

HAIFA, PORT CITY AND CENTER OF BUSINESS

My family first lived in a single-story stone house in Haifa, one of the few houses located on Sheikh Salim el-Khoury Street, a main street in Haifa's Arab residential quarter. Haifa was the main commercial center for all of Palestine, Transjordan, and Iraq, and its port was the largest on the eastern Mediterranean. Those three countries were mandates of the British Empire after the First World War. Farther up the Mediterranean coast, Lebanon and, to the east of it, Syria, were mandates of France. They included the ports of Beirut, Tripoli, and Latakia, which were important for the Allies during World War II.

In 1831 the French established the Foreign Legion, constituted of foreign regiments of the Kingdom of France. Recruits included soldiers from the recently disbanded Swiss and German foreign military groups of the Bourbon monarchy. Later, soldiers were recruited from colonies in Africa and became famous for their bad behavior when sent abroad. Their famous line, oft repeated toward the Arab population, was *mois civilizer vous*. Soldiers recruited from African colonies and sent to restless countries with little to no proper training were vicious and harsh. *mois civilizer vous* meant "I am here to civilize you," which they repeatedly shouted.

The British were, as always, modest with what they said. If you were a citizen of one of their colonies, though, you might interpret their words differently. "Your most obedient servant," which usually preceded the signature ending a letter, did not typically fit the content of the document signed.

From the end of the First World War, the British Mandatory government (a gentler word for "colonial rule") brought Jewish settlers by ship from Europe and Russia to the Port of Haifa. They were assigned to live in various areas of the country according to a plan which we knew nothing about. In Haifa they were allocated to its suburbs and assigned hilltop areas overlooking the city. This allocation naturally brought them closer to the Arab residents, and so, by plan or by chance, creating friction between them and their Arab neighbors. This situation—and the large numbers of new European Jewish settlers—led to the 1936 Arab Revolt against the British Mandatory government.

The Allies built oil refineries at Haifa to supply their armed forces and export to other fuel buyers. The refineries received their supply of crude oil from the Iraq Petroleum Company and the Mosul Petroleum Company through a pipeline connecting the oil sources in Mosul to Haifa's refineries. The importance of the city and the business opportunities there contributed to my father's resolve to move from Nazareth to Haifa. Given that the distance between the two towns (about thirty miles) is short, he considered commuting to work. However, the transportation and communication facilities were poor; he decided moving the family was a more practical option.

Haifa attracted businesses, professionals, and skilled and unskilled labor from all over the Levant, Egypt, Britain, and India. It had an atmosphere of freedom and easy interaction with others; different cultures came, settled, and mixed there. Moreover, infrastructural contracting in the Near East found Haifa to be a suitable base where financial and human resources were available and willing to venture.

As early as 1921, banking and accounting, two interdependent professions, found in Haifa and Jerusalem a welcoming environment. Early on, the men who worked in these fields were dedicated, honest, and hardworking. Their businesses not only flourished in a relatively short period, but they also provided others in the other countries of the Middle East with the incentive to do the same. Two of the pioneers were Abdel Hamid Shouman, who founded the Arab Bank, and Fuad Saba, who was the first to open an accounting office. Arab Bank, Saba Accounting, and the contracting companies building the oil pipelines and the roads connecting Palestine to Iraq, Syria, Jordan, Saudi Arabia, and Iran contributed to the fast development of the city of Haifa.

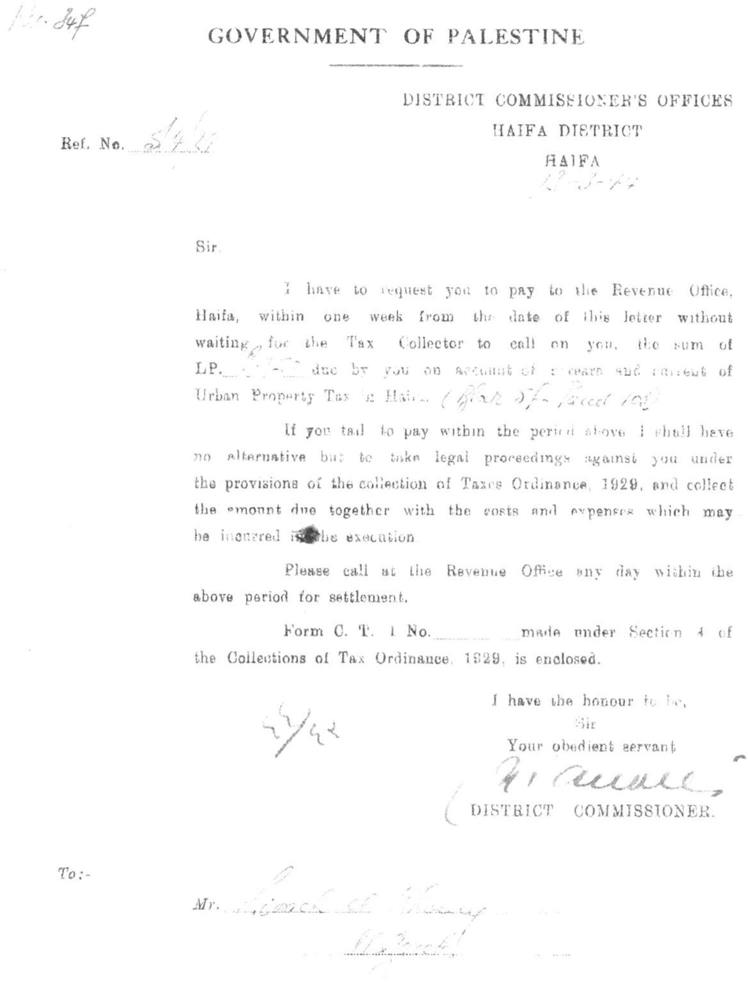

[Letter image with handwritten annotations]

GOVERNMENT OF PALESTINE

DISTRICT COMMISSIONER'S OFFICES
HAIFA DISTRICT
HAIFA

Ref. No. _____

Sir,

I have to request you to pay to the Revenue Office, Haifa, within one week from the date of this letter without waiting for the Tax Collector to call on you, the sum of LP. _____ due by you on account of arrears and current of Urban Property Tax in Haifa _____

If you fail to pay within the period above I shall have no alternative but to take legal proceedings against you under the provisions of the collection of Taxes Ordinance, 1929, and collect the amount due together with the costs and expenses which may be incurred in the execution.

Please call at the Revenue Office any day within the above period for settlement.

Form C. T. 1 No. _____ made under Section 4 of the Collections of Tax Ordinance, 1929, is enclosed.

I have the honour to be,
Sir
Your obedient servant

DISTRICT COMMISSIONER.

To:-

Mr. _____

British Politeness

OUR LIFE AND FAMILY AND MY FATHER'S WORK

In the early 1920's, probably as early as 1921, my father started an accounting business in Haifa. He did not pursue this field of work for long because he also managed agricultural land in Marj Ibn 'Amer. His clients were the Fahoum family of Nazareth and the Sursock family of Beirut; the total acreage under his management was about 6,000 acres, some of which he owned. His land management business went on from 1921 until 1939, but much of the Sursock's land was sold earlier to the Jewish Agency for the Zionist organization then in charge. My father retained his property until it was confiscated by Israel after the 1948 occupation, confirmed later as per The Israeli Absentees' Property Law 5701-1950.

Sometime between 1930 and 1931, at age forty, my father became ill by poisoning. We never knew why he was poisoned or by whom or even what the poison was. The medical knowledge at the time could not detect the type of poison. His sickness continued throughout the rest of his life. There was no medication to help him out of his intense agonies, but the intensity and severity of the pain slowly subsided with time. He lived his last years mentally able but physically weak. He passed away in 1956 at the age of sixty-six. When he moved to Haifa, he was healthy, and despite the poisoning while in Haifa, the move proved to be of practical value. The family stayed in Haifa until World War II, when the city became a target for the German Luftwaffe. It was then, in 1939, that the family returned to Nazareth.

I was born in the house on Sheikh Salim el-Khoury Street in Haifa. The house had a spacious entrance room with high ceilings, furnished with chairs and tables and used for non-family guests or people who stopped in for business or villagers from the areas where my father owned or managed agricultural land. The room led to a long and wide central room known as the liwan. All the rooms open onto the liwan; part of this room was also used as a dining area.

The main sitting room occupied the far end of the liwan, and there my father received guests when he needed some privacy and received his more important visitors, especially those from afar, which meant either Jerusalem or Beirut. He received sheep breeders and merchants from the cities of Damascus and Amman closer to the liwan entrance. Four bedrooms, two bathrooms, and a large kitchen completed the structure of our home. In addition, there was a small garden, a pantry area, and a servant's room with a bathroom. On the ground floor level was a khan (stable) for our and our visitors' horses.

Arabian horses were part of the household and our life; we used them for riding and traveling to the rural parts surrounding Haifa and Nazareth, such as Marj Ibn 'Amer. The Marj is the central agricultural expanse, in the north of Palestine.

The biblical name of Marj Ibn 'Amer is the Jezreel Valley which in Hebrew means "may God give seed"—a hint to the fertility of the plain and inland valley. Geologically, the valley acted as the channel by which the Mediterranean Sea at the northwestern end of the valley, connected to the Sea of Galilee, the Jordan Valley, and ultimately to the Dead Sea. The valley formed a more leisurely route through the Levant than crossing the hills on either side and was the site of many historic battles. Ancient caravans bearing merchandise and the innovations of far-off cultures of antiquity passed this way, and so did the armies—as evidenced by the famed ruins of some twenty-five cities, including Megiddo, Tel Jezreel, and other antiquity sites. My family always felt we lived very close to where generations past had made history.

Across the street from our house was a large parcel of land on which a kindergarten and elementary school were built, and it had a small number of students. The school was run by the government of Palestine. The building didn't take up much space, and the rest of the land was used for occasional municipal or government functions requiring a lot of space to accommodate the many guests. This provided me and siblings and friends with some occasions to watch official activities, even though we were not invited to the events.

It was fun to watch official ceremonies from close proximity, except on one occasion, when the guest of honor was the British district governor, the highest Mandatory officer in Palestine. A group of boys and I sat on the wall, and for some reason, we decided to throw pebbles at him and the other notables on the podium. Soon, the police started blowing their whistles and running toward the source of the stones, and by the time they found us, we were happily running away, but I was terrified. We each took a different route to our separate homes, making it there without getting caught. Later, we learned that the police knew who the culprits were, and the police told our parents to look after us and keep us on a "leash," the word my mother told me the police used. The police captains were British, and the lower ranks were Arab.

A barbershop and another road led downtown to the commercial area at Sheikh Salim el-Khoury Street. In the other direction, the road continued to the Arab residential area known as Wadi el-Nisnas (the Wadi). We owned a house in the Wadi and moved there a year or two later. At that time, Arabs and Jews were already partially separated as to the locations of their residences and partially segregated as to their national commitments. I say "partially" because the social and business interaction between them did not suddenly halt, willy-nilly; neighbors, business partners, government employees in all its branches, and professionals worked together.

We moved to our house in the Wadi just as electricity became available. We got electric light bulbs around 1936. One day, and to our amazement, a lighted bulb was on in the liwan. A press of a button and there was light! Suddenly we entered a new era. There was no longer a need to keep kerosene or oil lamps, a real daily chore for the person in charge of maintaining clean lanterns, refilling the kerosene, and trimming the wicks to keep the flame clean. My aunts decided that we should have electricity in every room and get rid of the kerosene lamps. I missed the lamps, with their chimneys made of thin glass slightly translucent or opaque and which came in different shades of green, blue, pink, lavender, and yellow.

I was about six years old when we moved from Sheikh Salim Street to Wadi el-Nisnas. Here, food and vegetable shops were nearby, a great relief for the women in the house. Our new home had two and a half stories, located at the intersection of the Arab and Jewish main streets, the Arab Wadi el-Nisnas and the Jewish Hadara Carmel. The location allowed us to communicate on both sides of the house with the two opposing groups; I can say that we enjoyed the relationship with our neighbors on both sides of the street.

In 1937, our family was composed of my parents, Ne'hme el-Khoury and Farida Atallah; my older brother Yusuf, born on July 20, 1929; three unmarried aunts, Amini, Marie, and Alice; and Uncle Eliyah. Our aunts did have suitors, but the suitors were not accepted because of sectarian differences. We were Melkite Catholic and the suitors were Greek Orthodox. In addition, I had two aunts who were married before I was born and continued to live in Nazareth; they were regular visitors, and I remember them with love. Soon, three additional brothers, Victor, Michel, and Emile, and two sisters, Thérèse, and Vera, were born to my parents, for a total of five boys and two girls. Emile and Vera were born in Nazareth, to which we, like many others, fled when World War II began and German air raids over Haifa became a constant threat. The British Army had a significant presence in Haifa, making it a target for the Germans.

The purpose of the German air raids was to disrupt fuel oil production in the refineries, the only source to supply the British Army in the eastern Mediterranean. To prevent the German planes from hitting their targets successfully, the British attached huge helium balloons to steel cables and floated them to about half a mile above the city. The balloons interfered with the paths of the planes and complicated the bombing raids for the Germans.

On account of these threats circling above, my father decided to move his wife, children, and sisters to the el-Khoury family's hometown of Nazareth. It would be a safer place. I had the impression that my father's inclination, my aunts' too, was to go back to their roots and settle where they had been born, and they were enthusiastic about the move. On the other hand, my mother was not happy to move from the city to a rural town.

My mother, Farida Iskandar Atallah, was born in Haifa in 1912 to a family of humble means, a circumstance resulting from the death of her father during the First World War while he was serving in the Ottoman Empire's army. Military service was compulsory, and he, like other young men, was conscripted. He came from Deir al-Qamar, a town in the Chouf mountains of Lebanon. My mother's family consisted of her mother, Labeebi, her sister, Wadi'a, and her brother, Majid. She was married to my father in September 1927, at the age of fifteen. Her education was limited to the primary school level, and, like other young women of her era, her new responsibilities of wife and mother took priority over other needs.

She was always a happy person, loving and energetic. Her life was easy, as my three aunts oversaw running the house, and later, when children were born, they took care of them. A full-time helper was also part of the family. My aunts and my mother got along well, and home life was smooth.

With little demand on her time, my mother was the socialite, visiting family and friends and enjoying whatever she did yet available at home whenever needed. She had no chores at home, since my aunts enjoyed working around the house and kitchen and handled household needs, while my mother enjoyed her freedom. I remember that one relative, an agent for a shipping line, had a very large house and hosted large parties. One of his friends played the piano, and the guests reveled in music and dance—I remember mention of the mambo and samba. And there were tea parties that about a dozen ladies would attend and take turns hosting. Life in Haifa, as in all coastal cities, was a socially open society, and in my mother's view, there was no reason to go back to the more closed, rural society of Nazareth.

We held onto the house in Wadi el-Nisnas, and my mother became less unhappy, as this indicated to her that the move was temporary. My father had a knack for getting consensus in family matters. I do not remember him making decisions on the issues that affected members of the family without their approval. Yet, nor do I not remember any who questioned his preferences.

OUR FAMILY ORIGINS

Our family originated in southern Jordan. We have a tribal affiliation to the Halasa clan, a branch of the al-Ghassasina tribe, which was spread all over the western parts of the Arabian Peninsula and north to the present frontiers of Turkey. The Ghassasina are a Christian tribe and were politically allied to the Roman Empire. Their lands acted as a buffer zone between land annexed by the Romans against raids by Bedouin tribes. When Islam took a firm footing in the area, many people converted to Islam. When an ancestor who was a priest married and started a family, he changed the name to el-Khoury in the tradition of naming family according to the name of the head of the family's profession.

My paternal grandfather, Yusuf Khalil el-Khoury, was born in Nazareth around 1850 and died in Nazareth in the late 1920s. I have scant information about my ancestors as in those days, as the churches, cemeteries, places of residence, and relatives together held the family memory. There didn't seem to be a need to draw up a family tree. But I hope one day I will search the church records in Nazareth.

My paternal grandmother, Martha, lived with us until 1936, when I was five. I remember her vaguely as a tall, thin, and strong woman. She was regarded as the head of the household. Mothers in Arab society are highly respected, and when they grow to an advanced age, families take care of them with deference, love, and respect. She died in Haifa in the Salim el-Khoury house where I was born. We moved into the house in Wadi el-Nisnas after my grandmother died.

My father was born in Nazareth, Palestine, in 1891. At that time, the Galilee and Nazareth were part of the wilayat (province) of Beirut of the Ottoman Empire. His birth certificate, which I keep, says he was born in the city of Nazareth, District of Galilee, wilayat Beirut in 1891; the certificate's heading is al-dawla al'alliya al-Uthmaniya, الدولة✟العلية✟العثمانية.

At the time of my father's birth, there were no geopolitical borders in the Near East. The whole region and much beyond were part and parcel of the Ottoman Empire. When the First World War ended, the victors divided up the Arab area of the declining Ottoman Empire among themselves to accommodate their needs and their greed. Great Britain and France were the new powers. They drew lines on a map to divide the landmass, creating several new nation-states, a novel concept to the people of the Ottoman lands: Palestine, Transjordan, Iraq, Syria, and Lebanon. By these lines on paper, our family became citizens of the

State of Palestine, which was destined to be emptied of its indigenous population and handed to the Zionist movement to become the home of the Jews of the world. The world cleared their conscience for the inhuman and criminal treatment of the Jews in Europe by offering Palestine for the taking.

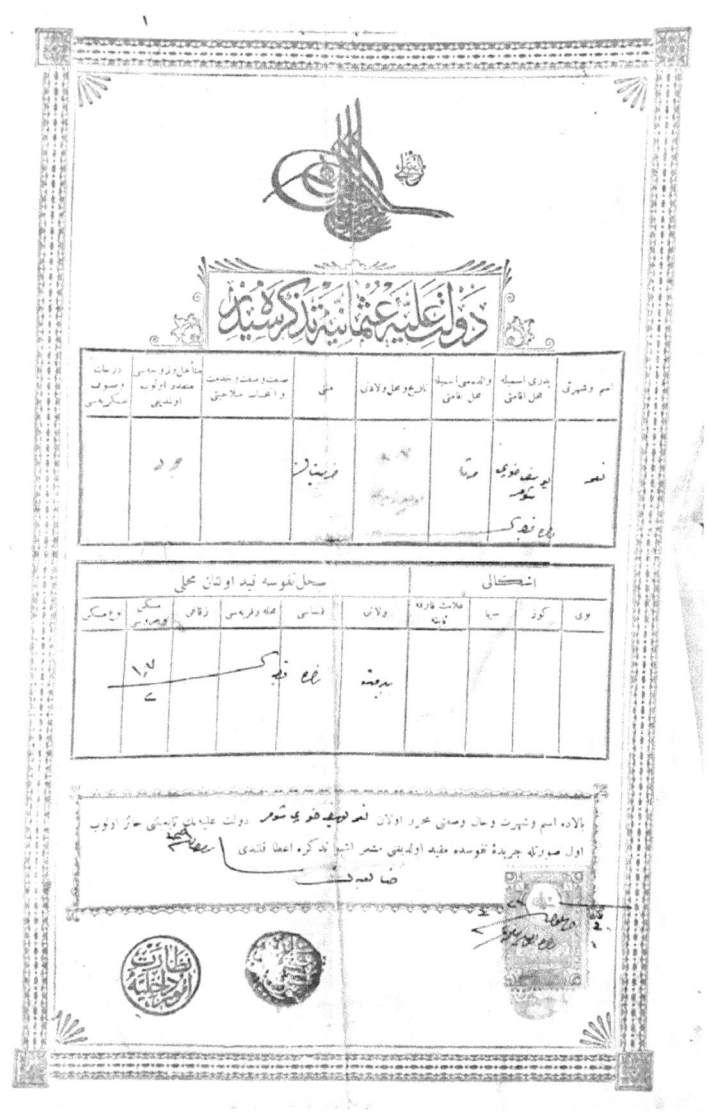

My Father's Ottoman Birth Certificate

We loved my maternal grandmother, Labeebi, because she was loving and kind, and we were happy when we visited her. Her house was small, with a gate that was too big for the size of the house and a small garden dominated by a huge, old olive tree. The house consisted of one multi-functioning room: a bedroom, a living room, and a kitchen that was also used for bathing on Saturdays. The outhouse was behind the gate. In summer and spring, my grandmother and family spent time on the small terrace, and that was where we had our meals and, on occasion, where all of us slept. I remember my visits quite fondly, especially that I was very well taken care of by my Aunt Wadi'a, Uncle Majid, and grandmother.

I remember my grandmother's weekly clothes washing day. She would boil water, add ash, immerse the clothes in a large pot, and keep stirring. Ash is a whitening substance used for washing clothing. When she considered that the cleaning process was complete, she would hang the clothes in the sunny garden to dry.

My maternal Uncle Majid worked as a clerk in the Port of Haifa; he had only a primary education, and the family's later flight to Lebanon left him with no job, no career, no prospects, and no money. He lived in poverty at a time when we were unable to help.

We had many relatives in Haifa on both my mother's and father's sides, and visiting family was a regular event. Teatime was the main function for women, and each hostess tried to outdo the others as to the number and quality of dishes and food items offered. I went with my mother to some of these outings to sample the sweets, but usually I preferred to join the men. Local politics was their constant topic of conversation. They met in a café, and when I joined them, I had the luxury of ordering ice cream or a cold drink, which did compensate for what I deprived myself of when I chose to absent myself from the women's parties. My recollections of our life during that period are scant. My description of the Salim el-Khoury house and its occupants are vague impressions supported by stories I heard from my aunts and mother. When we moved to the Wadi, we were close to the old house, and my recollections are also supported by what I remember seeing when passing by.

The British Mandate

Due to the political policies of the British Mandate, there was a national uprising by Palestinian Arabs in Mandatory Palestine in 1936. It demanded independence from Britain and the end of the policy of unrestricted Jewish immigration and land acquisition. The Great Arab Revolt lasted till 1939 and coincided with a peak in the number of Jewish immigrants, from 60,000 to over 300,000.

Government-owned land, known as *miri* or *masha'a*, constituted a large portion of the total area of Palestine. Sometimes these vast properties were administered by local authorities, and some lands were leased to farmers for a consideration or left untended, but the decisions on their use were determined by higher Ottoman authorities in Istanbul until the end of the First World War. After that, such decisions were made in London, the capital of the Mandatory power.

Rural Palestinians became landless and impoverished. One British policy was to give Palestinian government properties, which had been inherited from the Ottoman Empire and managed by the British Mandate, as gifts to the official organizations of the Zionist movement, with the stated goal of establishing a "Jewish National Home."

Israel was created in 1948. The new state took over all these lands and declared them property of Israel, even though these miri lands were not part of the Jewish allotted sections of Palestine as defined by the United Nations Partition Plan. On these lands Israel built settlements, some of which grew into cities.

The largest area of land to be occupied by Zionist forces was the Beersheba district in the Naqab (Negev) Desert. The population of 4,000 was primarily Bedouin Arab, and most lived in the northern part of the district, where land cultivation allowed a livelihood. The southern part is desert but is rich in archaeological sites. Historically, land ownership in the Beersheba district was held on the basis of tribal custom. On this basis, individual plots were sold, inherited, rented, or divided. In 1948 the Israeli government decided that the Negev was vital to its security and so waged battles against Egyptian forces stationed there and occupied it. The entire district of Beersheba came under occupation, thereby doubling the area of the State of Israel.

As a sign of belonging to the Arab cause, meaning they were on the side of the rebellion, men changed their custom of wearing a hat or a tarboosh (fez) to wearing the Arab headdress, the hatta, and 'ikal. The red fez made of felt usually has a black silk tassel attached to the top. Men wore it throughout the eastern Mediterranean region and North Africa; in some places it was common well into the 1950s.

Men in Haifa were not used to wearing the *hatta*, or *kufia*, the square piece of fabric folded diagonally and placed on the head. It is supported by the *'ikal*, a thick, round, black rope sufficient in length and weight to keep the hatta in place. The city men didn't always know how to wear the headgear, and some came to my father for help on how to wear it properly. The main reason their hatta slipped off was that they had bought silk rather than cotton fabric. Silk is slippery and slides off the head, while cotton does not, and so we, the children, had occasion to laugh at the city men's ignorance.

During that period, whenever a bomb exploded near or in the Jewish Hadara Carmel, a British police officer with a contingent of conscripted soldiers would gather all the residents of the Wadi and move them outdoors to a fenced area; they remained there until the police investigated each and searched a large sample of those corralled. These included everybody in each household: children, women, and men, of all ages. When released, a stamp on their hands showed that they could go home. I experienced this procedure three times between the ages of five to eight;

my friends and I must have posed a scary image to the armed men of the British Army or police. I could not distinguish between the army or police, as to me both appeared to be vicious and appeared to be enjoying what they were doing.

My memory sometimes plays tricks on me but living in Haifa left profound impressions; I cannot forget the Arab Revolt and attempts to suppress it and the consequent injury or death of many we knew. A relative of ours was in the crowded vegetable market, the souk, one early morning when a bomb went off. The explosion killed him in company of around sixty others.

From that time on, whatever we did was tempered by this new reality. It was further cemented when Great Britain withdrew as Mandatory power from its positions three days before the date declared by the United Nations for withdrawal, giving the Jews all the tactical advantage. The official date for the evacuation ushering in the end of the Mandate granted to Great Britain over Palestine by the League of Nations (the predecessor of the United Nations) had been set for May 15, 1948. However, the actual British evacuation started as early as May 13 and continued through May 15.

With prior knowledge of the early withdrawal and cooperation of the British Army, the Zionists were able to occupy all the police stations, government departments, and arms and ammunition depots left by the withdrawing British Mandatory powers, intact and unprotected. The Arabs did not know of this plan, and with that, the Zionists had a clear advantage. The Palestinians were at a disadvantage in the many battles in 1947 and 1948. They were unprepared to fight on May 15, the day the country was to have been officially partitioned in accordance with UN General Assembly Resolution 181—the Partition Plan of November 29, 1947, between the now-warring parties. So, the British and Jewish starting the war prepared one party to take over Arab land, leaving the Arab population in no shape to defend themselves. The fighting was not in the Arabs' favor; Palestinians lost the war before it started.

To encourage Arabs to leave their homes, the Zionists circulated rumors of actual and planned massacres. Their militias, the Irgun, the Stern Gang, and the Haganah, were well armed and well trained in Europe's World War. They made incursions into Arab towns and villages and slaughtered its residents. These events are well documented by the United Nations and the British and Israeli archives, but more importantly, the events are recorded in the memories of the Palestinians and also their archives.

Deir Yassin, a small village not far from Jerusalem, was the first but also the classic example of what the Zionist militias did in many small, populated villages. Irgun Zvi Leumi stormed Deir Yassin on April 9, 1948, and massacred all who were there. The number of unarmed villagers—men, women, and children—killed was between 250 and 320. The same was done in other villages, and news spread all over Palestine, putting fears of such killings in people's hearts, with stories from witnesses as well as by propaganda whose goal was to cause panic and induce Palestinians to flee. In some cases, to emphasize the seriousness of their plans, the Zionists inflated the tally of people killed.

The rumors and the killings succeeded in creating an exodus of major proportions. From 1947 through 1948, hundreds of thousands of Palestinians became refugees. Lebanon, Jordan, Syria, and Egypt, as host countries, have borne the brunt of caring for the "refugee problem" and have paid the price in political and social unrest, thus creating many untold other problems, the end of which does not look to be forthcoming. In addition, more Jews from all parts of the world immigrated to Israel over the decades, making it less amenable to allow Arabs back to where they lived, or even to live alongside Jews.

The Palestinians' dream of return still eludes the most optimistic of those who left the country for a promised fifteen days' absence—time to allow armies to fight the enemy, but the enemy won the war. The refugees discovered later that they were living in other countries with no hope of returning to their own land and homes.

Almost overnight, they became refugees, living in poverty in tents hastily erected for them by aid organizations and governments while waiting for a resolution of their miserable state of affairs. A solution has yet to be found, despite the international community's and Arab countries' strenuous and dedicated efforts to resolve the issue of Palestinians as refugees, making the status quo of life in camps a lasting solution. Instead, and with few exceptions, the refugees are still refugees and still live in refugee camps, but the dream of return to their homes is still paramount in their aspirations and plans. The children and grandchildren of those who were forced out of Palestine believe that their right of return cannot be denied and expect to return home one of these days.

In 1949, the UN General Assembly established the United Nations Relief and Works Agency (UNRWA) "to provide relief to all refugees resulting from the 1948 conflict." It took care of the refugee problems and settled the refugees in camps. My family tried to help relatives and friends, but our resources were small; the new State of Israel had confiscated our property as "absentee owners," as stipulated in its Absentee Property Law. Our family became "absentees" and lost everything we ever owned. My many relatives suffered terribly, and all of them lived and eventually died in conditions of poverty. My immediate family also suffered but we managed to reorganize our lives and avoid dependence on UNRWA for food gifts. UNRWA is unique in terms of its long-standing commitment to one group of refugees, the Palestinian refugees, and has had to continue its work for over 74 years.

DECEPTIONS

As I said earlier, military service at the start of the First World War was obligatory. When Britain, together with Sharif Hussein, ruler of Hejaz, started their advance from the western part of the Arabian Peninsula (now part of the Kingdom of Saudi Arabia) northward to Damascus, and eventually to the borders of what is now Turkey, the military deployment became necessary for the Ottoman Empire war effort. Recruitment became obligatory for any able-bodied Arab man anywhere in what is now Palestine, Lebanon, Syria, and Iraq. The Hejaz is where Mecca and Medina, the two largest and holiest cities of Islam and where the Prophet Mohammad declared his message, are located. Sharif Hussein was a descendant of the Prophet and a member of the ancient Hashemite house. He was the last of the Prophet's descendants to rule Hejaz.

Poor Sharif Hussein was deceived by Britain when he agreed with them to declare war against the Ottoman Empire and thus made it possible for Britain to easily occupy the Arab parts of the Empire. Promises given by Britain documented in the Hussein–McMahon Correspondence and appended to this story were not honored by Britain. The legendary and controversial Lawrence of Arabia appeared to help Sharif Ali, son of Sharif Hussein, in his assault on behalf of his father against the Ottoman's Caliph Abdel Majid II.

In that same year, 1917, Britain's foreign secretary Arthur James Balfour released a statement in one paragraph, declaring Britain's support for "the establishment in Palestine of a national home for the Jewish people." Many years later and in 1955 during my work in Jordan as the general manager of the Jordan Phosphate Mines Company, I met some Jordanians who knew Colonel Lawrence personally. Some parts of the movie of Lawrence of Arabia were being filmed in Jordan, and I got to meet the main actors. They stayed at the Philadelphia Hotel near the Roman amphitheater in Amman. Some friends and I used to visit them, have drinks, and chat when they returned to Amman from shooting various movie scenes in Aqaba, Wadi Rum in the southern desert of Jordan, or other locations on the road to Damascus. Wadi Rum is a particularly beautiful valley cut into a landscape of layered granite and sandstone hills, showing off colors of red, orange, and brown. It is a popular tourist destination.

The story of Lawrence of Arabia was well researched. I learned a lot about the Arab-Turkish war from the film crew and the actors, who had been well briefed about the characters they were portraying. I learned that they had to study the topography of various location in the desert, army positions, local and Arab tribal warriors from the south, skirmishes, and battles. They also studied the railway system connecting Mecca in the south and Damascus and, further north, to Turkey through Aleppo. They shared this information with us, and that is how I learned more about the war and its major participants.

Wadi el-Nisnas

Our new house in Haifa's Wadi el-Nisnas was two and a half stories high, built on a slope. The lower half comprised a kitchen, ample storage space, a bedroom, and an indoor bathroom for our house helper, Mohammad el-Saleh. He worked for us from his early teens. He was treated like a family member because his father had worked for my father on a farm and died young. His mother remarried a short time later, and so my father offered to take care of Mohammad.

On the first floor were three bedrooms for my three aunts and me and my four siblings, a reception area, a guest room, and a dining room. A large, open space outside the house was used for family gatherings, to receive guests informally, and for the three Arabian horses we owned. Next, accessed by an external staircase to the second floor, were our parents' rooms. An entrance room on the second floor led to a bedroom, a small kitchen, a bathroom, and a relatively spacious balcony facing the Hadara Carmel, a Jewish section of the city. My brother Yusuf and I spent a lot of time on that balcony to communicate with our Greek friends nearby in the Hadara Carmel area.

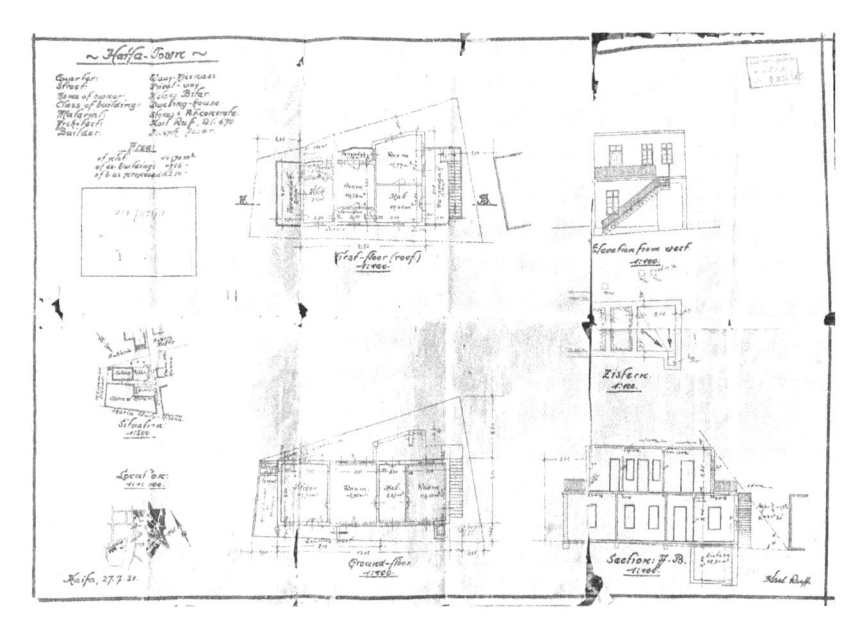

Architect's Plan for the Haifa House

Mohammad worked for my father until we moved to Nazareth in 1939, but he did occasionally surface in Nazareth. My father employed him to be responsible for a parcel of land called el-Khalleh (Khallet el-Deir), with an area of sixty-three dunums (about sixteen acres). It was so named because of its topographical characteristics: slopes on each side, with a flat bottom area that is about two-thirds of the total area and wet most of the year. Vegetables and lentils were the main crops. Later, before we moved out of Nazareth, my father decided to plant it with olive trees. I never saw it after leaving town in the second half of 1946I never went back to Nazareth.

Mohammad resurfaced in Amman, Jordan, in 1956. One day he came to my office at the Jordan Phosphate Mines Company (JPMC), where he sought refuge after being ordered by the Israelis to leave his home in Palestine. I was able to employ him as chief of my office guards, and he retained this position until the mid-eighties, long after I left my job at JPMC.

EXPERIMENT WITH MY BROTHER YUSUF

One day, my brother Yusuf and I were playing on the balcony on the second floor. I was seven years old; he was nine. Dangling from the wall was a long thin, strong rope. I suggested to Yusuf that we take turns hanging each other by the neck to find out what happens. I told him to go to the rope first. The idea of hanging was common at the time; hanging men for committing "crimes," which the British governors punished with a death sentence.

I tied the rope around my brother Yusuf's neck, but by a stroke of luck for him and me, Mother appeared, saw what was happening, and came to the rescue. After that, I do not remember ever getting a beating, but this time was the exception.

Our horses were my father's pride and joy. Many visited just to admire them. One was a Saklawi and two were Imm 'Arkoub, a rare breed. I never rode a horse in Haifa due to security issues related to the Arab-Jewish and British conflicts. The exchange of fire between the parties was a common occurrence. Even when going to school, we had to be accompanied by Mohammad el-Saleh, and on occasion, we came home early when dead bodies of people shot in the night were left unattended in the streets. It was a frightening sight.

WE ATTENDED PAROCHIAL SCHOOL

My mother sent me to the Besançon school, Rahibat al-Mahabba, also known as Sisters of Charity, which was run by Catholic nuns. I stayed at that school until I was five or six, and then I was sent across the street to the Jesuit Frères School.

Rahibat al-Mahabba appeared enormous to me as a child. It had many large buildings, with red-tiled roofs, surrounded by gardens on all sides. We had lunch in the school's dining room every day, joined by the nuns and the teachers.

The nuns very effectively used lunchtime to instruct us in both religion and table manners, including how to converse, what subjects were suitable with others at our table, and how to hold the fork and knife and how to use them. We were encouraged to converse during lunch but in low voices. I learned a lot about enjoying food and company and allowing others to do the same. We said prayers before and after each meal. At four in the afternoon, we had hot drinks such as tea or cocoa and cakes or biscuits in the same dining room, but we were spared the lectures and instruction of the lunch table. I learned later that my mother herself had been a student there as a child and was eager for us to learn what she had learned.

The Frères School, across the street from Rahibat al-Mahabba, also had many large buildings as well as edged, manicured gardens with trees planted in straight lines. Though we ate our lunches the same way we did at the nun's school, the supervising priest in charge was very strict and expected everyone to be "good." His definition of "good" sometimes annoyed me. On many occasions, I left the dining room because of offenses such as talking before prayer or laughing or speaking Arabic when I was supposed to speak French.

At the Frères School, students were not allowed to speak any language other than French. The idea was part missionary zeal and hope to spread the French culture; it also must have been the best way to teach the language. I know that encouraging the use of French was the policy. English was becoming popular, and the French did not look with favor at the competition. A student caught speaking Arabic was given a small, rectangular piece of wood called le signal. He would hand le signal back to the teacher in charge at the end of the day, and in exchange, he received a minor punishment or a deduction from his grades for French. Because of this closed-minded teaching method, I lost interest in the French language, and as soon as I moved out of the French system to another school, I abandoned French in favor of English. However, when I was preparing for my matriculation examination at the University of London, which was the equivalent of the high school certificate plus the university freshman class, I took French as a second language. I passed the exam with flying colors, thus making use of that long-forgotten experience and knowledge.

My brother Yusuf and I stayed at the Frères School until 1939 and the outbreak of World War II, at which time my family decided to leave Haifa for Nazareth. My brothers Victor and Michel and my sister Thérèse were born in our house in Haifa. Victor joined us at school, but Thérèse and Michel were still too young for schooling.

In Haifa, we owned a small parcel of land on Mount Carmel overlooking the city and the Mediterranean Sea; there, my father planned to build another family home. It was a very nice area with strict building regulations. The house would be a hundred feet from the famous Baha'i Gardens, where members of Baha'u'llah Abbas Effendi's family, the leader of the Baha'i sect, were buried. The Baha'i Gardens have nineteen terraces with beautifully manicured gardens, waterworks, and small sculptures. The plan of building a house in Haifa never materialized because we lived in Nazareth throughout the war, and in 1946 we moved to Beirut.

My father's business connections and our extended family's connections kept the household happily busy. However, life was marred by my father's illness. He was sick most of the time. As I mentioned earlier, doctors suggested that he was probably poisoned with arsenic, though that was never confirmed.

We were financially settled and had lots of friends, both local and regional. As a child, I was impressed every time a notable visited us but more so when a Bedouin prince arrived on horseback with his retinue. This was not a common occurrence in a city like Haifa, and the occasion was colorful and drew a lot of attention. I remember Emir Mohammad el-Saleh (carrying the same very common name as our house helper) dressed in Arab garb, wearing a sword, and carrying a rifle. He had a goatee and was trim and tall and remarkably distinguished. His visits were seasonal, and he and his party would spend a day or so with us. I remember that the purpose of these visits was to settle joint business issues relating to trade in livestock between Palestine, Syria, and Transjordan. His visits with his retinue meant the women in my family had to do a lot of cooking; the number of men in the accompanying group varied between seven and twelve, and the horses also needed attention and feed.

Our guests from Beirut provided a contrast to the Bedouin visitors. They were always impeccably dressed in European clothes and were remarkably well educated and spoke French. They were usually representatives or managers of the wealthy Lebanese Sursock family, who owned a lot of property in northern Palestine. My father managed the Sursock property and farmed their huge land holdings, maybe as large as five thousand acres in Marj Ibn Amer. The Sursock family received most of their property holdings in Palestine through land grants from the Ottoman rulers in appreciation of the family's hospitality to their high officials and services rendered to the Ottoman officials. They sold this property to the Jewish Agency in the early 1930s, making it the first large parcel of land in Galilee to be acquired by the agency. My father once gave the Sursocks a beautiful Arabian mare he had promised to me, and I was very upset.

In the seventeenth century, members of the Sursock family served as tax collectors and held other key positions on behalf of the Ottoman Empire. As a result, they benefited greatly from the 1858 Ottoman land reforms, during which they acquired large tracts of fertile land in Palestine and Syria, in addition to extensive holdings from Egypt to Beirut.

For us young children, it was exciting to get attention from visitors and to see people coming and going. I remember little else other than school experiences, a busy household, and the problems of fighting during the 1936–1939 Arab Revolt. I was eight when my family left Haifa for Nazareth.

My father's health deteriorated further during this period, making the move from Haifa to Nazareth inevitable. The decision was made when World War II was declared—and we were, in fact, ready for the move to our hometown. We sold our house in Haifa some years later. Religious leaders, both Christians and Muslims, encouraged people to leave Haifa. They suggested that it was a difficult time and, since Haifa was the site for the British military headquarters and oil refineries on the Palestinian coast, it was likely to be attacked by the German Luftwaffe (which it later was).

Beirut, this twenty fifth day
of November 1932 by Nicolas
Hanna Karnath

before me
[signature]
British Vice-Consul

IT ALL STARTED IN NAZARETH— A MEMOIR

*Sealed, signed and delivered
at the British Consulate-General
at*

Left and right: My Father's Power of Attorney to Manage Sursock lands, 1932

This chapter would not correctly close without mentioning that very pleasant memories of a good life still linger in my mind. We often went to Mount Carmel overlooking Haifa, or to Acre, a coastal city just north of Haifa. At other times we went to the beach with uncles and cousins or other family. We played in the sea and always gathered around ice-cream sellers to enjoy what they were offering. Ice-cream carts were plenty and sold individual portions in biscuit cones. After a few visits, we discovered that sellers had different mixes and every seller was eager to promote his goodies, so we each chose different flavors and quarreled about "tasting" other siblings' flavors and thoroughly enjoyed those trips. On very special occasions, we accompanied the family to lunch in a restaurant.

Nazareth

OUR LIFE IN NAZARETH

Even today, I remember that I come from another place, a good and hospitable place where I lived a very happy childhood. I was born in Haifa and left it before I grew up. In Nazareth, I lived a full life for a teenage boy, the age when one's character is being formed and when one starts to grasp what is going on. Nazareth was a special town, and the contrast with life in Haifa makes it more poignant in my memory.

Our move from Haifa to Nazareth was very significant, both emotionally and socially. Our lives changed to a simpler way, with different social values and mores. In the late 1930s, urban and rural, though separated only by short distances, were separate worlds.

Haifa has a natural deep-water harbor, and a port was built there, inaugurated by the British in 1933. The port allowed Haifa to grow, and in 1936, the city had over 100,000 inhabitants. Later, the port became the gateway for thousands of Jewish immigrants to Israel. Haifa was also the terminus of the Mosul-Haifa oil pipeline, which was also built by the British. The city was open to the western world, where the latter found what its ambitions and commerce needed. The British and other Europeans brought their social, cultural, and business customs and styles, and the local urban Palestinian population adapted, for commercial gain, to the new ways.

F. 35.

GOVERNMENT OF PALESTINE

حكومة فلسطين

ממשלת פלשתינה (א"י)

ANIMAL ENUMERATION BILL

تذكرة تعداد الحيوانات

תעודה לספירת הבהמות

133701

Book No. / رقم الدفتر / מספר הפנקס		Bill No. / رقم التذكرة / מס' השובר		
Kind of Animals / نوع الحيوانات / מין הבהמות	Number of Heads / عدد الرؤوس / מספר הראשים	Tax / الضريبة / מס Mils / مل מיל	Total of Tax / مجموع الضريبة / סה"כ מס L.P. / ج.ف. / פ"מ (א"י)	Mils / مل מיל
Sheep / خراف / כבשים		48		
Goats / ماعز / עזים		48		
Camels / جمال / גמלים		120		
Buffaloes / جواميس / תאים	17	120	10	500
Pigs / خنازير / חזירים		90		
		Total / المجموع / סך הכל	10	500

I certify that the animals enumerated in the village of .... in .... District in the name of .... are numbered as above, and the amount of the tax is L.P. .... mils.
Date ....
Enumerating Official. ....

اشهد ان عدد الحيوانات التي تم تعدادها في قرية .... من اعمال لواء .... باسم .... هو كما ذكر اعلاه وقد بلغ مقدار الضريبة المستحقة عليها ج.ف. .... مل
التاريخ .... مأمور التعداد ....

הנני מעיד בזה כי ספירת הבהמות שנעשתה בכפר .... מחוז .... על שם .... במספר כמבואר לעיל, וסכום מסיהן מגיע ל .... פ"מ (א"י) .... מיל
תאריך .... פקיד הספירה ....

Government of Palestine Tax

Unlike in Haifa, people in Nazareth were closer to each other through family ties and through the land they farmed. They had similar needs, and they lived according to customs that did not change for a long time or maybe even for centuries. Nazarenes did expect conformity to socially accepted conventions. Marriages, for example, occurred very much among one social tier of families and sects. In Haifa, there had been more leeway.

There were no conveniences to accommodate travelers and visitors, such as restaurants and hotels, which meant that homes doubled as points of service providing meals and often a bed. Visitors appeared frequently, with no advance notice sent or received; thanks to minimal communication facilities, surprises were the order of the day. Families on whom visitors descended were required to be hospitable, no matter the monetary cost or the inconvenience incurred. Our family—with a fair number of relatives, business associates, and workers spread over cities, villages, and farms—was always prepared. It was customary for the host family to first serve the guests and then head to the dining room after the guests had their fill. Although it took my urban mother quite a while to adjust to these customs, she had no choice but to be cheerful, while my father and aunts, whose hometown was Nazareth, actually enjoyed seeing people and offering hospitality.

Nazareth's location makes it cool in summer but quite cold in winter. It sits in a natural bowl at an elevation of 320 meters, surrounded by a crest of hills about 500 meters high. It is about 25 kilometers from the Sea of Galilee and about nine kilometers west from Mount Tabor, where I often rode my horse. The pleasant summer weather was another inducement for visitors, with a consequent demand on our resources. As I said, we were expected to be welcoming and show pleasure in the visitors. But I do remember my aunts' and mother's many comments when the guests finally left. With few exceptions, there was always a sigh of relief.

CHURCHES

Nazareth has a long Christian history and many churches and mosques. The oldest mosque is the White Mosque, located in the

"Mosque Quarter" حارةالجامع† in Nazareth's Old Market. A close friend of mine from childhood, Atef el-Fahoum, administers the mosque and its waqf. Under Islamic law, waqf typically involves donating a building, a parcel of land, or other assets for Muslim religious or charitable purposes, with no intention of reclaiming the assets.

Each Christian sect has at least one church in Nazareth. I remember those I passed by frequently or attended services in. I am sure I saw dozens more churches, though do not remember much of what they looked like on the inside.

I remember the Church of the Annunciation because my Uncle Iskandar Shahtout was the organist, and I felt free to be on the church's grounds, which were out of bounds to other little brats. It lay adjacent to our original house, which was later bought by the Vatican and physically merged with the church, which was at the time the largest church building in the Middle East. In Roman Catholic tradition, it marks the site where the Archangel Gabriel brought good news to the Virgin Mary of the future birth of Christ.

I remember the other Annunciation church, that of the Eastern Orthodox community. Some of my ancestors are buried there, from when the family belonged to the Eastern Orthodox Church.

Among my paternal ancestors, there was at least one priest. As I explained earlier, that is how we got the family name el-Khoury, which means "priest."

I remember the Melkite Greek Catholic Church because some ancestors became Melkite after the family and the Orthodox church had a misunderstanding some 300 or more years ago. While the Melkite Greek Catholic Church's Byzantine liturgical traditions are shared with those of the Eastern Orthodox, the church has officially been part of the Catholic Church since the reaffirmation of its union with the Holy See of Rome in 1724. This is the church where my family attended Mass on Sundays. I also remember the Basilica of Jesus the Adolescent run by the Silesian religious order. It sits on a hill overlooking the town of Nazareth, where I often visited on my mare Khadra.

THE LAND

My father owned agricultural land near Mount Tabor in Marj Ibn 'Amer. Grain was the main crop and provided the family with its primary source of income. The total area of land was probably about three hundred acres, mostly in one parcel. He owned another small but separate plot, around two or three acres encircled by a stream, a beautiful place to visit. We had fruit trees—pomegranate, fig, plum—and vegetables for our household's use. We must have owned other properties in the Galilee, but I have no memory of where they are except for the plot just on the Nazareth southern city limit called al-Khalleh and the adjacent lot of three acres parceled into thirteen lots, which my father had earmarked to sell as lots to build homes.

I enjoyed my childhood. I had all that I ever wanted. But more significantly, I was close to the ones I loved. My father and I were very close, and we shared many interests. He treated me like a friend and took me wherever he went, to work and to the villages where we had an interest, especially Dabburieh. He managed our farm property and the properties of others. We rode horses together, and we talked about issues of work as well as politics. My father was an accomplished equestrian, and I learned from him the finer points of horsemanship. I was proud of the trust and attention he so generously bestowed on me. My father helped me build self-confidence and created the traits that made me who I am today. No other relationship gave me more.

When I accompanied my father on his rounds on the land, I had some interesting experiences. One was the tradition of communal morning coffee. In the villages of rural Palestine, as well as Lebanon, Syria, and Jordan, mornings began with a call to gather in community. The village's sheikh—the respected elder—began the day by roasting coffee beans over an open fire. Once roasted, he pounded the beans in a mortar and pestle, to a distinct rhythm of his own. Other sheikhs pounded coffee beans to different rhythms, and the sound traveled over the village and woke everybody up just before sunrise.

When the men in the village heard the soft sound of the wooden mortar and pestle, they knew they were called to share coffee with their elder. They joined together, sipped coffee in silence, and then headed to their work, taking the tools of their trade with them. When evening came, the men returned to their homes. On occasions, the villagers assembled and feasted together, and usually, the sheikh provided the food and shared the occasion of the feast with them.

Women were not included in the dawn ritual; they had chores, of which there were many, according to the day's events, such as preparing food for any guests, and they were responsible for caring for the children and the home. There were also seasonal duties: working in the fields or collecting olives or other fruit from trees. All the village responded to the ritual of a communal early morning cup of coffee. Ritual produces a bond between people. It contributes to the welfare and the security of each person. It assures all community members that they are part of a whole that will look after them in health issues, crop failure, suffering from bad weather, and any problem that may arise. The support is mutual, and so everyone feels secure.

Unlike mine, my older brother Yusuf's interests were elsewhere, more on the cultural side. He enjoyed music and reading books in literature and philosophy and had friends who enjoyed and shared the same interests. He did not care about business or horses, and he had no reason to resent my close relationship with my father.

Life in Nazareth and its surroundings was beautiful; I loved it, and above all I felt free. I traveled in town and in the neighboring towns carefree, on horseback. Having Khadra made me the envy of many. My horseback riding was a joy to my father, and the people's admiration made him proud.

I rode at least once a week from Nazareth to spend a day around Mount Tabor. The distance to Mount Tabor and the village of Dabburieh is about fourteen kilometers on a dirt road. It took me about two hours on horseback to get there or sometimes longer, depending on the weather and the detours I made. I knew some of the people living along the way, and I enjoyed talking to them. They combined the familiar with the unfamiliar and spoke in dialects different from ours, and I learned a lot from them about the area.

OUR HOUSE AND HOME

We owned a house in Nazareth in which my Aunt Fairouz, married to Raji Lahham, lived. It was adjacent to the Church of the Annunciation. As I mentioned before, the Vatican had reason to believe that the building rested over the place where biblical Joseph was a carpenter and where he lived with Mary and Jesus. To avoid family problems, my father did not ask them to vacate the house and instead rented a very nice, large home for us. Sometime in the early 1950s after we left Nazareth, Aunt Fairouz sold the house to the Vatican.

The house, built sometime in the nineteenth century, had ceilings six or seven meters high. A Lebanese pilgrim-artist had painted the ceilings with figures representing angels, coastal cityscapes with ships at sea, and horse drawn carriages approaching the city. There were scenes from Acre and Haifa and other locations. The artist signed his work on a ribbon drawn around an angel's torso, with the name Saliba Yohanna, dated 1889. The murals were detailed and beautiful. Local government officials such as the district governor or the mayor of Nazareth invited visitors from abroad to show them the art. Also painted were the undersides of balconies (entresols), which could be seen from the street below. Ours was one of probably a dozen large houses in Nazareth with painted ceilings. The flooring throughout was a pattern of white marble tiles separated by narrow black tiles, similar to floors found in Catholic churches, which added to the character of the house.

Painted Ceiling

The main entrance from a narrow street opened onto a staircase leading to a balcony, with two doors to the interior. The first door led to a liwan, which in turn led on the right to the family quarters and on the left to a large balcony covering the space between the house and a newly built suite of two bedrooms, a sitting room, and a kitchen. The second door on the balcony led directly to the living quarters so the family could come and go without being seen by guests or visitors. This sitting room was separated from the liwan by colored glass doors. The roof of the house was covered with red tile.

Sometime over half a century later, my daughter Leila visited Nazareth and phoned me from the house. I asked her whether the ceilings were as high as I had remembered them and whether the art was close to what I had described, and she assured me that they were. My granddaughter Nadia also visited more than once and enjoyed being in touch with one of her roots. In my time, Nazareth's population was about twelve thousand, a quiet town with cobblestone streets. The town's center was its souks.

CHILDHOOD GAMES

I took very quickly to the new way of life. I made friends and enjoyed the simple lifestyle; it suited my temperament. The freedom in Nazareth was very different from the many constraints I had experienced when I lived Haifa. Moreover, the 1936–1939 Arab Revolt was over, and there was no apparent conflict between Arab and Jew or British, at least not in Nazareth. With the threat of the more significant conflict of World War II on the horizon, local enmities receded by themselves.

One day my father told me to take the horse of an overnight visitor to my Aunt Fairouz and Uncle Rajis's stable, as we had no room in ours. Sure enough, I rode the horse down to their house, tied her there, and gave her some barley.

I was carrying some firecrackers to use later with my friends. While I was preparing to leave, I realized I had a good place right there to test my firecrackers. Three camels were tied near the horse. I lit one firecracker, tied it to a few more, quickly lifted the tail of one camel, and inserted the lot there. The noise, the furious camels, and all the saddlery— halters, bridles, bits, and tack—flying off the wall were a sight to be seen. I was thrilled with the commotion, but I forgot that my Aunt Fairouz and Uncle Raji were upstairs. They, as usual, interfered and created a problem for me which really hurt my reputation.

The guest horse to which I had provided barley was enjoying her snack and did not show any interest in what was going on. This was the first of two incidents in which my father became very upset with me. My friends and I played in the town's narrow streets. Our house was on the line of demarcation separating the Greek Orthodox neighborhood from the Melkite Catholic area. We boys on both sides played war on weekends and during vacations and whenever weather permitted. On "war days," we gathered on each side of the line, collected stones as weapons, exchanged challenges, and started the battles by throwing stones at each other. Our house was the meeting place for our gang, consisting of my brothers except for our older brother, who did not see the fun in what we were doing and did not join in. We also had the Fahoum boys, our neighbors and good friends, ready, willing, and sitting with us on the balcony overlooking the battlegrounds, and we decided together which side to support.

The only doctor in the combat zone lived on the first floor of our building. Dr. Leo Less was a German Jew, the one and only Jew at the time in Nazareth, welcomed and respected by everybody. He always cared for the wounded in these combats and told us not to fight when he was out of his clinic. Dr. Less, a marvelous man, lived and died in Nazareth.

My childhood activities were similar to children's activities elsewhere. I relate one story because it left a mark that still graces my forehead. I was about twelve when I fell from the third floor of our neighbor Dr. Less's house while helping myself and the gang to grapes from his garden.

My friend Atef el-Fahoum, one of his brothers, and two of my brothers were playing in the alley by our house. We realized that the grapes in our neighbor's garden were ripe, and we agreed that it was time to sample them. We divided into two groups: one to keep watch, the other to get the grapes. Two were to watch the paths leading to the garden to alert the grape collector of impending unbidden passersby and, especially, to keep an eye out for Dr. Less. I chose to climb over the wall and pick the grapes because I was the most willing gang member. My reputation at the time and my knowledge of the ins and outs of that garden also recommended me for the mission.

To enter the garden unseen, one needed to jump from the landing at the top of the staircase of our house onto the flat roof of Dr. Less's clinic, a distance of probably less than a meter and a half.

In the garden was a wooden bridge leading directly to the grapes. Dr. Less's roof was three stories high, on the side of a hill. I had made this run frequently in the past with the approval of the good doctor, as I kept a rabbit or two in his garden, so it was no remarkable feat to make it down to the garden and up the grapevine, which climbed on a wall and was tied well to it and then back to safety—or so I thought. Suddenly, I heard Dr. Less entering the garden. I panicked, jumped from where I was perched, ran over the wooden bridge and up the neighbor's roof, and jumped toward our landing. Alas, I missed our landing and fell back into the garden and hit my head on the only rock on the ground.

I remember waking up on the doctor's examination table with my mother watching, but none of my friends were there; they had disappeared into thin air. They claimed later that the doctor did not come through any of the alleys. He must have been in his clinic, and he must have heard some noises and come out to investigate. It took some time to dress my head injury and empty my shirt of grapes tucked in for safety and temporary storage. My mother grounded me for a few days. I stayed in bed for those several days because the doctor was afraid, I might have a concussion, but that proved not to be the case. Dr. Less never mentioned the incident again. He was the same doctor who attended to my injuries later, when the attack on our house resulted in severe wounds to my chest and face.

Another pastime I indulged in was the sale of small stones, which I collected from a cave in the Church of the Annunciation. My customers were the pilgrims and tourists, whom I charged one shilling for every stone, and so my pocket money budget did not need family support. Some of the monks noticed this enterprise but said nothing when they saw me going in and out of the cave. The pilgrims valued these tokens of Jesus's hometown, and I reaped the benefits of their faith. The supply and demand principle played in my favor.

OTHER NAZARENE FAMILIES

On the northern part of Nazareth is a hilly area known as Jabal el-Freihiyeh, the hometown of the Farah clan; the hill faced our house, and we had a clear view of each other. The Farah clan numbered a few hundred strong, all Greek Orthodox and mostly well educated. One older member of the Farah family, a friend of my father's, graduated from the University of California, Los Angeles, with a master's degree in agriculture in the mid-1920s.

Some members of that family were eccentric, and one or more were quite crazy. One man used to walk around town barefoot and talk to himself and to anybody who would listen, but nobody made fun of him. One day a snake bit him in the foot, but because his feet had been hardened from walking barefoot and by exposure to the elements, the snake could not get its fangs out, and so he walked around with it wriggling on his foot until someone helped get it off.

Another member of the Farah family is my friend Elias Farah. I knew him throughout my life, at school and later at university. He had a remarkable memory. On one of his regular visits to Beirut, he said he had memorized all entries under the letter A in the Encyclopedia Britannica. He said he would soon study and memorize the content under the letter B. His claim was actually true; I tested his knowledge in words starting with the letter A: he really had memorized all the entries, which is the most extensive letter section in the encyclopedia after entries with the letter E.

Our next-door neighbors were the Fahoum family. Yusuf was the head of the prominent family. He was instrumental in discouraging the

Nazarenes from leaving their homes when the Zionist militias initiated the Palestinian diaspora in 1948. As a result of Yusuf's power of persuasion, most Nazarenes remained in Nazareth, whereas those who left for neighboring countries sadly became part of the "refugee problem." He became mayor of Nazareth in the early 1950s.

Yusuf el-Fahoum's stand to encourage Nazarenes to remain in their homes came at a price. Israelis forced him out of town and placed him in confinement in the village of Dabburieh for three full years.

Yusuf's oldest son, Atef, was my best friend. Though we have not gotten together since 1946, I have many pleasant memories of this friendship and hope to see him again sometime before one or both expire; today, he is a successful businessman and in charge of the waqf of the White Mosque in Nazareth. We did talk on the phone in early 2019. When he picked up the telephone he said, "Before we continue, I need to be sure it is you who is calling." I replied, "Go ahead and check." He asked, "What was the name of my father's mare?" and I replied, "Asmahan." I passed his test, and we had a wonderful, long chat. The last time he and I said the name Asmahan was in 1946, a very long time ago to remember, but our childhood interests are thus revealed. My memory gets a cheer.

Asmahan is an unforgettable name. There was a beautiful, musically talented girl by that name. Born in 1912 to Syrian Druze nobles, she was a princess by right. She was raised in Cairo, and performed at the Cairo Opera House at the age of seventeen. Among the rumors surrounding her life was whether she was a spy for the British or for the Germans and she died under mysterious circumstances in a car accident at the age of thirty-two.

WE ATTENDED GOVERNMENT SCHOOL

Those were some of the most enjoyable years of my life at home and at school. At first, I attended the only government (public) school in the Nazareth district. It covered classes from elementary to the second secondary. Higher education up to and including the fourth secondary, which completed the secondary school curriculum of Palestine (equivalent to high school plus the freshman class at college) was only available in Jerusalem. One had to either apply to one of the two schools in Jerusalem to complete secondary education or seek schooling outside Palestine.

Students from Jerusalem and those environs generally attended the schools there. In contrast, students from the northern areas usually went to schools in Lebanon, and those from the south and Gaza went to schools in Egypt. Interestingly, students who graduated from secondary schools in Jerusalem generally continued their college education in Egypt, and those from the north continued their education in universities in Lebanon. The significance of this experience became noticeable as time went by. The two groups developed different cultural identities; Lebanon, a multicultural liberal society, provided one culture, while Egypt provided a unilateral and religiously strict culture. Gaza is a stark example of the Egyptian cultural influence, while the West Bank's political and cultural stances provide a clear contrast.

The school in Nazareth that I wanted to attend was a single large building housing all classes from the fifth elementary class through the second secondary. The playgrounds were ample, and teachers supervised every activity in the classroom and on the playgrounds. The teachers were outstanding. The school principal, Hanna al-Khazen, a Lebanese with an exceptional teaching and school administration background, was highly respected in the community and by the Department of Education of Palestine. Despite his strict disciplinary methods, he was well liked and respected by the students. I was lucky to be a student there. However, my plans to join did not materialize until one year later, and the reason for this was a complete surprise to my parents and me.

CLERICAL INTERVENTIONS

When my family first arrived in Nazareth, the principal of the Haifa Frères School, a monk, came all the way to our home to tell my parents that he had arranged everything for the Khoury children in the Nazareth

Frères School. He said my brother Yusuf and I had been accepted into the classes we were to join in the Haifa school and that we need not consider any other school. He and a fellow monk stayed for lunch and then left for Haifa, happy to know that we would continue studying at the Jesuit Frères School. My father thought it was strange for the Haifa school to worry about us in Nazareth, but he thanked them for their concern and unsolicited help. He himself had been a student at the Frères School at the elementary level around 1895. The school administration had not changed much since he was a student, and those still alive were still there and knew him well.

My mother was happy that we would continue our education at a parochial school. She was a religious person and a practicing Catholic. Like other religious establishments, the Catholic church did not want to lose students to other schools and would go to any extent to keep the young ones under their thumb in the hope that they would remain members of the church into adulthood. I hated the idea of being coerced into a particular type of education, no matter how good it was, and I made no secret of it. I started cutting classes and showing displeasure in every way I could. Nevertheless, I had to stay for an entire year before I could switch to the government school. I pressured my father to register me there, and I kept insisting until he did. Finally, I was accepted into the fifth elementary class and my brother into the sixth.

My brother Victor, who is two years my junior, did not attend government school. One day, the bishop of Galilee, later to become the patriarch of the Melkite Church, came to visit. He suggested that one of the five sons of Ne'hme el-Khoury should attend the Institute of Melkite Greek Catholic Church in Jerusalem to study religion and become a priest and serve the church. My parents accepted the suggestion, and by the time my father and mother agreed, Victor seemed happy to be out of home discipline and off to another—hopefully more exciting—life. He only lasted for two years of training for the priesthood, and then he changed his mind and headed home to lead an everyday life. We, his brothers, had missed him and were glad he came back home.

SUMMER JOBS

During our summer vacation, which lasted for three months, I found a job in a haberdashery owned by Bermans Iskandar, a family friend. The Iskandars had about twelve children, and their names all started with the letter J: Jamil and Jules are the two I can remember. My wages were a shilling a week. The owner's older son, Jamil Bermans Iskandar, also worked in the store, but we had different jobs and different pay. His wages were one and a half shillings per week. My task was to use a specialized machine to make buttons by pressing fabric onto the metal button base. It was a mechanical job, but the variety of fabrics, sizes, and shapes of the button bases made the job entertaining, and the one shilling coming at the end of the week kept me interested.

My colleague Jamil had no defined job. He was always walking between the shelves and singing, and sometimes he asked me what I was doing. I guess, being the son of the owner, he thought he was my boss. I did not mind it, as we were friends and remained friends until he passed away in Beirut more than half a century later. I had another part-time job with Jamil's uncle, an older man who commuted from home to the haberdashery store on a Cyprus donkey, a costly, high-quality breed. My job included fetching lunch for the two brothers and their employees. I always tried to borrow the donkey to fetch the lunch, which sometimes they allowed, but other times they refused to give me this pleasure. My absence when riding the donkey was more prolonged than when I did this job on foot; I took longer detours. The donkey was big, and my various friends who were roaming the streets would look at me with envy. At the owner's house, I was welcome and treated very well; I was always given sweets and, on occasion, a piece of cake, and therefore, my trip was not a bother.

The following summer I had the same job, but the third summer I got a job in a pharmacy next door to the haberdashery, still for one shilling a week but with a lot of authority. The pharmacist was an older man, and he was prone to taking the occasional long nap. He told me how to run the pharmacy and use the laboratory to mix the compounds as described in a prescription. I tried my best, but I sometimes approximated the required weights. My most significant tests related to people coming to the pharmacy, telling me about their aches and pains, and expecting the pharmacist, me, to have the answer. I always tried to help.

Having a job became less enticing when my father finally gifted me Khadra, the mare my father had promised me before we left Haifa. Now I had less time for school and work but doing well in school was a condition to keeping Khadra. Thankfully, I was a good student. Khadra was a beautiful, light-golden yearling when she became my friend and associate; she was an Arabian Saklawi.

THE BOY SCOUTS

During my first year in the government school, I joined the Boy Scouts. The teacher in charge was a fantastic fellow who planned wonderful excursions, mostly long hikes. He took outstanding care of all of us. He took us to historical locations all over Galilee and thus we learned firsthand about our country, especially about Nazareth. We brought food and were taught how to make a fire using whatever material was available, cooking and eating with no utensils.

Sa'id Bushnak, our scoutmaster, was also a history teacher specializing in ancient Egypt. He made the subject interesting, though he made us memorize the many Egyptian dynasties by the name of the pharaoh in the dynasty and the period of his rule, back to the third millennium BC. I made him happy by learning the lessons assigned and memorizing the pharaohs' names.

Sometimes, other teachers joined us on excursions; they talked to us about our studies, themselves, and their families and prepared meals for us. It brought us into a more personal relationship with our teachers. They helped us in our studies and alerted us to less fortunate students who could not afford the time for school and had to work in the fields as unskilled laborers to help support their families. On one occasion, when one of my friends had to leave school, he came to the classroom and announced that he was leaving to help his father in the fields; the teacher asked us to shake hands with him individually. We wished him good luck.

This is a moment that kept surfacing in my mind. It made me remember how lucky I was, when others among my peers were not so fortunate. I went through the elementary grades with minimal effort and learned a lot. I am convinced that during those two years I built my understanding of the intricacies of the Arabic language. It gave me an advantage even in my university days and, later, in the world where I lived and worked.

The eighth grade (equivalent) started well, and I was happy to see my friends and classmates after the long summer recess. But I was to leave this school after the attack on the eve of March 8, 1946, which left me crippled for a long time. This was an event that changed our life.

My brother Emile and my sister Vera were born in Nazareth, and the family grew in numbers. Together with my aunts and uncle, we were thirteen living under the same roof. My mother was always busy doing one thing or other, visiting with family and friends, while my aunts were the ones who took care of the house and of us children. They were a special gift to my brothers and sisters and me.

My mother and father were also loving and never failed to show their love, but sometimes, due to their social involvements and other time-consuming duties, were happy for my aunts to take over.

I am lucky to have been raised in this very warm and caring family. Our house was open to visitors all the time. Rare were the times we ate a meal without a guest. I learned how to relate to all types of people. Even on Sundays, when guests were least likely to appear, the extended family, on returning from church, would gather over lunch and talk about, among other topics, World War II and its progress. Some sided with Britain, but most sided with Germany since Britain was in occupation of Palestine.

A CRAZY ACT THAT I REGRET

One day, walking down the cobblestone streets with our horses in tow, I asked my father if it would be all right for me to gallop in the town's streets, and he said that he did not see anything wrong with it if there was a pressing need and when safer alternatives were not available.

However, he said sometimes one must take risks, and riding a horse with iron shoes covering the whole hoof on cobblestones was quite risky. He always put his advice in positive words, but I did not always obey his suggestions or advice. It was not much later when I neglected this advice and did something crazy.

The story goes like this: One day, I was at the top of the hill overlooking the town and was enjoying the view and occasionally galloping or just walking and talking to Khadra, something I always did when we were alone, and she always understood me. A friend of my father's suddenly appeared, riding one of his purebred Arabian horses, and pulled up beside me and we talked about horses. Then he complimented me on Khadra and suggested we gallop down the hill and see which was the faster horse.

The road to the market was long and narrow. I knew that galloping on cobblestones on an iron-shod horse was crazily dangerous. Yet I accepted the challenge and rode at a gallop through the alley down to the town center, around 80 meters. I made it without any damage to myself or my mare. I hate to remind myself that while I was riding, I was so scared I did not know whether I was still galloping or having a nightmare. It was a good lesson learned and one I never forgot. In fact, this act reminded me of advice I had received from my father—but at that moment I just forgot. The advice was specifically aimed at not doing what I had just rashly done.

Everyone was astounded to see what this foolish boy was doing. People in the market were aghast and all activity ceased. Storekeepers stood in bafflement where my gallop ended. They left their shops and shopping and gathered to see what had happened.

Stories spread about the how and why this boy raced his horse down a cobblestones hill, how he did not fall when he galloped and did not break his neck, how Khadra survived this run without breaking a leg. My or my mare's physical harm or death weren't my concern, but my parents' attitude toward me was. Would they allow me to keep Khadra? Maybe I was not worthy of their trust and separation of me and my mare was the wise solution.

When my father and mother heard the news, my father was shocked yet very proud, which he did not show openly. My mother, on the other hand, was about ready to faint. She was furious and told me that if I wanted to kill myself, it was my business, but I should do it in a civilized manner. I did not understand her attitude, but I guess she was worried and thought that reprimanding me in this fashion would prevent me from attempting other similar crazy and dangerous acts in the future.

The main risk in this run was the type of horseshoes my mare wore. Horseshoes at the time were complete metal coverings of the horses' hooves, unlike the shoes used in the West, and therefore.

the slippery cobbled road and the slippery horseshoes used made the gallop very risky.

My father's friend did not participate in galloping down the hill; he was a better judge of the risk but a poor adviser and challenger.

CHANGING TIMES

Our happy life was not to continue for long, as in the spring of 1946 several incidents occurred, culminating in the attack of March 8th in our home. As time passed and the effects of the changes and the shooting were evaluated, a decision seemed in favor of sending us children to Beirut, where it was safe, and the schooling system was sound. We rented and furnished an apartment, and the children were to start a new life in Beirut. One of my aunts would live with us, and the rest of the family would visit from Nazareth. The distance between Nazareth and Beirut was a three- to four-hour drive in the automobiles of the period.

Were the unfounded rumors that Ne'hme el-Khoury was buying land in Nazareth on behalf of the Zionists a reason for our departure? In those early days, selling land by Arabs to the Zionists was considered an act of betrayal to the Arab cause. However, the Jewish Agency tasked with buying land offered people higher prices than the market justified, and some families did sell their property. Lebanese and Syrian landlords owned much of the property sold. For example, the Sursocks of Lebanon sold 20,000 dunums of land (approximately 5,000 acres) in the late 1920s in Marj Ibn 'Amer. With the substantial proceeds, they built the horse-racing track and facilities in Beirut. The racetrack was part of the golden age of Lebanon in the 1960s, when royalty, presidents, and officials who visited Lebanon would attend the races. Some Palestinians probably did sell land, but people close to the government centers in Beirut, Damascus, or Istanbul held the most significant properties.

Very few Palestinians had much influence or clout with the Ottoman bureaucracy to justify land gifts, which was the main path to becoming owners of extensive holdings. Major landholdings were generously given as gifts to people valuable to the Sultan in Istanbul or his district governors. The Sursock's influence came from their European and Ottoman contacts. They were very close to Istanbul and the District Governor in Beirut. Besides the land granted them, they bought prime property, including 5,000 acres in Marj Ibn 'Amer, at low prices, so this property was not an outright gift by the Sultan or his functionaries. Another source of land ownership was the Ottoman governors' sale of tax-delinquent properties to close associates or friends for nominal figures.

Most ordinary people did not trust banks, so keeping large sums of money at home was generally an accepted concept. One such rumor must have surfaced that my father sold land and kept the cash at home, making our home the target for robbery. My father rarely sold land to anyone, Jewish or otherwise. Whenever he could, he bought small parcels with water or road rights to consolidate and, if possible, expand the property he owned in the Marj and make it free from small outside interests.

The last days in Nazareth were not so happy for me, though family and friends hosted us and treated us lovingly. I hoped my father would reverse his decision to move to Beirut, but my parents, especially my mother, were adamant. My mother, I thought, had a good feeling about living in the big city, but this is just a thought, and I may be wrong.

LEAVING NAZARETH

Our move to Beirut was to become permanent, and the search for an identity and a home was to become a quest which slowly started to become a life endeavor. In Palestine, we faced physical danger. In Lebanon, we did not know that we would face terrible times when we were near poverty and vulnerable. In hindsight, the move to Lebanon was no better or worse than staying in Nazareth. The relocation constituted a significant decision affecting every detail of our new life. Whether it had a specific purpose or whether my father was involved in any activity that prompted it, the reason for the move to Beirut was for me, at best, a guess. Those were times of upheaval in Palestine. I know my father was concerned about the various incidents here and there, on farms, occasional shootings, but probably he believed the unrest was temporary. If that was his opinion, then the decision to make such a substantial change in our life was not justifiable.

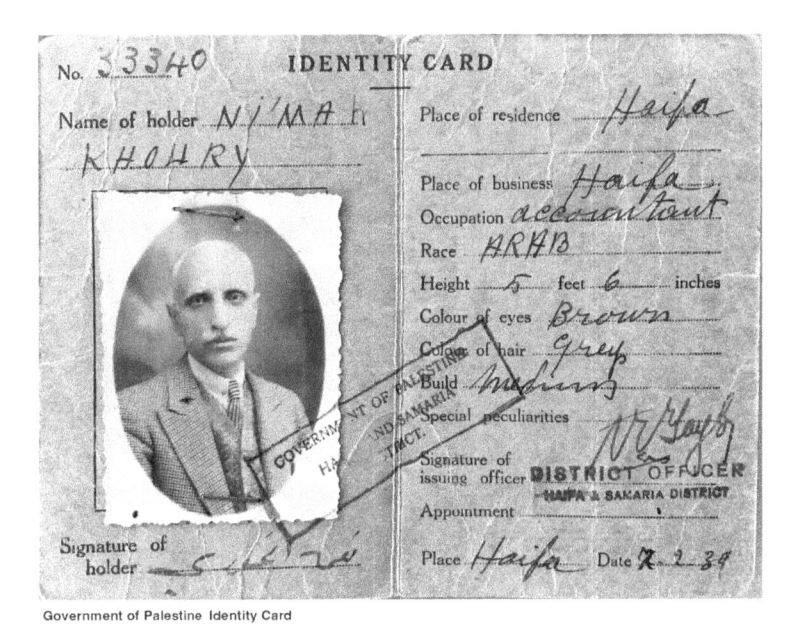

My Father's Palestinian Identity Card

I clearly remember the trip by car from Nazareth to Beirut. As we drove away and reached a hilly spot overlooking the familiar Nazarene scenery, I cried, turned my face away, and never set eyes on what was home again. Of all the troubling thoughts, emotions, and feelings, this moment is the most vivid in my mind. I remember the drive out of Nazareth, the scene below, and the moment when I turned my face away. Yet, no matter what happens, Nazareth will continue to be my home or a dream of one. It also keeps my thoughts and feelings about roots alive.

History: The Sykes-Picot Agreement

When the British and the French emerged victorious at the end of the First World War, they partitioned the eastern region of the Ottoman Empire to accommodate their needs and greed. Essentially, Mr. Sykes, Colonel Sir Tatton Benvenuto Mark Sykes, 6th Baronet, an English traveler, Conservative Party politician, and diplomatic adviser, particularly with regard to the Middle East at the time of the First World War, and Monsieur Picot, François Marie Denis Georges-Picot, a French diplomat and lawyer, negotiated the Sykes-Picot Agreement. They were appointed by their victorious governments to draw borders and create states in the Arab area of the Ottoman Empire.

The resulting states were Palestine, Transjordan, Iraq, Syria, and Lebanon. When drawing the lines, Sykes and Picot did not consider the ethnic, sectarian, or tribal composition of the population in each new state; they just drew straight lines separating what Britain and France wanted to control and exploit. These new states' geopolitical locations and material resources were necessary to the victors to control global commerce. Oil, a ready and abundant source of wealth and a great source of power, was a significant bounty which the mandate of the United Nations bestowed on them. The Sykes-Picot Agreement was one of the worst political arrangements from which the Arab world had suffered since the brutal invasion of Baghdad by the Mongols in 1258.

The agreement was a secret deal which proposed that Britain and France, and later Russia and Italy, would divide up the Arab territories between them. Britain took mandate over Palestine, Transjordan, and Iraq, and France received Lebanon and Syria. The mandates continued until close to the end of World War II. The British were also in control of Aden and parts of mainland Yemen, the Trucial States, Kuwait, and Bahrain.

Mandatory Britain's promise to create and establish in Palestine a national home for the Jews was fulfilled by the infamous Balfour Declaration, creating mistrust of Britain and France in the Arab counties. Lives were upturned, uprooted, and destroyed by the new and sudden reality. Britain, under whose auspices the State of Israel was created, has faded as a great power. The result of its promise though, is still reverberating today in the Middle East, most visibly in the refugee status of so many Palestinians.

Well into the twentieth century, Jews were part of the indigenous populations of Palestine and many other Arab countries and lived with other religious and ethnic groups and other minorities for centuries in relative peace until the country was shattered in 1948. Prior to the creation of Israel in 1948, approximately 800,000 Jews were living in lands that now make up the Arab world. Jewish poets, architects, and scientists were revered like other groups throughout Arab history.

The Jews in anticipation of Arab revenge against them, gradually left Iraq, Egypt, Yemen, Morocco, and other Arab countries, where they had lived in peace with their neighbors and fellow citizens and emigrated to the newly established State of Israel. In contrast, others chose to migrate to more settled and more convenient countries in the West. In Lebanon, Morocco, Iraq, and Yemen, sizable communities decided not to emigrate.

Two hundred and sixty thousand Jews from Arab countries immigrated to Israel between 1948 and 1951, accounting for 56 percent of the total immigration to the newly founded state; this was the product of a policy change in favor of mass immigration focused on Jews from Arab and Muslim countries.

In retrospect, I always wondered why we were destined to move so frequently. Wars, revolts, and coups d'état all provided good reasons; still, sometimes I reflect on the past and feel that fear for our family's safety and well-being was exaggerated. It is painful to leave friends and family behind, start over again, build relationships, and hope that life will continue to be what you want it to be. Our uprooting to Lebanon resulted from the creation of the State of Israel and the partition of Palestine. We involuntarily started a new life, one in which we endured hardships. I am still not sure that the circumstances necessitated our uprooting.

We are one family among hundreds of thousands who suffered psychological and material damage from Britain's policies. The creation of a Jewish state at the expense of the Arab population culminated in a significant Palestinian wave of emigration to neighboring countries where they sought refuge. Every day in the decades since 1948 and the official declaration of the State of Israel, the refugees continue living in camps with few if any civil rights. Some parts of this story will not make sense unless one is familiar with prevailing conditions.

It is interesting to consider that my wife Grace was born in Mosul, which is now in Iraq, and I come from Nazareth, then in Palestine and now in Israel, all originally part of the Ottoman Empire. My parents and Grace's parents were born and lived until early in the third decade of the twentieth century as Ottoman subjects. There were no states of Iraq, Palestine, or Israel. The Sykes-Picot Agreement placed Mosul and Nazareth in two separate nation-states. Grace and I both lost our ties to and connections with our roots. We also lost all that we owned.

One more recent disaster is the war waged against Iraq by the USA, ostensibly to "introduce democracy" and get rid of the dictator Saddam Hussein. The aggressor's failure to introduce democracy cannot be ascribed to the Iraqis but rather to how the invaders occupied Iraq, removed all its civil society and government structures, ruled Iraq, and finally turned it over to Iran to reap the benefits and bounty of the wealth of Iraq. George W. Bush did the legwork and Barak Obama administered the coup de grâce. The brain of Donald Trump added insult to injury and gave away what was not his to give, Jerusalem and the West Bank, to Israel and cut all aid to the Palestinian refugees. I wonder whether Israel will reap long-term stability and peace in land and property that does not belong to it.

To me, the grand picture looks like everyone in this region will again find themselves rearranging their lives and relying on their previous experiences to learn how to limit their losses; this will not be limited to the ones who suffered in the past or are suffering today, but certainly will include some of those who are creating the mental and physical infrastructure for this impending tragedy.

Beirut

EARLY LIFE IN A NEW CITY

Beirut was fantastic and breathtaking. I had never been in a city so alive. It was busy day and night, and streets were always bustling with people. The atmosphere, the historic buildings downtown, the big and beautiful tree-lined squares, and the incredible variety and abundance of goods in the marketplace astounded me. It was quite a culture shock.

We spent our first night at the Hotel America in Martyr's Square, downtown where the central government buildings, shops, cafés, restaurants, and hotels were located. It was very different from what I knew in Nazareth or Haifa. As I had never spent a night in a hotel room before, the experience was exhilarating. We arrived in the late afternoon and went to our rooms; we unpacked whatever was necessary for one night and then went to the lounge, a busy place with guests and my father and mother waiting for us. My mother was delighted to see us and was mainly concerned with the state of my health. We had tea and cakes of many kinds. My brothers and I indulged and enjoyed the occasion. Later, we had a very good dinner in the same dining room. The following morning, after a sumptuous breakfast of fried eggs, cheeses, and jams, manakeesh, and croissants, we went out, on our way to Sanayeh and our apartment.

Sanayeh was a desirable residential quarter. Its centerpiece is a public garden, beautifully planted, with a large fountain in the middle. As time went by, the quarter was developed with residential high-rise buildings, and at the time of this writing, it is overbuilt though still quite lovely. Our apartment was on the first floor of a three-story building and consisted of three bedrooms, a sitting room, a dining room, and a kitchen. After leaving the hotel carrying our substantial luggage, we entered the apartment and were assigned a bed in one of two rooms, the third being for our aunts.

Our presence in Beirut gave members of our extended family the motive to visit without worrying about the cost of the stay. They spent nights at our house and wanted to tour Beirut, eat Lebanese food, and enjoy the souks, the seashore, and the mountain villages. They paid for their transport from Palestine to Beirut and back and accepted my father's generosity to fund their touristic plans in Lebanon. We continued the open-house way of life we had in Nazareth or Haifa, which my family accepted without knowing what the future held for us.

After a year, we left Sanayeh and moved to a new apartment in Wardieh Square. It was spacious, on the fourth floor of a building at the end of a dead-end street overlooking the Mediterranean and surrounded by land used by its owners to grow vegetables and from whom we bought fresh produce. There were four bedrooms, two sitting rooms, a dining room, a large kitchen, and two balconies. We spent many summer days on the large balcony accessed from the sitting room. A smaller balcony in the back connected to the kitchen and the dining room. Sixty-five years later, Grace and I lived close to Wardieh Square, not far away from the house we had rented in the 1940s. That building is still there and still occupied.

Our house in Nazareth continued to be the family's primary residence until the war of the '48 started. Then, early in 1948, my father decided that we should all be together in Beirut. As I said earlier, my father was sick, and he was unable to manage his property. My mother, understandably, wanted to be with her children in Beirut, visiting Nazareth occasionally. Only one aunt remained in Nazareth. The move to Beirut was completed early in 1948, probably in February. It was good for us to all be together, and life felt normal again.

Welcome as it was, the move to Wardieh was to become a precursor to untenable financial problems and a lot of hardship. Of course, none of us would ever have thought that being in Beirut would deprive the family of access to our financial resources. But the new Jewish state confiscated all our assets in Palestine, and our family, like every other Palestinian family, was not allowed to return or claim any ownership.

Under these conditions, we also had to accommodate extended family members who had lost their homes. I remember my mother having to host as many as a dozen people, and some stayed for as long as a few months with us and sharing whatever we had or could afford. But soon, our ability to help friends and family deteriorated. Our attempts to draw on available resources in Palestine not yet in possession of Israel, such as our bank accounts, also failed. Whatever savings we already had in Beirut were insufficient for our new and expanding needs.

The Absentees' Property Law, enacted on March 14, 1950, established the Office of the Israeli Custodian of Absentee Property. As enacted, this law allows free management and expropriation of property. Absentees are persons who resided in Palestine at the time of the occupation and left the country after 1948. Property includes immovable property, movable property, money, a vested or contingent right in property, goodwill, and any right in a body of persons or its management.

ADJUSTING TO PROPERTY AND FINANCIAL LOSSES

My father tried to get cash from his bank in Haifa through the church. I accompanied him when he visited the Melkite patriarch Maximus Sayegh Hakim, bishop of Haifa and Galilee. The bishop was free to travel between Israel and Lebanon. My father asked him to cash a check from the Ottoman Bank in Haifa. The patriarch accepted and promised to bring the money on his next visit to Beirut. The check was for a substantial sum, and we waited anxiously for the patriarch's return. Some weeks later he returned, but my father could not reach him by telephone, and there was no word from him about the money. I believe that this patriarch kept our cash for himself. My father tried many times to see him but was told that the patriarch was not available. Finally, he did receive us; he was very friendly but said that the bank had declined to cash the check. Of course, patriarch Hakim said he would return the check but was not carrying it right then. After that, we never saw him or the money or the check again. This patriarch was the same old Bishop Sayegh who had visited us in Nazareth and took my brother Victor to school to become a priest. In Palestine, he had been one of our regular guests.

For two years, 1948 and 1949, we were able to manage on our meager funds. We accommodated family and guests, paid rent, and bought food. Then, when we failed to pay rent, the court issued an eviction order and gave us one month to vacate. We started to look for some solution but miraculously, and just during the last week before the date for the eviction, I found a job that gave me enough money to pay an advance on a new rent. The new apartment was on Hamra Street, an excellent residential area that later became very fashionable. It was on the first floor of an older building, but we could afford it. We lived there for just about one year and then moved, yet again, to another apartment on the same street, where we stayed for several years until all family members moved out or passed away.

It was a difficult chapter in our lives. No one in the household was of working age except, with a stretch of the imagination, me. My father encouraged us to keep the faith, but he was sick, and friends and wealthier family members conveniently disappeared.

The 1948 war in Palestine uprooted hundreds of thousands of people and sent them to seek refuge anywhere but in their homes in Palestine. Many fled to Lebanon, especially people like us coming from the north in Galilee and Haifa. This immigrant's problem did not find a solution, and the refugees who arrived in 1948 are still living in camps. The Refugee Problem, as it came to be known, turned into an international political issue. In the 1970s, in a war in Jordan between Palestinian guerrillas and the Jordanian Army, Palestinian refugees in Jordan were pushed out into Lebanon; in 1975, a fifteen-year civil war started in Lebanon involving Palestinians and Lebanese factions. To add insult to injury, both Syria and Israel got directly involved. Other countries such as Iraq and Libya supported a faction, thus adding fuel to the fire and extending the hostilities and the consequent suffering for fifteen years. The casualties estimate of those killed in the civil war in Lebanon is around two hundred thousand, with over a million displaced.

MAURICE N. KHOURY

Ni'mah Yusuf Khoury
c/o: P.O.B. 250
American University of Beirut
Beirut, Lebanon.

Beirut, July 2nd, 1951

Commandant Delseries
President de la Commission mixte d'Armistice
Libano-Israelienne
Hotel Normandy
Beirut.

Dear Sir:

We have sent to your committee a letter months ago which contained an application for a permit to enter Israel, since laws and regulations applying to refugees do not apply to us as we are Palestinians but not refugees; we received no answer from your Committee. Knowing that conditions were then unsuitable for you to help us, we have refrained from calling on your office to expedite your reply. Yesterday, July 1st, we heard from radio Israel, and read in all major papers, that the Israeli government has allowed non-refugee palestinians (i.e., those who are in Israel, and those who are non-refugees in the Arab countries and thus not legally barred from entering Israel) to the free use of the property they have in Israel. This means that I, being a non-refugee from Palestine, have the right to enter Israel and manage my property for a minimum of a month, and thus enable my family of a decent living here, as I am the head of a family composed of 15 persons who get no rations nor receive any help, because we came here before hostilities started and remained here for educational purposes, and we are not allowed to work in Lebanon.

I am the bearer of Palestine Passport no 200744 issued in Beirut on the 24th of February, 1947, in replacement of my old passport which expired on the 11th of February, 1947. I also have a residence permit (Lebanon) starting from mid-July 1946 to date, and a Lebanese Identity card for strangers no 14052. Thus I am a Lebanese resident from 1946, 2 years before hostilities started. I am a landlord, owning lands, houses, bank credits, and notes and accounts receivable.

I wish to ask you to present my case to the mixed committee as soon as possible, to interfere to give me permit to enter Israel to remain in Nazareth for a month or two where I shall stay at the house of my sister Feyrouz Khoury Lahham. I wish to take with me my wife, Farida Atallah Khoury, who is included in my passport.

For references in Israel, I can name Mr Yusuf Fahum, Mayor of Nazareth; Mr Habib Hakim, merchant in Haifa; Horatio Khoury, member of board of trade and agriculture company of Galilee, Nazareth. In Lebanon: Mr Salim Bichara, ex-mayor of Nazareth, Beirut; Maitre Milhim Ghurz Dine, Lawyer, Beirut; Mr Jaques Tannous, owner of Jeanne D'Arc Press, Beirut.

Attached is a list of my property in Israel, with numbers of the necessary documents. I hope that you will try to help me in securing the permit, and I shall remain, Sir,

Yours Truly,

IT ALL STARTED IN NAZARETH— A MEMOIR

Attached list

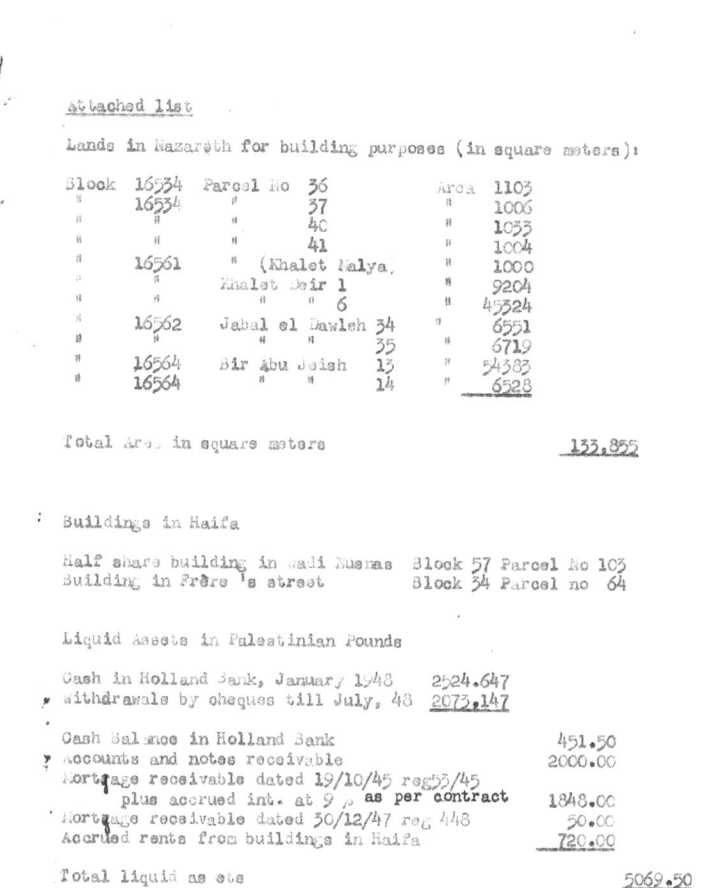

Lands in Nazareth for building purposes (in square meters):

Block	Parcel No		Area
16534	36		1103
16534	37		1006
"	40		1033
"	41		1004
16561	" (Khalet Nalya)		1000
"	Khalet Deir 1		9204
"	" " 6		45324
16562	Jabal el Dawleh 34		6551
"	" " 35		6719
16564	Bir Abu Jeish 13		54383
16564	" " 14		6528

Total Area in square meters   133,855

Buildings in Haifa

Half share building in Wadi Nusnas   Block 57 Parcel No 103
Building in Frère's street   Block 54 Parcel no 64

Liquid Assets in Palestinian Pounds

Cash in Holland Bank, January 1948   2524.647
Withdrawals by cheques till July, 48   2073.147

Cash Balance in Holland Bank   451.50
Accounts and notes receivable   2000.00
Mortgage receivable dated 19/10/45 reg53/45
   plus accrued int. at 9 % as per contract   1848.00
Mortgage receivable dated 30/12/47 reg 448   50.00
Accrued rents from buildings in Haifa   720.00

Total liquid assets   5069.50

Left and right: My Father's Letter Requesting Permission to Return to Nazareth, With Attached List of Assets, 1951

When we moved to Beirut, I was fifteen years old, and we were unprepared for what was to come. We experienced violent uprooting. From the minute the family decided to leave Nazareth, I felt lost. Whatever motivated my family to move, and irrespective of how I felt, I always needed to have roots and missed my Nazareth.

The many experiences and memories that crossed my mind were pleasant. This chapter of my life did not fade away over time. It is no exaggeration to say that the family at the time did not consider Beirut as a permanent home; to all of us, it was a transit point, and all of us waited for something to occur and allow us to go back to where we belong. But that was not to be; we were to remain in Lebanon, and our elderly members who passed away were not laid to rest in Nazareth.

The first two years in Beirut were fine, and much as I craved to visit Nazareth, I was happily discovering the city and making friends at school. I missed Khadra very much. There, everything I wanted I had in abundance, and whatever I wanted, I expected to have. Before Beirut, I did not know that there was another side to life and that it may be unpleasant. I learned how harsh life can be and that taking anything for granted is not wise.

On the other hand, schooling, work, and handling ongoing home needs helped provide me with the maturity and clarity of vision that made my life out of home tenable. Then, in Beirut, I met my love and future wife, who returned my love and provided me with the support, encouragement, and stability I very much needed. First, she was the loving friend and later, the loving wife, the person I turned to when the chips were down and with whom I celebrated our successes. Grace was and is my love.

Academic and Other Education

I JOINED THE INTERNATIONAL COLLEGE

In 1947, I joined the International College (IC), which at the time was part of the American University of Beirut (AUB). Two decades later, it became independent but remained on the original premises, so graduating students did not feel the change when graduating into AUB.

The school occupied a substantial area west of AUB, separated by a narrow street and steep steps going down to the sea. In effect, both campuses were one, and we spent time on AUB campus playing, swimming, or attending cultural activities in the various well-planned facilities. Like the AUB campus, the IC was beautiful, overlooking the Mediterranean Sea and having several large buildings, spacious, well-manicured gardens, and playgrounds. The school had two academic sections, one English and one French, both teaching Arabic as the mother language.

I was admitted to the English section and to the second class in high school. I was able to follow courses without undue effort. In the public schools of Palestine, I would have been admitted to the sixth elementary class, not to the secondary level. The IC, a private school, and the Palestine government school systems differed, and therefore I did not question the classification and the course I was to join. I was good at school but especially in the Arabic language and mathematics. My teachers were all outstanding; they were devoted, and some published textbooks in their fields of interest. I still have one or more of those books autographed by their authors, my high school teachers. I skipped two years and had more time to finish university and start working. At the time, our financial situation was not yet in a dismal state. My brother Yusuf was one year ahead of me, and Victor was a year behind in the French section. These two years of schooling influenced my life positively and enabled me to make friends. And those friendships were to last a lifetime. Time passed rather quickly and uneventfully, I was happy, school absorbed all my energies, and it was a pleasant change from the preceding period.

However, my health gave me trouble, and my ability to participate in some activities, like basketball or even swimming, was limited. My wounds still bothered me and occasionally opened to expel pieces of bone embedded in my cheeks or chest muscles. The last health problem I experienced related to the shooting was a minor chest surgery in 1985 to remove a foreign body, a small piece of cloth from a shirt I had been wearing at the time of the attack.

My mouth wounds gave me trouble too. I have spent many hours of my life in dentists' chairs. I had many surgeries, including one on my tongue to remove a piece of a tooth embedded there. For a week after this surgery, I had a problem with speech and I absented myself from school, staying home until my tongue healed and my speech impediment disappeared. I had movable bridges made to fit my changing gums, and those were replaced every three to four years. When a replacement bridge was called for, it took time for the dentist to fit it, and it took my mouth time to adjust to it. The nature of the wound, which had removed most of my upper gum and part of the bone in the jaw, made it difficult and costly to make a bridge.

In one instance, the mold was sent to Switzerland to produce an acceptable and usable bridge. Decades later, and thanks to advances in oral surgery, I had implants in all my upper jaw while the remaining teeth covered part of the lower jaw. Eating became a pleasure again; juggling food in my mouth with the not-so-well-fitting movable bridges had been embarrassing and tiring. Now, this is in the past and nearly (I say almost) forgotten.

When we lived in Sanayeh we used to walk from home down to Hamra Street, which at the time was not fully paved, then through what is today Abdul Aziz Street to Bliss Street and then to the main gate of AUB or the IC; the narrow paths were lined with cactus plants. In summer, the roads from home to school were dusty and in winter mostly muddy, and sometimes we had to walk in puddles that made our shoes damp and dirty. There was little car traffic, and the Hamra area lacked the needed infrastructural amenities. There were a few modest stone houses with some land for planting and some small homes built by AUB for teachers.

CHALLENGES AND EARLY JOBS

Our third year in Beirut was difficult. The family's finances started to deteriorate further and expectations of drawing on our reserves in Palestine disappeared when the Absentees' Law of Israel was under review and later enacted.

As I wrote earlier, the Israeli government confiscated all our assets, including our bank accounts, as it did to all who were outside the Israeli-occupied areas of Palestine. Israel called us Absentee Owners, with no rights whatsoever to our properties. The problem started to weigh heavily on all of us, particularly on my father, who continued to be ill. I loved my father and felt it my responsibility to find a way to secure an income for us all. I started looking for work with enthusiasm, and in a small way, I succeeded. My older brother Yusuf was absent from family life, and the rest of the siblings were too young to assume responsibility.

I was a year away from enrolling in the American University of Beirut as a freshman as I looked for part-time jobs. There were jobs available in teaching, and I signed on for as many hours as possible. I was surprised that the total income from various part-time jobs totaled more in salary than I would get in one full-time job. Just being an International College student contributed significantly to my résumé. Opportunity and need worked in tandem to make me work hard, reach out for more, and make more money. Work became an obsession, and my work and study combined schedule ran into a dozen hours a day.

While studying and working, I discovered that I could prepare and sit for the London Matriculation Examination then offered by London University, England. It was the official secondary school certificate of Great Britain and a requirement for admission to British universities. By passing this exam, which I did in January 1949, I was entitled to admission to the AUB sophomore class, thus skipping the freshman year.

The certification helped me get more and better part-time jobs at a much-needed higher pay. I was able to pay the rent for our apartment, and the added income allowed for a slightly better quality of life. At that time, I was eighteen.

The United Nations Relief and Works Agency provided an exciting and rewarding job. Founded in December 1949, UNRWA supports the "relief and human development of Palestinian refugees in the Near East." UNRWA asked me to teach middle management staff a course in bookkeeping, a subject I knew nothing about at the time. Classes were agreed to be conducted in the morning from 4:30 a.m. to 6:30 a.m., six times a week. It was a challenge to teach a subject not familiar to me in a classroom of older men and women. However, the money, the only inducement I needed, was perfect. So, I spent many hours studying bookkeeping and initially made it easy for my students, as my early preparations were insufficient to go deeper into the subject.

Once I read and reviewed more, I recognized the concept's simplicity, making it easier for me to learn and teach. I was always one session more prepared and ahead of my students. Thank God, I was judged by UNRWA to be a good teacher. More teaching hours at UNRWA meant I could drop other, less-well-paying part-time jobs.

From these classes, I learned a lot. Being young, inexperienced, and faced with many challenges, I wanted to succeed at whatever I was doing. Hard work and determination helped me develop a keen sense of understanding of all that was happening around me and instilled confidence in my abilities, shown in the money I earned and the happy smiles that appeared at home.

As life improved, my view of the prospects changed, and I became more optimistic. Through teaching older adults, I learned how to express myself clearly and concisely. Preparing well for my classes became an obsession, and I took the same approach later in life in conducting business or social meetings or in negotiations with third parties to work a contract or award one. Lessons I learned while teaching adults were valuable, as many of my adult students were experienced and attended my classes because that guaranteed a job with UNRWA. Of course, I also blundered at times in my approach.

For example, one day while teaching a bookkeeping class in the early hours of the morning, the performance of an elderly student was unsatisfactory. He appeared to barely understand what I was teaching. I made a harsh remark toward him and carried on with the class. At the end of the session, he asked to talk to me. I still remember our conversation clearly. "Young man," he said, "I know you are trying to teach us as best as you can, but I am not a young man and I would hope you will understand those older than you. It is not easy for us to remember or focus, not anymore." He asked me my father's name, and I told him, and he immediately said, "Do you know that your father and I were in school together in Nazareth just before the beginning of the First World War?" I apologized for my harsh remark and felt terrible that I had been thoughtless. Afterward, I tried to be more careful about passing judgments on others. The incident and the observation never left me. Learning comes in unexpected ways, and this opportunity came to me early in life.

With my family's finances on stable footing again, late in 1950 we moved to a larger space, a nearby fifth-floor apartment that overlooked all the western part of Beirut and the Mediterranean Sea. We stayed there until members of my family over the years moved individually to other places, got married, or passed away. Then, about three years later, I moved to Jordan and set up a home there.

I JOINED THE AMERICAN UNIVERSITY OF BEIRUT

In 1949–1950, I entered the sophomore class at AUB. The year was no different from the previous ones, as I knew most of the students in my various courses. My IC friends were a year behind me in the freshman class. Nevertheless, we all attended classes in the same buildings and gathered in the same outdoor places and, in brief, kept in daily touch. I kept my teaching jobs and was always very busy.

It is notable that by 1948, AUB was already famed for the statesmen and doctors among its 15,000 alumni. That is how many of us became friends and acquaintances with movers and shakers in the region.

DEAN HARVEY BATY

One man who influenced my life was the dean of students at AUB, the Reverend Dr. Harvey Baty. Dean Baty came from Montana, in the United States of America. He was a good man who cared about the students and encouraged them, and when we sought his help or advice, he made himself available to talk to us. Hundreds of students at the university in the years to follow found in him the adviser and helper they needed. His value to me and all other students became evident during the academic years to follow. His outlook on life and ideals were admirable and infectious.

Harvey Franklin Baty was born on Feb. 14, 1909, in Coalgate, Oklahoma, and passed away on Feb. 14, 2004, in Missoula, Montana. He was the fifth child of eight siblings. He graduated from Montana State University in 1931 with a major in sociology and received his divinity degree from the Colgate Rochester School of Divinity in Rochester, New York, in 1934. He began his professional career as pastor of the First Baptist Church of Montana in Helena in 1934 and married Emmalou Neffner that same year. In 1938 the family moved to Missoula, where Harvey became director of the School of Religion. After completing his doctorate in student personnel administration at Columbia University (in New York City), Harvey, Emmalou, and their children ventured to Lebanon, where Harvey became dean of students at the American University in Beirut. After seven years there, the family returned to Montana, where Harvey founded the International Cooperation Center at Montana State University in Bozeman.

The following year I registered for the junior year class in business and economics. However, I could not make enough money to pay tuition, provide for the family, and pay the rent. I never told my parents of my dilemma, but somehow, they felt what I was going through. I tried to find a way to tackle this obstacle, but time was not working in my favor. It was too late for me to register, as classes had already started. I felt frustrated and defeated but refused to give up. I knew I had to find a solution.

DR. STEPHEN PENROSE AND ME

I missed my classes in the first month, which was bad news for me, as the jobs I held depended on my being a student in good standing at AUB. As a last resort, I decided to appeal to the president of AUB, Dr. Stephen Penrose, for help. I asked for and got an appointment with him and described my predicament; he listened and said he would see what he could do. Days passed, with no word from President Penrose.

Meeting him again was no simple feat, so I decided to sit outside his office's back door and wait for him to finish his morning work and leave through this door to walk to the president's residence in Marquand House. As soon as he emerged, I walked by his side until he reached his residence, which was less than a hundred feet away, and asked about finding the funds I needed. Marquand House, still the residence of AUB presidents, is a beautiful house with a large garden on the upper campus. This game continued daily, and the delay in getting my finances in order put me in a precarious situation. Classes were progressing, and I became fearful that I would not catch up with the rest of the students. So, I raised the pestering level and suggested that he give me a job, any job on campus now that financial aid was not in the offing.

My persistence paid off. One day he told me to check with the vice president in charge of finance, and to my great surprise, I found that a Point Four Scholarship, the most generous of all scholarships, was waiting for me to sign up. The scholarship covered the university fees, the cost of books and accommodations, and a sizable discretionary fund for me to use liberally. Dr. Penrose also made an exception to allow me to return to class an entire month after courses had begun. This scholarship was good for the duration of my studies at AUB, which is how I paid for my education. Dr. Penrose allowed me to learn, and I made full use of it. I am indebted to him for his patience as well as his help and support.

Dr. Stephen Penrose was an impressive, good-looking, generous, and charismatic man. It was my privilege to have had the opportunity to meet him, talk to him, and walk him home every day before lunch. He was a brilliant administrator and orator. He passed away in his mid-fifties while on the job. I once sought him out to ask, among other subjects, if my daily walks with him had been annoying. His reply was both honest and complimentary; he answered that they were annoying, but he was proud to have a student eager to learn. He said to forget those daily encounters, especially since they had solved my education problems.

Stephen L. Penrose was the fourth president of AUB. He was born and grew up on the Whitman College campus, where his father was president, in the state of Washington. He graduated magna cum laude from that college in 1928, majoring in Greek and chemistry. On his father's advice, he went to AUB, where he taught physics from 1928 until 1931. He went back to the US for a PhD in philosophy from Columbia University, and then he returned to AUB in 1948 as its fourth president. He played vital roles during his days in office in the fundraising campaign, Point Four Scholarship program, and in establishing the School of Public Health, which became the Faculty of Health Sciences. He passed away in 1954.

My junior year at AUB was quite testing but enjoyable, and many things happened during the year. Dean Baty and a select number of students—three of us including Grace—decided to set up a student cooperative whose aim was to provide jobs for students with financial needs. The jobs were to be within the university. We elected a committee to run the co-op. I was elected chairman and Grace Saaty, later my fiancée, became secretary. Dean Baty prepared the grounds with the university authorities and got the official approvals. Later, I learned that President Penrose thought my appointment as chairman of the cooperative was a plus for this Point Four Scholarship recipient.

We discussed the organization of the cooperative, its range of activities, and a rapid expansion to help as many students as possible. After that, Dean Baty never interfered in the co-op's administration but always was on the watch and always helped steer it in the right direction. I will never forget Dean Baty, an AUB professor and a good man. During this time, I met and fell in love with Grace, my colleague in the management of the cooperative and a student of sociology at AUB. It was a wonderful time. However, I discovered that courting was an expensive activity. Before I met Grace, I might have a cup of coffee and savor it. Later, with Grace I would order two cups of coffee plus two pieces of cake. Restaurant lunches, going to the cinema, and trips to the mountains were what we usually did. At the time, these outings were quite costly for me.

AUB: INCUBATOR OF IDEAS AND IDEALS

AUB's liberal atmosphere encouraged the development of ideas, and many of them found expression in political parties. Al-Urwa al-Wuthqa Association, an Arab cultural society founded in AUB in the 1920s, grew to become the focal point for all Arab nationalist movements. Music, social issues, and literature also found expression in societies and associations on campus.

Three revolutionary organizations created at AUB were the Arab Nationalist Movement; the Ba'ath Party; and the Syrian Social Nationalist Party, known as PPS. These three groups had a long-term impact on the region's politics and life in the Middle East. Most of the Arab uprisings in the twentieth century and in 2011 drew on the original ideals, beliefs, and outlooks of one of the parties that was founded in the liberal atmosphere of the university.

The Arab Nationalist Movement's thoughts and beliefs were conceived by Dr. Constantine Zureik, who was a history professor at AUB and for two years its acting president. George Habash, a medical student, became the main disciple of Zureik's thoughts and was the one to create the movement. Wadi' Haddad, another Palestinian and AUB colleague of George Habash, and others such as Ahmad al-Khateeb from Kuwait participated in its development. All were friends of mine and Grace's, and we were to meet George and Wadi' again in Jordan, to which they moved to practice medicine, and I moved to look for work.

The PPS founder Antoun Saadeh, a charismatic Lebanese, succeeded in creating a sizable following quickly. I met him twice; he impressed me with his personality and his logic, but I did not join his party.

The third and most influential Arab national party, al-Ba'ath, was created by a group of Syrian intellectuals, the founder was Michel Aflaq. The Ba'ath party—not as it was originally conceived—in time became the ruling party in both Syria and Iraq. Aflaq's ideas were convincing and patriotic, but the politicians who later took over the party had different plans. Aflaq was expelled from Damascus by the new party leaders and died in Baghdad. He and his wife were frequent visitors of ours in Beirut before their move back to Damascus. Aflaq was a shy person and his wife an introvert, but we managed to have interesting discussions when they visited us in Beirut. His ideas and ideals, later adopted by many, were the declared ideals of the rulers of both Syria and Iraq.

Students at AUB participated in rallies, and the central issue for most demonstrations was Palestine. The Palestine problem manifested itself in turmoil in the Arab region and frequently in coups d'état. There was the belief among the Arab populations that their regimes were corrupt and needed to be forcefully changed. This fact, they claimed, justified a change in the status quo; coups d'état were the sure paths to save Palestine. However, these methods and this cause supported attempts to take over countries and change regimes that had often nothing to do with Palestine.

Through the history of political upheaval in the Arab world, a coup hardly ever produced a positive result for the Palestine cause. New strongmen such as al-Assad and Saddam Hussein prevented honest and capable individuals from effective participation in governance in the new regimes. In brief, coups d'état became a frequent occurrence. Examples are many and various, especially because governments of the day were wary of what the public wanted their government to be and do. As in many other countries around the world, students became the political force.

On one occasion, I checked my AUB mailbox number 250, which Grace and I shared, to find a letter addressed to Grace signed by the dean of women students. The letter said that an American naval vessel was visiting the port of Beirut and that she would appreciate it if AUB women students would entertain the sailors. Dean Kerr did not mean it in a bad way. She was a very good and religious woman who spent her life serving AUB and its students.

I took the letter to the main gate, where students congregated at noontime, read it to the crowd, and suggested we go on strike and later demonstrate. The atmosphere became one of anger, and by evening a strike was declared at AUB, and by morning all of Beirut participated in the strike and related demonstrations. It took three days of negotiations with AUB administrators and the intervention of Sa'eb Salam, the prime minister, to bring calm and allow for apologies to explain that Dean Kerr's intentions were innocent, and the issue was finally resolved.

While at AUB, I studied for an external degree in law from London University, completed the course requirements for the intermediate level, and then gave up. I needed a full academic year to meet the requirements for the degree of bachelor of laws, but time constraints made it too difficult to attempt. However, I did try to sit for some professional exams in accounting and became a fellow of two accounting bodies, both in England. One day I got a letter to say that I had been selected to be a Fellow of the Royal Economic Society. The membership entitled me to use the "F.R.Econ.S" letters after my name, and I used them on some occasions.

AUB STUDENTS' COOPERATIVE

As mentioned earlier, the students at the university, with the support of the dean of students, started a cooperative whose purpose was to help students pay their university fees. The initial capital subscribed and paid amounted to seventy-five Lebanese pounds, equivalent at the time to about twenty-five US dollars. With the support of the university, the co-op started on a solid footing.

Grace Inaugurating the Co-operative

    The support of Reverend Dean Harvey Baty and the amused indifference of President Penrose helped the cooperative grow and become successful. We achieved our objectives rather quickly. The immediate success was noticed by the faculty who became supporters of the co-op, and some helped us with the work. Within one academic year, the co-op was fully up and running and offered employment for about a hundred students, and that was just the beginning.

    We set up a dining hall in West Hall, and a Chinese AUB student worked as cook. We rented two buildings across the university's campus on Bliss Street, which we divided into about sixty bedrooms for students. We started an evening school for out-of-university students to attend courses AUB students were offering. The space for the school was provided by the university on the first floor of College Hall, eliminating rent payments and supplying reliable cash flow; the fees collected were used primarily to pay the teachers, and any profit was in turn reinvested in the cooperative.

    We bought produce from the wholesale market in downtown Beirut early every morning. and set up a fruit and vegetable retail outlet at the co-op, where we sold produce to university staff, friends and family. A bookshop, which occupied space in the main administration building on street level inside the university, was also set up to sell stationary and standard textbooks, usually used books, to students.

AUB sometimes employed the cooperative to do legwork for its various departments and paid for the work rather generously. The biggest AUB job we got was moving the main library from College Hall to the newly built Jafet Library facing the north side of College Hall. Students managed everything and were paid handsomely.

First Anniversary of AUB CO-OP

At its high point, and before the university decided to take it over in 1955, the cooperative employed about 450 students. The total student body of the university then was less than two thousand. The cooperative provided room and board at nominal prices for more than sixty students in the building across Bliss Street.

The wholesale purchase of fruits and vegetables required us to buy a pickup truck, which we used daily to drive to the market downtown and transport the goods to AUB. We sorted the goods following orders taken the previous day and then carried them to the buyers' homes and collected the money.

I learned how to drive a car when we bought the pickup; I would wind my way through the narrow streets of Beirut in the early hours of the morning and back to AUB. A friend and classmate of mine was my driving instructor. During the weekends, we toured as much of the countryside as we could, a pastime we could not otherwise have afforded had it not been for the availability of transport. The pickup had difficulty climbing the mountain roads, as it had a small engine, but we enjoyed our trips, nonetheless. As chairman of the cooperative, I had the choicest of jobs, and together with the Point Four Scholarship, I made enough money to pay my expenses and support my family. I also could afford to invite Grace and sometimes her friends out for a cup of coffee or a movie.

OTHER JOBS AND CONTINUING TO A MASTER'S DEGREE

President Penrose recommended me for a job as a translator to the Associated Press's Middle East correspondent. I remember working for the correspondent in his apartment close to AUB when we heard the news of Gamal Abdel Nasser's coup in Egypt. The correspondent allowed me to write the first draft of the story and paid me handsomely for work done that night in July 1952.

In June 1952, I graduated with a Bachelor of Arts degree in economics and decided to go out into the world and seek my fortune. The decision was easy to make, tough to implement. Jobs were still in short supply, and my support costs were higher than what the marketplace offered a recent graduate for a full-time job. But, on the other hand, I was deeply in love, Grace was still studying, and I thought it would be nice if I could stay at the university, keep close to Grace, study, and work. Moreover, the scholarship President Penrose had secured for me covered up to two years of graduate study. And the cooperative jobs were still available.

To make a long story short, I changed my mind, took the line of least resistance, and registered at the university for graduate studies in business as a student in economics, a path that was in line with my scholarship's terms. In addition to the minimum course requirements in the Department of Economics, I took all the courses then offered at the Business School, and thus I thought I would qualify for an MA or an MBA.

It took me two years plus two summers to complete the courses and write the dissertation. That was the era when getting through the American University of Beirut requirements for graduate work was a feat. We had more professors than students, and in one memorable seminar I was the only student, with two professors. I felt like my teachers were competing to make me suffer, and they could easily claim total success. I wrote my dissertation, which I wanted to title on a difficult subject that satisfied the requirements of the two faculties of business and economics. When I started my research for the dissertation, there were very few references available on my chosen subject; it took me a very long time to complete the dissertation. Originally, the subject, "the accounting treatment of intangibles," related mainly to intangible assets, which were difficult to define and for which the accounting treatment was therefore always debatable. To compound the problem, this subject, when completed, satisfied the business administration requirements but not those of the economics department. The long and short of this story is that I suggested tackling the problem by looking into "The Economic Significance of the Accounting Treatment of Intangibles", and that became the title of my thesis.

The big day for my master's defense arrived, and six professors sat on the podium to test my understanding of the subject while some students came to watch me suffer. The oral examination lasted for about seventy minutes.

Immediately on being dismissed from the examination room and before the panel decided on whether I had passed the exam, I went to Uncle Sam's, a café across the street from the university's main gate, to see Grace. Later, I learned that the supervisor of my thesis went around trying to find me to tell me the result, and it took him some time before he located me. I had passed the oral examination with flying colors—and why not? I knew more about this tricky subject than all the professors sitting on the podium combined. In October of 1954, I graduated with a master's degree in economics and immediately started to look for a job.

Our university days were full days. We had to work to get through, but we also participated in activities of the student body and the university. Grace was one year my junior in college. She graduated with an MA in sociology in June 1955, and we decided to get married. Grace's family wanted a prosperous man for a son-in-law, and in fact, they already had an Iraqi fellow in mind. Grace's mother looked down on me as a Palestinian refugee with many obligations who, she thought, was financially unprepared to give her daughter the life she deserves. Mothers are entitled to make this kind of demand. I visited my future mother-in-law in Mosul, though initially, my welcome was not what I expected. On the other hand, my own mother wanted me not to make a hasty decision to marry a Protestant, but my father was happy for me. He liked Grace very much and encouraged me to get married soon.

Job availabilities were still meager and offers ranged from accounting, to audit work in the Arabian Gulf, to part-time teaching in Beirut; salaries offered were way below my needs, and I could only turn the jobs down. So, I decided to become self-employed and moved to Amman, Jordan. I had some friends there; Amman is close to Beirut, where Grace was at AUB, my family lived in Hamra, and I could easily travel to see them all.

I set myself up in business, which I will explain later. I must say that my choice of Amman proved to be my best decision, the future looked promising, and life became rosier. I was a good worker and an ambitious one, but my success in Amman was also a stroke of luck. A new chapter in my life opened. I never expected Jordan to give me what it did. Several Jordanian families took me into their fold. My stay in Jordan, short as it was, completed my education and prepared me very well for what I would be involved in.

Jordan

BEGINNINGS IN AMMAN

Arriving in Amman, the first thing I did was to settle down in a hotel in the center of the city. The Sawalhas, a Christian family from the southern Jordan city of Madaba, owned the hotel I stayed in, and we got along very well. Permanent guests usually paid weekly for room and board, but the Sawalhas offered me a convenient and generous arrangement: I paid when I worked. The spirit of this verbal agreement was to pay when I could. So, I thought the conditions for my stay in the hotel were fair.

I had access to a sitting room in the hotel frequented by interesting and sometimes highly placed government officials or businessmen who met there to chat, and I was sometimes invited to join them. This was a good beginning to get to know locals and expand my list of contacts, which was a short one at that time.

Later, we discovered that the Sawalhas and my family are tribally related and that our families have one common tribal root in the south of Jordan. We all were Ghassasina, and because of this bond, the Sawalhas considered me family. As a result, my life became easier, and the month or two of unpaid rent because of my lack of income passed with no stressful incident. For all that the Sawalhas did, I am grateful.

Grace and I were married in Beirut in 1955, and we left for Amman shortly after. I could not afford to rent an apartment, so we decided to stay at the Amman Club Hotel, one of the two best hotels in the city.

The hotel was owned by the Mua'sher family, good people who took a liking to us, and assigned the best and only suite to us. We spent about five months there, and Sa'id Mua'sher refused our payment of the accumulated hotel bills. He even helped me financially later in life when political and other issues sent us out of Jordan. Sa'id Mua'sher came to Beirut after my ousting from Jordan, especially to give me a temporary loan to help us.

That loan remained unpaid as Sa'id refused to accept a repayment. The Mu'ashers were, by the standards of the day, a well-to-do and influential family. They originally come from Salt, a town about sixteen kilometers west of Amman, and they also were Christians.

GRACE, HOME, AND FRIENDSHIPS

Grace Saaty and I had decided it was time to start our family, make a home, and settle down. Grace was a beautiful and intelligent woman with bright, blue-green eyes and a joyful smile. We were married in Beirut at the Franciscan Church in Hamra Street on Sunday, December 4, 1955, and friends and family attended the wedding. We received congratulations in church and then left for our honeymoon at the Sheppard Hotel in Bhamdoun, a summer resort about twenty kilometers east of Beirut. While leaving the church, we got a telegraph message that David Saaty, Grace's nephew, was born that same day in London.

Our honeymoon was a short, three-day event. The budget for the honeymoon was not sufficient, so we decided to splurge frugally. Our hotel was very good, and expensive too. Our stay was enjoyable, and though the hotel was not full, the service was good. Bhamdoun is a summer resort, very busy during summer, but in the cold winters of the mountains, when we were there, few visitors arrived in the city or its hotels.

What we had in cash, we discovered, was not sufficient for our honeymoon. Early the following day, I traveled back to Beirut to borrow some money. I thought of one friend, a businessman whose son was my classmate at the International College. It was an awkward situation, but

Fares Dagher did not ask questions. I asked for 150 Lebanese pounds as a loan, and he gave me the money and told me to forget about it. It was a kind gesture which I hoped to return one day, and which years later I did.

Grace and I enjoyed the rest of our stay, paid the bill, and went back to Beirut. It was a memorable week, ending with a visit to my parents, and then we both proceeded to Amman, where I had already arranged for us to stay in the Amman Club Hotel. The Mua'shers reserved a suite for us, where we received friends who were all eager to meet Grace. Our hotel stay exceeded four months, and the owners and their families spoiled us. On occasion they sent us home-cooked food, which was always welcome and very good, especially as Grace was new at the skill of cooking.

The first apartment we rented in Jabal Amman was also convenient, as it was close to downtown and close to my office and my clients. Later, when I started to work for the Jordan Phosphate Mines Company, the apartment was also close to the company's main office. The life we settled into was active, pleasant, and rewarding. Grace got involved in social work and had a busy social life, as many of her friends from school and university were Jordanian, and the relationships continued uninterrupted. When we rented our first apartment, we were neighbors of Said Pasha Mufti, and Grace got to know his daughters.

She also spent time visiting Palestinian refugee camps in and around Amman, together with one of the most dedicated figures of the Palestine cause, Dr. Wadi' Haddad, who later became an internationally known activist. Other women also participated in this humanitarian work; the one Grace mentioned most was the wife of the German ambassador to Jordan, who worked closely with her.

Our apartment became a meeting place for some of the nicest people we knew then and throughout our life. Some were influential and made decisions of government or addressed political issues there. The Arab Nationalist weekly, al-Ra'i, the organ of the Arab Nationalist Movement, was a secretly published and frequently banned weekly newspaper, and the lead article was often written at our home. Grace acted as secretary to the writers' group. They included Hamad el-Farhan, George Habash,

Mohammad Touqan, and sometimes, but not always, Wasfi el-Tell, an occasional contributor. al-Ra'i has passed the test of time; now, about seventy-five years later, it is still published and maintains, according to the editorial staff, the same political and social outlook.

A year later, we moved to a larger apartment on the second floor of a two-story building on a narrow street in the First Circle in Jabal Amman. We had four neighbors: the Iraqi Embassy; the Saudi Embassy; Bahjat Talhouni, the prime minister; and the building owner, who was chairman of the oversight arm of the government. We lived there until I became persona non grata, at which juncture I had to look for a place to live and work outside Jordan.

Jordan, as I noted earlier, was still in its infancy, with no resources to speak of except phosphate, which was marginally exploited. The country's budget was humble and subsidized by Great Britain and the US. Amman, the capital, had a population of no more than 120,000, a large proportion of whom were Palestinian refugees who had fled Palestine during the 1947–1948 Arab-Israeli War.

From the day we moved to Amman to the day we had to leave the country, our time was one of our life's most interesting and challenging periods. I am grateful for what Jordan offered me and for what our Jordanian friends offered in friendship, kindness, and support. The government and the private sector entrusted me with some of their most intricate and important projects, which allowed me to build confidence in myself and my abilities. When Grace and I left Jordan late in 1958 and moved back to Beirut, I was again without a job for about nine months. The political issue with Jordan was not something to disregard, and so all my applications for work were turned down, stating that I was "overqualified."

Within a year, the political atmosphere in Jordan changed, and a good friend, Hazza' Pasha al-Majali, was appointed prime minister. On his first day as prime minister, he called me in Beirut and asked me to return to Amman immediately to see him, which was a good sign and a change from the status quo. What happened in that meeting is written in detail later in the story.

Hazzaa' al-Majali was born in Karak in 1917, the son of a sheikh of the Majali tribe. He studied law in Damascus. He was appointed by King Abdullah I as chairman of the Greater Amman municipality and then served as the minister of agriculture, twice as the minister of justice, and twice as the minister of the interior. He first served as prime minister in 1955, when King Hussein tried to join the Baghdad Pact, but quickly resigned following popular protests. He was reappointed as prime minister in 1959. He selected Wasfi el-Tell to be his public relations advisor during this term. Sadly, Hazzaa' was assassinated at his office on 29 August 1960.

ANECDOTES FROM JORDAN

I will recount anecdotes of events that I was fortunate to have experienced. Some were pleasant, others less so, but most were occurrences with an edge. One event, which did not seem of any importance, turned out to be an incredible moment in history for us.

THE DEAD SEA SCROLLS

This must be one of the most unusual experiences I ever had. One evening in 1956, Dr. Abdul-Karim Gharaybeh, the director of the Department of Antiquities in Jordan and a friend from university days in Beirut, came to our home in Amman carrying two large sacks of smelly, rolled parchments. He said that the Bedouin who had brought the sacks to him told him that he found them in jars in a cave in the hills east of the Dead Sea. The Bedouin gave his find to Abdul-Karim, who paid him one Jordan dinar for his effort, which was worth one pound sterling. It was a Thursday, the start of the weekend, and government offices were closed. Abdul-Karim asked if he could leave the sacks with us for safekeeping until Saturday, when the museum opened for the week. He told Grace that he didn't have anywhere else to store them and asked her to take care of them for a few days, when he would return and pick them up, and she accepted.

Abdul-Karim predicted that the parchments from the caves in Qumran might have some historical value, and that is why he wanted to keep them in our custody. The two sacks spent the weekend in our house waiting to be picked up and taken to the museum, but Abdul-Karim did not come for them. Their nasty smell permeated our small apartment. Grace decided to call Abdul-Karim and remind him to collect the parchments; otherwise, she told him, she would dispose of them, as they smelled bad.

It took more than one call for Abdul-Karim to come, but he did. He took these sacks to the museum in Amman, where they were kept in an underground storage area. When the specialists finally inspected the content, they knew that these were Dead Sea Scrolls!

The Jordanian antiquities department moved the scrolls to the museum in Jerusalem, where they waited for future study. Then, in 1967, the Israeli army occupied Jerusalem, museum, and all, and took whatever it contained. The news of the scrolls went public when they were cleaned and their value established.

SIR JOHN BAGOT GLUBB, ARAB LEGION GENERAL

Another anecdote has nothing to do with discovering history. It is important because of who was involved and why. It is an admirable example of the willingness of someone to adapt the habits and traditions of the society in which they live and be willing to pay the price when necessary to gain their admiration and loyalty. One such person was Glubb Pasha.

Lieutenant-General Sir John Bagot Glubb, KCB, CMG, DSO, OBE, MC, known as Glubb Pasha, was our neighbor in Amman. Though we never had the opportunity to visit him, we heard many stories about his relationships with his Bedouin friends.

He was the commander of the Transjordan Army, also known as the Arab Legion, from 1939 until 1956, when he was dismissed from his position by King Hussein. Before that, he was its deputy commander, and in this post, he spent years living with the Bedouins. He brought the Bedouins into the army and founded the Desert Patrol. He knew the Bedouins and their customs very well, and his book The Story of the Arab Legion shows his knowledge and the affection he held for them and they for him. Stories abound about his life in the early period of recruiting and staffing the Arab Legion.

General Ali Abou Nuwwar, a Bedouin himself, served under Lieutenant-General Glubb and knew how influential he was with the army. He told me that the general lived with the Bedouins and adopted their habits. At the start of his service, the Bedouins were not clean; water was scarce and generally not available in the desert, and bathing was not one of the daily activities of his soldiers. Some had lice in their hair and their clothes and would scratch all the time, and when someone caught a louse, he would kill it by squeezing it between two fingernails. Glubb Pasha did the same. He was never an outsider to them; he spoke the Arabic dialect they spoke, ate what they ate, and behaved the way they did. That relationship explains how he so easily but efficiently commanded the army.

REFLECTIONS ON MY EARLY YEARS

As I write the story of my life, I remember the abundance that life gave me, but it took from me plenty too. The past is the past, and one may think one should forget it. However, I believe that the past provides suitable lessons and may dampen future dreams, but to forget the past is not a good idea.

The Arab region has been troubled politically and socially since its inception. Political influences dictated much of what happened to me, my family, and others. Our choice did not frequently play a significant role. Like everybody of my generation, we lived the unique life experience of the early century, the hope and optimism after the end of World War II, and into the technological decades and advances that followed.

My business was most interesting, challenging, and satisfying. I lived well, and so did my family but much of my work was repeat work. Our clients kept us busy. When new job types came our way and required new and different approaches and techniques, our combined staff of English, French, Swedish, Americans, and Arabs worked together well. We and our associates sometimes used different methods to accomplish a job, and our cooperation helped us understand each other's different approaches, social needs, and constraints.

LIFE AND WORK IN JORDAN

My best bet in Jordan to start earning my keep and in the absence of a suitable job was to set up office as an accountant. I had some accounting qualifications and an MA in business and economics, which were in short supply in the area. I rented an office in downtown Amman and started looking for clients—and I very much needed a client, if only to feel that I was doing something. I borrowed money to buy furniture, employed an office boy to run errands, and started contacting the business community and government departments to sell my services. In a short period, I had my first client, the government of Jordan itself.

In the mid-1930s, maybe earlier, a company had formed to mine copper in the south of Jordan. It was a partnership between the public and private sectors. According to historic hearsay, copper had been extracted in those early times, and the company had retained its mining rights. The owners of the company, convinced that the rumors were believable, decided that costly feasibility and geological studies were therefore unnecessary. Even though traces of copper were present in the mine, the effort to begin to find the main lode or some worthwhile reserve met with no apparent success. The project teetered on financial failure, and the company's liquidation was the only realistic option. The government of Jordan appointed me as the company's liquidator. It was a great opportunity, one which laid the foundation for my Jordan career.

The relative ease by which I got my first job related primarily to the help, support, and recommendation of Hamad el-Farhan, the director general of the Ministry of Economy. We were close friends, and the relationship continued for several decades, until he passed away some fifty years later. He was an Arab Nationalist with charisma and courage and was prominent throughout the Middle East. He had substantial political clout and influence, especially in Jordan.

Hamad el-Farhan was born in al-Naima in 1921. He completed his schooling in Jordan. He received a scholarship to study physics at the AUB, where he graduated in 1941, and took jobs as a teacher in several schools in Irbid, Salt, and Amman. In 1944, he studied economics in London. He worked in Jordan's Ministry of Works and the Ministry of Education, was appointed secretary of the Council of Ministers. In 1955 he was offered the position of deputy minister of economy, which he refused because he had not been consulted about his appointment. In 1958, he established the Arab Shipping Company, of which he was general manager. Hamad's plans and perseverance helped Jordan achieve progress in industry, in mining potash and phosphate, and in infrastructure planning.

Another close friend who helped advance my career was Mohammad Touqan, mayor of the City of Amman. Mohammad came from a wealthy and influential Palestinian family originally from the ancient city of Nablus. Some of his family had established homes in Salt, northwest of Amman, so they settled in Jordan before the First World War. Our friendship was to last until he passed away in the early 1980s. Mohammad was a gentle and generous person, liked and respected by all those who knew him. Later, when I got my job with the phosphate company, he became mayor of Amman.

I was very young when I arrived in Amman, twenty-five years old, and all my relations, social or work, were with older men; I got along very well with them and formed lifelong friendships. Grace's arrival in Jordan changed my life. We became a favorite couple, socially sought in Amman and elsewhere in Jordan. We established very close family relations in Jordan and Palestine, which made life more enjoyable and more meaningful. Work started coming my way, and it covered a wide field and needed multiple skills, some of which I did not possess; every job I got or worked on was new to me, starting with the Copper Mining Company.

The Jordan Phosphate Mines Company

A SHORT HISTORY OF THE COMPANY

The Jordan phosphate mines company, a shareholder-owned company, was granted in 1953 a concession to mine phosphate rock permanently and exclusively in all the Hashemite Kingdom of Jordan.

Amin Kawar, a pharmacist and avid geologist, first established JPMC in 1935 following his rediscovery of phosphate in the railway cuttings near the town of Rusaifa. His discovery led to the establishment of the Trans-Jordan Phosphate Company, which by 1939 was exporting to the outside world through the Port of Haifa. Exports were suspended during World War II. After the 1948 Arab-Israeli War, phosphate was exported via Beirut and eventually to Aqaba.

Operations were started by the concessionaire, Amin Kawar, who produced small quantities of the raw material to sell abroad. The cost of exploration was more than Kawar could afford. Nevertheless, he tried hard, and at its apex in 1955, when I took over its management, the company produced thirty thousand tons of raw ore a year. At the market price then prevailing, the project was at best marginal. The losses incurred were not substantial, but the company could not afford to expand its capital base and continue without guidance and possible public help. New and sizable investments could have made the project feasible; however, such assets were unavailable from private sources or from banks. Venture capital, new to the banking system, did not exist in Jordan. The banking community was in its infancy, and large sums of money were for company, at best, a dream.

The only other source of financing was the public sector. Though also in its infancy, this sector was eager to develop the country and find sources of income to finance its own needs. Jordan was politically dependent on the support of its former Mandatory power of Great Britain and had to live within the financial constraints.

The phosphate reserves were the main natural resource in Jordan. Mining phosphate was viewed as a solution to create income, by exporting a raw material in demand worldwide. It would create jobs outside the mining industry, and secondary services would sprout all over the areas where mines were active. The roads along which trucks loaded with phosphate would travel, from the mines to the ports of export in Aqaba and Beirut, would also provide an opportunity to set up facilities to service the flow of transported minerals. Thus, the whole country would benefit from new industries and services. This dream required a feasibility study to judge the degree of success it might attain, which the government, through the Ministry of Economy, ordered. The project was judged feasible and therefore accepted.

CONSULTING FOR JPMC, 1954–1955

My appointment as consultant to the Jordan Phosphate Mines Company deserves special mention, as it impacted my life in no uncertain way. I had other clients, including the municipality of Amman, the Potash Mining Company (organized to produce potash from the waters of the Dead Sea), the Jordan Electricity Company serving the city of Amman and suburbs, and the legendary Hejaz Railway. All my jobs, both in the private and government sectors, were in the management field and not in the accounting or audit fields for which I had set up business in Amman, and I had no reasons to complain.

When I worked at JPMC, it was the only substantial exporter of local products. So, to enhance the company's abilities, increase its production, and generate jobs, the government never denied the company any request.

The national transportation infrastructure that JPMC needed to move phosphate from its mines to the ports required the building of a road from Amman to Aqaba. The existing route could not handle substantial traffic; it was narrow and not all asphalted, and to rebuild or upgrade would have required a lot of money which the government could not provide. It took time until the International Bank for Reconstruction and Development provided the financing, and the road was completed just when the need to transport the raw materials became apparent.

When traffic along this road increased, small industries, shops, secondary service industries, and production centers appeared, to service the traffic from Amman south to Ras el-Naqab and, later, to Aqaba. Soon, small villages sprouted along the newly constructed road to make use of the new opportunities the route provided. In the case of Aqaba, it grew from a small fishing village to a major Red Sea port and later into a bustling business and tourist center. It took many decades to grow to what it is today, but life in the town started changing when phosphate mining grew into a significant industry.

I needed the support and cooperation of the government to approve the construction of roadways and to make improvements to the railway equipment and tracks. Such upgrades were necessary for the development of the industry. I was for a long time the one who came up with ideas. I always discussed them with friends in government and the private sector and created an atmosphere of acceptance and support through hard work. However, work was not always pleasant, as political and tribal resistance to the company always caused complications. JPMC's property and mines covered a large area near the town of Rusaifa, north of Amman, and negatively affected the lives of its residents. Mining dry phosphate produced a lot of dust, and on windy days the air was full of this dust and pollutants.

The desert area through which the Hejaz Railway, and hence the phosphate, travels is government land, and all lands east of the railway tracks were assigned to Bedouin tribes or clans to use freely for their lifestyle needs. The authoritative figures in Bedouin communities are the tribal sheikhs and princes. As the phosphate mines were in proximity to these areas, a tribal intervention was always there. The Bedouins complained about the dust and polluted air to which they were constantly subjected. They were neither aggressive nor too demanding, yet they persevered in their demands for employment priority over villagers closer to the mines. When Bedouin sheikhs visited to talk about individuals, they wanted us to employ, they made their visits long. As they talked and sipped coffee, they enjoyed the office atmosphere and the attention. As a result, it was not easy to terminate their visits.

In most cases, I had Bedouin assistants to receive them. However, visiting sheikhs insisted on seeing the boss, and they expected that I would receive them personally. I handled most of these demands well, but it was time consuming, and on occasion I had to ask the government to send support to do some of the talking and negotiating. Thankfully, the government response was primarily positive.

JPMC was, outside the oil industry, probably the biggest employer in the Middle East region and in Jordan was second only to the government. Today, JPMC is a large company producing over seven million tons of phosphate a year, as well as fertilizers for the local and export markets. I was, in a sense, lucky when I started work in Jordan, and as I said earlier, my efforts were fairly rewarded. The most important contribution of all this success and consequent social exposure was that it helped me further build my confidence in myself and prepared me for a more challenging career in the Middle East, mainly in the Gulf States and Saudi Arabia. I happened to go to the Gulf when oil started gushing, and international companies had plans and dreams to get their "fair share" of the developing markets. The pace of development was dizzying.

This feasibility depended on the quality of management to take over and the availability of the necessary financial resources. As a job-creating entity, it opened many new avenues. This resource, phosphate, was a national wealth; the government also deemed it worth exploring. The fact is, a detailed feasibility study was superfluous. The ore was there and could be anywhere south of Amman, the capital of Jordan, and the world needed phosphate to produce fertilizers. What was needed was to define and set up a sufficient organization, estimate and provide the investment required, write the necessary production targets, and use the country's engineers to prepare a detailed list of the equipment requirements for every year included in a five-year plan.

I participated in the study and the recommendations made. One million dinars was the estimated capital requirement in 1955; the government approved the investment and funds were reserved for the project. We planned the capital to become available in four installments, with the first available at the front end. The only proviso set by the government was to reorganize JPMC, to upgrade its management to the level needed to run the expanded project efficiently. I wrote the section of the plan about management, but I spent most of my time moderating and interfacing between government departments and private investors until the project was approved and funds reserved.

Over time, the company issued one million common shares, each with a face value of one dinar. Both government and private investors participated. The government became the majority owner and, therefore, the single decision-maker. A Jordan dinar at the time was equal to a pound sterling or about US$4.50. The board of directors tasked to oversee JPMC consisted of twelve men, ten of whom were elected in a general assembly of the shareholders meeting and two members of ministerial level, representing the government, appointed by the Council of Ministers. I suggested that we should not let government officials run the company but rely on businesspersons who possessed both the experience and the motives to run it efficiently. We gave the private sector this opportunity, and it succeeded. When I took over, I made good use of the directors' time and knowledge, and they were happy that I recognized their abilities and therefore, initially, cooperated fully. That interface gave me a lot of knowledge, and that is where I learned my first real lesson in management.

The Ministry of Economy, which worked on and promoted this project, selected me to reorganize JPMC. Being selected was a pleasant surprise, but it carried a level of challenges that gave me sleepless nights. It was my first significant job, and in a field way out of my knowledge or interest area. The company's original owners, Amin Kawar,

Mohammad Ali Bdeir, Abdul Rahman Abu Hassan, Aboulwafa Dajani, Jawdat Sha'sha'a, and others, were respected business leaders who were happy to guide me. They also oversaw the project in its new upgraded role and plans, and they remained directors throughout my tenure. They welcomed my appointment, even though I was very young to be entrusted with such a significant project, the likes of which was not seen in Jordan before. They later terminated my appointment when they had to accept political intervention.

In my search for information, I found that the company did not even keep good books of accounts, let alone cost-accounting records or production control methods. However, as I started reporting to the board and the ministry about what I found and intended to do, I found both government and private sides to be encouraging and supportive. The board continued to receive the detailed information, as in the past, plus new, relevant, and more detailed information. The government was pleased as the plan was taking shape, and when I needed intervention, they promptly intervened and facilitated my work.

I discovered internal jealousies and differences between the original owners and those appointed afterward. However, everybody found in me a willing listener and poured their stories into my ears. The knowledge I gained about the internal strife, differences of opinion and sometimes outlook, and knowledge of some details about the company's management not shared among board members gave me a decisive edge. Consequently, I found that I could easily make decisions and get approvals from the board.

I learned how to write my requests so that I left room for maneuver, and nobody objected. Hamad el-Farhan, director of the Ministry of Economy was the person who decided to have a feasibility study of the needs of JPMC conducted, so that the company could continue and progress and have the means to do so. He was the man who initially recommended me to manage the company and its resources to achieve the goals that were approved.

Six months later, I found myself in a position where I knew more about the company, its problems, needs, internal conflict, and personal interests than anybody else. I knew who was benefiting from what and in what way. I instituted the necessary regulations to encourage transparency. I did get government support, sometimes from the highest of levels. In most cases, the approval by government representatives on the board was sufficient. Understandably, some board members became more careful and less cooperative.

TERMINATION OF SERVICES OF THE FINANCIAL OFFICER OF JPMC

The manager of the Industrial Bank in Amman, whom I will refer to as N.I., retired late in 1955. As passed on to me by a member of the JPMC board of directors, his reputation as a manager was outstanding, and I offered him the job of chief financial officer. This offer was welcomed by many but, most importantly, by the board. N. accepted the offer, and we agreed on a procedure for him to reorganize the accounting department and later spend more of his time helping me with the company's finances and its financial control and oversight. We spent hours going over his job description and the accounting charts and systems I devised. It took us over six months to get that department functioning satisfactorily.

The accounting methods used by traders and service industry were financial accounts to show the bottom line. In the JPMC case, the introduction of a cost-accounting system was essential. For example, we did not know what a ton of phosphate cost to extract, dry, clean, and transport to Beirut or Aqaba for eventual loading on vessels we chartered. We used to divide the total company costs by the tonnage produced to establish the cost per unit. I was eager to know in the minutest detail the cost of production by every mining area and the relative costs FOB (free on board) for Beirut and Aqaba, so we would be able to optimize our mining plans and the ports of export. That done, I could do a better job to support the case to develop the Aqaba port which, even in the collected cost figures before upgrading the accounting system, was more advantageous to JPMC.

Everything went well until one day I allowed for payment of a minimal amount of money to a charity. Having been in a meeting, I wrote my financial chief a note to pay the money. A few minutes later, I received my message back with N"s handwritten remark telling me he was not authorized to make the payment. I wrote back to say that I allowed him to make the payment, and he sent me a negative reply, so I fired him on the spot. I suspected that the decision would create some problems, but discipline was prime in my mind at this stage. I thought this action would be a lesson to all and that even this high an officer was not above the company's discipline and rules. I never expected this to become a focal point in the administration of the company.

There were immediate repercussions, some of which I expected and some I did not. I received calls from the chairman and members of the board saying that I could not fire such a high official and a well-known individual. To make a long story short, the board quickly convened and called me to the meeting. The chairman advised me of my limited authority and said I should rescind my order. I refused. They said that I was not authorized to fire him. I suggested they read my employment contract before they talk about the extent of my authority. Seeing that I was unwilling to negotiate, the chairman of the board took me aside and said, "Do you know who this man is?" I said that I was sure I knew who he was; he was the man I had appointed to a job and fired that day. Then, I was politely advised that he was the brother-in-law of Tewfik Pasha Abul Huda, the prime minister of Jordan.

I knew this fact very well, but that was an argument I did not accept as a good reason to rescind my decision. In no vague terms, I told the board that they should think of the company's welfare and not their own. I suggested they should start looking for my replacement if they insisted on their request. I then submitted my resignation verbally and told them I would put it in writing immediately. I left the boardroom straight to my office and dictated my resignation, spelling out the reasons for this decision. My office manager took it to the board and soon returned it, saying that the resignation was not accepted.

An impasse it was, for sure. I volunteered to tell the board that they should support me, and that the company's welfare should be our only guiding principle. If they felt the prime minister would take issue with this decision, then the board had to put the prime minister in the know. The board refused the resignation, on the condition I resolve the matter within forty-eight hours.

I had two options: either insist on my resignation or find a solution. I decided to go directly to the prime minister and tell him what happened, and I did. He listened to my story, and before I gave him the name of the person I had fired, he said, "Why do you come to me with this story? You are running the show for Jordan, and if I were you, I would terminate his services; we cannot play games with discipline." He continued, "If you do not take such an action, I will ask the board to terminate your services."

He told me that he knew and was aware of my appointment to the phosphate job. He hoped that I would prove to be strict but fair and lead JPMC into new horizons. I thanked him and told him that I had fired his brother-in-law, to which he replied: "I thought you knew me better; the person does not make any difference. Good luck and tell your board not to consider people's feelings when entrusted with the country's interests and future." I had a field day reporting back to the board of directors, and in fact, they were happy with the outcome.

I do remember, with respect, that after my termination of his post, N.I. did not try to create problems for me; in fact, he continued to communicate with me and on occasion he and his wife came visiting and were pleasant and the subject of my decision was never brought up. This outcome really boosted my morale and gave me faith in human judgment.

In an unconnected, sad event, Tewfik Pasha, the prime minister, was found not much later hanging by the neck from his bedroom window. Nobody knows whether he committed suicide, as the official story goes, or whether a crime was committed at the highest levels of government.

He was a well-educated, well-connected, efficient administrator who served the monarchy for over two decades. I cannot say he was loved by the Jordanians, but he was respected for his honesty. His influence was seen by the Hashemites as a threat to their continued control of the country and so he had to be eliminated.

APPOINTMENT AS GENERAL MANAGER AT JPMC, 1956–1958

The completion of my consulting work was when the government appointed me to run JPMC. I then managed the most significant single private sector entity in Jordan. Because the government wanted a new and clean start, it terminated the services of every employee on the high managerial levels one day before I took over. The clean slate meant that I would run the company with no benefit of experienced help. It was a challenging job, and for some days, I wondered whether I would be able to function correctly. The official job titles I assumed were the best way to explain the difficulties I faced and had to overcome. I was general manager of the company and acting manager of every single department. As I remember now, the acting manager title covered local purchasing, international sales, land transportation, ports, shipping, accounting, mines, personnel and industrial relations, government relations, international relations, and undoubtedly other jobs that I have forgotten because of the passage of time. It took two years to fill all the managerial positions I assumed temporarily.

It was a learning period par excellence, significantly so when the other ex officio informal consulting (e.g., potash company, railway tracks manager) and positions I held outside my jobs in JPMC were added to my expected functions. For the first few weeks I was overwhelmed, not only because of the range of job functions I needed to perform, which were primarily alien to me, but also because of the unfriendly attitudes of those who had lost their jobs. The feedback was simple: they were waiting for me to blunder or, better, to fail. All those managers came from influential local families, and it was wise not to show any hostility to any of them.

The work routine started early morning in the Rusaifa mines and as early as 8 a.m. in the office. It involved endless and relentless meetings with government officials discussing the economic progress of the country and the role of phosphate in it, board directorships that came with the job like the potash company, the Hejaz Railway, and more. I traveled inside Jordan when roads were terrible and going south to Aqaba on desert roads meant I had to travel for more than ten hours each way—another strain on my schedule. Once I lost my way and had to wait for hours before getting help from a passing Jordanian camel company, an army unit called al-Hajjana. All this was the kind of a challenge that I vigorously pursued, and I was always determined to succeed. My appointment as general manager of the Jordan Phosphate Mines Company had come as no surprise. The board was already well established, and I had a reputation as a hardworking and efficient young individual with leadership qualities.

I was pleasantly surprised when within a week of being offered the phosphate job, I got another offer from the World Bank in Washington, DC, to be in charge of the Jordan, Syria, and Lebanon desks, which were lumped together as one. I found myself in a dilemma; how could one choose between these two spectacular prospects and offers?

I must say I deliberated for what seemed to be a long time about the pros and cons of both possibilities, but the pros and cons of each were challenging to establish and difficult to compare. At last, I decided to stay in Jordan and remain in the job in which I was already involved. The phosphate offer was generous and socially desirable. It also kept me in the proximity of my family in Beirut. The government of Jordan was then in the process of acquiring JPMC. My job put me again in direct contact with the highest governmental authorities.

The undeclared policy of the government at the time was to acquire faltering companies, organize them properly, participate in planning their growth, collaborate with private investors, and facilitate capital funding. When such companies became profitable and stable, the government sold them back to the private sector. Jordan was still in its economic infancy, and this policy proved to be a success. I am proud to say that I participated in making this policy and actively participated in its implementation. I am sure it was a unique approach to development, especially when resources were scarce, investment capital nonexistent, and any decision to invest risky.

Jordan had no experience in anything beyond the ordinary. Being a newly formed state and poor in resources, it needed everything— food, medicine, medical services, education, public services, roads, water, and basic infrastructure. The needs had to be prioritized, and government intervention was welcomed by the private sector, which saw this public support when banks and other institutions did not provide a blessing. These hard circumstances and lessons changed the country's attitudes and especially encouraged the private sector to invest in the banking sector.

The most potent business grouping in Jordan, referred to as the "Tuesday gathering," met weekly in total secrecy in one of the member's houses over dinner to consider the economic and business developments planned for Jordan. The eight members constituting this gathering were Yaseen Talhouni, Mohammed Ali Bdeir, Abdul Rahman Abu Hassan, Mohammed Madi, Jawdat Sha'sha'a, Farid el-Saad, Ibrahim Mango, and Toufiq Pasha Qattan. I happened to know about the gathering—but not its regularity or purpose—because all its members either were on the JPMC board of directors or had direct business with JPMC or one of the companies for which I consulted. This gathering must have been the nerve center for the private business sector and must have influenced some government decisions. Later in life, when I learned more about this Tuesday gathering, I wondered whether the support I got from the private sector had been recommended or approved by its members.

CANDIDATES FOR MAJOR POSITIONS AT JPMC

Dr. George Habash was an activist politician and a recognized leader of the Arab Nationalist Movement in the Arab world. He resided in Jordan after graduation as a medical doctor from AUB and worked together with Dr. Wadi' Haddad, who was also an activist. They set up a clinic in downtown Amman and had their sleeping quarters in the clinic. Both were unmarried, and both were outstanding doctors.

For about two years, Grace participated with Wadi' Haddad in humanitarian work in the Palestinian refugee camps. They brought food, clothing, and medicine to those in need. The group of volunteers grew over the time period. Due to their political involvement and the flow of people coming from other countries to discuss political issues and ask for advice and sources of support, George and Wadi' had little time to see patients who could pay for services, and therefore they were very short of money. Hamad el- Farhan, another leader of the Arab Nationalist Movement in Jordan was undersecretary of the Ministry of the Economy. He called me one day and suggested that JPMC hire George Habash as the physician at the mines to attend to the laborers in Rusaifa, a town just north of Amman. Hamad wanted to provide George, with a source of income. George was not popular with the establishment, nor was I able to terminate the services of Dr. Mustapha Khalifa, the mine's physician who had held the job since before the formation of the new JPMC. Dr. Khalifa also happened to be the president of the Jordan Senate and therefore quite a powerful man. It was a tricky issue, to sneak George into this job.

I decided to call Dr. Khalifa at his office at the mines, to meet with him and try to find a solution. He came to my office and was curious to know why I had called the meeting. I told him that I wanted to appoint Dr. George Habash as the mine's medical doctor and asked if he would be willing to act as an adviser to the company's management on health issues. I offered him the job at a higher monthly salary than the one he had been receiving. He accepted, saying he appreciated my offer, which he felt showed my appreciation for his long service to the company. I then called George and gave him his letter of appointment, and he was happy too. He stayed with the company for about six months, and then politics started to play a violent role in his life and the lives of others.

Wasfi el-Tell, at the time, was assistant director of the Income Tax Department in Amman; his monthly salary was about thirty-eight Jordan dinars. JPMC needed a mines manager, and with the approval of Hamad el-Farhan, I suggested Wasfi for the job. He was well educated, with a degree in physics from the AUB. He had been an officer in the British Army during World War II and later a colonel in the Palestine Liberation Army. He was fit, and he looked aggressive. And at the age of thirty-eight, a Jordanian with Bedouin roots and an army career, he was used to maintaining discipline. In Jordan he was well-known and, all in all, the right man for the job. The board did not decide that day; I thought they had referred the matter to some higher authority, maybe the prime minister. When the board convened a week later, they told me to look for another candidate. Later, when Wasfi became prime minister, some members of the board of directors told me that they had not consulted anyone regarding his employment; they had decided they did not want to have such an aggressive personality around.

Wasfi was born in 1919. He served as the fifteenth prime minister of Jordan for three separate terms between 1962 and 1970, until his assassination in 1971. He was born in Turkey to the prominent Jordanian poet Mustafa Wahbi el-Tell, and the family moved to Jordan a few years later. He graduated from the AUB in 1941. He then joined the British Army in Mandatory Palestine after being trained in a British-run military academy and joined the irregular. Arab Liberation Army to fight against Israel during the 1948 Arab Israeli War. He served in various positions in the Jordanian government, rising to higher positions after his abilities captured King Hussein's attention.

KING HUSSEIN'S SPECIAL VISIT TO RUSAIFA MINES

One early morning in the spring of 1957, I met with mining engineers and some mines management chaps in Rusaifa to plan new production goals. I had already signed a contract with Jugometal, a major Yugoslav mining company, to train our engineers in using explosives and other mining techniques. Dynamite would replace manual digging which, besides being laborious and slow, was very bad for the laborers' health. The cost to us of this arrangement was attractive; compared with other non-communist European engineers, the price was way lower, and it was just marginally higher than salaries we paid to our local staff. The individuals seconded by Jugometal were enjoyable, efficient, and in no time, they struck up friendships with our local teams. They continued working with JPMC for a long time after I lost my job with the company.

When the agreement between the JMPC and Jugometal was made public, the BBC reported on it. The story was that I had signed a contract with Yugoslavia, a communist country, in preference to other European or more qualified providers. The BBC did not mention that a private business entity (JPMC) signed the agreement with a capable mining and engineering company that just happened to be operating out of a communist country. The relevant governments controlled each of the two companies.

My father happened to be listening to the BBC Arabic broadcasting service, and he heard the news and my name mentioned. He was a happy and proud father. The fact is that he was very happy to know from a source like the BBC that one of his children succeeded in surmounting the many years of worry that had impacted the family, which to him was enough compensation for the difficult times in his life.

On April 17, 1957, there were violent confrontations at the large army barracks in Zarqa north of Amman between royalist, mostly Bedouin, units loyal to King Hussein and Nasserist Arab Nationalist units. On that day, something went wrong in one of the tunnels under the main road connecting Zarqa and Amman. We did not know about the confrontations when we were in the mines. On that day, King Hussein traveled to Zarqa using the Amman-Rusaifa-Zarqa road, which passed over many of the JPMC's tunnels. The king's trip was unknown to us, and he was to meet with his generals.

At about 7 a.m., one of the Rusaifa mines' military guards came running from the road, breathless, saying that the king (usually referred to as *sayyidna*) was walking down the dirt road to our offices. We all went out to meet him and expressed both pleasure and surprise about this unexpected honor. He was pleasant and asked if we had coffee to offer, which we had, and he asked about our plans and chatted. Unfortunately, he did not mention anything about the confrontation in Zarqa, and like everybody in the country, we learned about the details from radio bulletins. His visit to the Rusaifa mines was not in the news; they were never published.

When he started to leave, he asked me to lend him some tough guys to help him lift his car out of a trench in which it was stuck on the main road. One of the tunnels under the street had collapsed while our employees were practicing using explosives in the mines. We realized that while dynamiting under the road, something had gone wrong and caused the road to collapse. Later, the road sank even lower than when the king's car had passed over it in the morning. We were aghast but he said to everybody, "Keep up the good work and do not make similar mistakes in the future." He never mentioned this incident with the car privately or publicly or on the day when it happened.

During my official term of service, which ended abruptly after three years, the production of phosphate increased manyfold. Then, in February of 1956, my father passed away. I wanted to see him, talk to him, and make him feel happy that he did not have to worry about money matters, a wish that left me with regret that I had failed to visit more often. Maybe I should not hesitate to admit that, when sick and moneyless, my father had to be satisfied to eat bread dipped in water. We could not afford more.

THE MONARCHY IN JORDAN

In Jordan, King Hussein was the monarch who began his political life while accompanying his grandfather King Abdullah when he was assassinated in Jerusalem in 1952. Hussein's father, King Talal, was forced to abdicate in favor of his son Hussein due to health reasons (reported as schizophrenia) on August 11, 1952. His cousin in Iraq was overthrown in a coup immediately after Iraq and Jordan formed the Arab Union in defense against the United Arab Republic formed by Egypt and Syria in 1957.

King Hussein's family ruled the Hejaz for centuries as descendants of the Prophet Muhammad but were ousted in the early 1920s by the Saudi dynasty. His great-grandfather Sharif Hussein of Mecca declared war against the Ottomans after an agreement between him and Great Britain. known as the Hussein-McMahon Correspondence. The Hashemites would replace the Ottoman rulers in the Arab countries. As mentioned earlier, this agreement later was not honored by Britain.

King Hussein's uncle, Faisal, was declared king of Syria at the end of the First World War, only to be ousted by the French in less than a year, and later he was moved to Baghdad, where he was declared king of Iraq! This family lived in suspended tension for at least the period between the two wars. The Middle East continued to be a dangerous area for the various regimes, and King Hussein had to stay the course that in his mind gave him safety. It was not an easy life for him or his subjects, who had to live under very strict political rules for decades. He died a natural death in February 1999 after ruling as monarch for forty-seven years. He was succeeded by his son, Abdullah II.

The Road to Aqaba

I traveled inside Jordan many times with mining engineers to plan for explorations of the mineral deposits. I traveled with experts on jobs and internationally, to meet with the financing bodies and the like. I struck an arrangement with the Jordan Air Force to lease planes for our travel from Amman to Aqaba, thus avoiding the time-consuming land transport on desert roads. In addition, Jordan railways allowed me to use a special train to travel in the areas north of Ras el-Naqab, which was then JPMC's southernmost phosphate storage terminal.

The phosphate was unloaded at Ras el-Naqab onto an open area, where it was reloaded onto trucks. These trucks transported the cargo down the cliff, using a winding and treacherous road that led them to bottom. From here, they proceeded down the British-constructed road to the Port of Aqaba, where the phosphate was loaded onto ships for export. The 88-kilometer trip from Ras el-Naqab to Aqaba took the drivers a full day to navigate.

Later, we moved the storage terminal to Aqaba on the Red Sea. In the meantime, we loaded phosphate on vessels anchored some distance out at sea. Phosphate was deposited in sacks, loaded onto small boats alongside the anchored freighters, and then manually loaded on board to empty into the freighter's storage compartments. We reused the sacks a few times before replacing them. The process was painfully slow, inefficient, and costly; we lost over 10 percent of the total exports to the sea.

Clearly, a port needed to be built, and we dreamed a lot about building one. In 1952, by royal decree, the Aqaba Port Authority was established, and ancillary facilities were added to the port. We participated in designing the building dedicated for storage and loading of raw material onto vessels for JPMC. I spent considerable time with Zublin AG and other consultants to ensure we got our fair share of the project we had initiated.

In order to transport the phosphate from Rusaifa to Aqaba, a rail line was also needed. Since the mines were immediately beside the Hejaz Railway lines, a plan was put in place to transport the cargo south using the existing rail lines, which were constructed in 1942 ending at the edge of the escarpment. Here, the town of Ras el-Naqab and the rail station came into existence. This station was soon heavily used for other goods, and passengers also started arriving.

Together with the board of directors of the Jordan railway, I participated in the reorganization and operational strategy of the Hejaz Railway within Jordan. The railway served Jordan's new transportation needs, mainly the transport of phosphate and industrial and agricultural products. A port at Aqaba and the railway were to be built to serve this purpose.

Many years later, both the railroad and the road were completed. The port is an important transit point for the export of phosphate, fruits, vegetables, and other agricultural products. Some of the produce comes from the fertile Jordan Valley, which lies between 100 and 400 meters below sea level, allowing all kinds of farm products to be ripe, outside the normal season, for export at higher prices.

All aspects of production, transportation and handling in the port were successful. However, exploration for more phosphate deposits was successful in finding major deposits northeast of the Aqaba area, rendering all that was built in roads, railroads, and ancillary services of no use to phosphate transport, but it did provide Jordan with the necessary infrastructure.

In the meantime, I needed to travel on business to Europe. The Yugoslav government invited Grace and me to spend a month in

Yugoslavia. So we did, leaving our daughter Rania with my mother and aunts in Beirut. We were entertained and visited many exciting areas in the country. Of course, we enjoyed all the sites, but outstanding in my mind is the time we stayed in the town of Bled (today in Slovenia) in the foothills of the Alps. The view of the beautiful lake is unequaled. We also spent time in the southern part of the country and on the shores of the Adriatic Sea. At the end of this trip, we were given an album tracing our travels during the visit and two artist-signed oil paintings.

The job kept me busy but most importantly, it kept me busy learning about skills that had never occurred to me, that I had not heard about or learned about until then. The scope of work and the fields it covered were fascinating and prepared me for the consulting work I had to start later.

THE INTERNATIONAL BANK FOR RECONSTRUCTION AND DEVELOPMENT

Sometime in 1957, the International Bank for Reconstruction and Development (IBRD) sent a delegation, at my request, to survey the financial and operational needs of JPMC. The primary and most crucial issue was the transportation of raw phosphate from the mines to the ports of Beirut and Aqaba. Aqaba was the natural port for Jordan, though the Jordanian front on the Red Sea at the time was very short. The core of the study was how to build the port and its ancillary facilities and prepare it to handle exports, and Jordan's sizable imports.

During the First World War, Aqaba was a strategic fortified Turkish outpost. It was bombarded by the British and French navies and captured by Arab irregulars led by T. E. Lawrence in July 1917. After the war, the status of Aqaba was in dispute; Britain claimed an outlet on the Gulf of Aqaba for its newly created protectorate of Transjordan (technically, part of the Palestine mandate), while the Kingdom of Hejaz (later Saudi Arabia) based a counterclaim to the town and regions to the north, on the former political subdivisions of the Ottoman Empire.

When King Abdul-Aziz conquered the Hejaz in 1925, the British placed Aqaba and the Ma'an district under Transjordanian authority;

this de facto situation continued when Jordan became fully independent in 1946. Saudi Arabia had never agreed to these frontiers, which were a matter of dispute until 1965. A boundary agreement between the two states was signed, giving to Saudi Arabia desert territories in the interior that were formerly part of Jordan; in return, the Saudis officially recognized Aqaba as part of Jordan and gave Jordan additional frontage on the Gulf of Aqaba and now it is twenty six kilometers.

Anecdotally, King Hussein personally asked King Sa'ud for the frontage and was given it, as a neighborly gesture, in return for desert land. Thus, Jordan now has a sufficient coastline for its needs.

Using the Aqaba port as the primary point for export was preferable to transporting the cargo by road to the Port of Beirut, which necessitated crossing two international borders, and possible political conflicts in inter-Arab relations. Syria was always a source of problems in transit issues.

The railway connecting the Rusaifa mines, on the northeast outskirts of Amman, to Ras el-Naqab some 243 kilometers to the south was the means of transport that we planned to study as a priority. The cost of transport by rail was substantially lower than by road. In fact, there were no roads yet when the study was underway. The section between Ras el-Naqab and Aqaba and Mecca had been destroyed during the First World War, and we dreamed it would be rebuilt.

All in all, we found we had to deal with three separate issues: the lack of roads from the north to the south of Jordan, a narrow-gauge railroad that connected the north to Ras el-Naqab but not to Aqaba, and a port that was still an idea. At the time, as mentioned earlier, the seafront was used in a primitive way, with a loss of about 10 percent of the loaded phosphate to the sea.

Every one of these problems was to be somehow managed using Jordan's local resources and capabilities with some help from IBRD. However, the mere presence of the International Bank and the way the members analyzed the situation and suggested possibilities that we had never thought of or had not been available before was enlightening.

One option was to extend the railway from Ras el-Naqab to Aqaba, which faced a topography that made it difficult to achieve. Ras el-Naqab is an escarpment at 900 meters elevation, and the descent to sea level was steep This was to become a two-tier study: the first and most urgent part covered the improvement of the present and already existent railway; the second required a specialist approach to the topographical problem south of Ras el-Naqab. Therefore, we recommended to the board and IBRD that we engage a consultant who could help us find a solution to this problem.

The IBRD representatives and I decided to make a quick survey of the needs of the present railway and ways to expeditiously improve its performance. We proceeded to examine the current line and visit the various train stations between Amman and Ras el-Naqab. During our visits to the stations, we discovered in one of the stations near the Ras el-Naqab terminal two locomotives only three years old, in mint condition, clean, and ready to roll. They had never been used and somehow, they were not on the books of the railway company. As a result, our project needed less financing, and I convinced the IBRD delegation not to report this significant oversight. If I remember well, the railway got its loan and started the long process of modernizing.

It is interesting to note that the railway and JPMC met in Amman prior to the completion of the survey. They discussed how it should be conducted but agreed that the railroad needed three additional locomotives, each costing about $750,000. I participated in writing the application based on the official records of the railway books and documents. IBRD agreed to provide long-term soft loans and help in the introduction and implementation of operational systems as well as staff training. When the facts changed to include the existence of the three brand-new locomotives, our financial needs became smaller, and the IBRD representative was accommodating. The option of building roads from Amman to Aqaba was not discussed because it was not part of the negotiations of this visit, nor was the study relevant to the Port of Aqaba.

The Muslim Brotherhood

Life in Amman was very good to us, but some occasions brought unexpected turmoil. The problems I experienced were occasionally life-threatening but, overall, bothersome situations causing tension in my day-to-day work. I was so busy that I had no time to think about anything except the day-to-day twelve-hour work schedule I lived. However, one memorable incident related to a confrontation I had with the Muslim Brother- hood, the fundamentalist Sunni Islamic party.

In 1956 the Brotherhood, then supported by King Hussein of Jordan, was well entrenched in the country. They mainly focused on the Jordan Phosphate Mines in Rusaifa, the mines closest to the city of Amman, to achieve two goals—for two obvious reasons which at the time were not known to me.

First, JPMC was an excellent place to target for job availabilies, especially for the unskilled labor of whom the Brotherhood had plenty. In secrecy, they succeeded in penetrating the local mines' labor recruiters and found jobs for many of their members. They also succeeded in getting jobs for clerical and low-level supervisors they needed and wanted to influence mine laborers to join the Brotherhood. I was not then aware of their manipulations, but even if I had known, I would not have taken action because JPMC needed laborers, who they supplied. On occasion they also were able to pressure their laborers to work harder to meet production goals.

IT ALL STARTED IN NAZARETH— A MEMOIR

Second, their infiltration in the labor ranks, where they fit perfectly and discreetly, gave them some power in preaching their beliefs and recruiting and efficiently and quickly enlarging the membership and the party. The mines influenced neighboring towns and Bedouin clans, as both communities depended on the mines for jobs for their unemployed men. I discovered later that some of the Muslim Brotherhood members were labor leaders in the Rusaifa mines and took a significant role in labor/management relations. Their leadership, I discovered relatively late in the game, was not among the higher ranks. Most were just above the unskilled labor groups, and I was surprised by the seriousness of the problems I was to face when they planned a political move under cover of defending labor rights.

On one occasion, mine laborers organized a peaceful strike and demonstrations, asking for an increase in wages. Laborers in the mines were underpaid, and naturally, they asked for but did not receive an increase in wages. Their serious and determined efforts made to convince the board of directors to act failed. Understandably, labor declared a strike and demonstrations ensued, which appeared to be peaceful and well-controlled for a time.

As I wrote earlier, the amazingly well-conceived plan found my management ill prepared. I had a chance later in the game, after settling the issue, to talk to the demonstration's organizers, who were proud of the plan they had worked hard to do, and they willingly shared it with me. What I found was worth my while. The Brotherhood did not need assistance from outside. The whole plan had been prepared exclusively by the local branch within the mines. None of the organizers held any middle management jobs. They were all just over the rank of unskilled labor but proved to be overqualified for their hired jobs. I will relate in some detail the story and the background of what happened.

I decided to leave Amman, go to the Rusaifa mines, sit with the labor leaders, and dissuade them from continuing their demonstration. The talks went well, and I promised to help increase the wages if they stopped the protests and went back to work. However, I did indicate that I would need about three days to convince the board of directors

113

to approve the raise and that my position would support their demands. The demonstrators' leaders knew that I had already asked the board for a wage raise, but it had not been approved.

As the demonstration built up steam, participants became less peaceful and soon got out of control. I was still in the mines, and the talks were still in progress. At that time, I started to doubt the reason given for the strike. The workers knew that my promise to raise wages would be honored. They had a strong sense to see that I did not go back on my commitments. Despite no proof, I decided that there must be some political purpose behind the strike. I just smelled it. The Brotherhood members' presence in the mines and their reason for their demonstration got a lot of support from all workers. Their plan, cleverly wrapped in a fair labor demand, began to get violent.

The Rusaifa mines had central dynamite storage facilities. The explosives used in all mining processes for extracting raw phosphate or for testing occurrences of the mineral elsewhere, were stored in those facilities. We were exploring for phosphate deposits outside Rusaifa, especially in the south. We also stored some dynamite for the army. The quantities of TNT stored could be substantial and would have been dangerous if breached; the building code for the storage facility was sufficient and satisfactory. Specially trained guards provided the security we needed, and I arranged for them to have ready communication with an army unit stationed just outside the Rusaifa mines proper. I assumed that these arrangements would make the area and the explosives safe.

In an unprecedented move, the Muslim Brotherhood demonstrators moved in the general direction of the dynamite stores—or this is what I was afraid was happening. I tried to dissuade them from taking violent measures and restrict the strike and demonstrations to a peaceful protest outside the mines, away from the sensitive explosives' storage area, but all my attempts failed.

It was common knowledge that I supported the wage increase and that I tendered my resignation when the board resolved not to give wage raises. I thought I had the credibility to intervene and spent most of my time with the demonstrators. When it transpired that the demonstration had become political, I decided to terminate the employment of the six leaders of the protest. I was surprised when I later discovered that the leaders whose services I had ended were the Muslim Brotherhood party leaders in the mines and the neighboring towns.

The demonstration lost its leaders and slimmed down to a size and a location that was easy for our guards and the army unit joining our staff to control and thus the demonstration ended. Being a Christian in a Muslim-majority country and earning the salary of a well-paid executive, I provided them with an unchallenged target. The Brotherhood lost no time to start a many-fronted defamatory as well as sectarian attack against me. The attack took the form of appeals to various bodies and the government. The first was to reverse my decision to terminate the employment of the six culprits. The second was a similar direct appeal to my board of directors, knowing that the board was the party that did not agree to any wage increase. Finally, the third appeal was to the Speaker of the Parliament to punish me immediately after I reverse my decision.

The Brotherhood printed a story about the attack by the guards on the front pages of their newspaper, which resulted in my name becoming known throughout Jordan, which was good, but my social classification, that I was part of "the establishment," was not one I wanted. "The establishment" is a term used to mean that the affiliation was with the regime at a time when all the political talk blamed the establishment for all failures in the Arab world.

The cabinet formed a committee of three ministers to talk to me and settle the issue of the individuals I had fired earlier. I was called to a meeting, but I refused to attend. I took the position that I would discuss company business only in the company's offices and not elsewhere. They did not object and came to my office. The discussions were heated, and I stuck to my position that I would not reverse my business decisions. One of the ministers, a fellow Christian, took me aside and told me that we should avoid any trouble with the Brotherhood and not create a sectarian crisis. I still refused to accede to pressure brought on by the government.

The following week, the parliament also formed a committee of three. I repeated the story, and I did not budge. The newspaper attacks became more vile, but I still did not budge. I took the stance that a reversal of my decision would result in my willingness to be juggled by anybody who had access to higher authorities. Yielding to political parties with specific interests and people interested in getting a business advantage would make me less efficient and too conciliatory.

However, the most severe and scary aspect was the direct threat in a letter Grace found at our home: a piece of paper with a drawing of a skull and bones. After we spotted armed men just outside our apartment, for the first time since we had left Palestine, I bought myself a handgun. I did realize that this acquisition would make no difference, should there be an attempt on my life, but carrying the gun gave me a sense of courage. I was too young to understand the gravity of the situation and the uselessness of carrying a weapon.

I was under pressure from the government, and the threat on my life and the challenge of conducting business in a usual way was formidable. Still, I tried, and business as usual was how I behaved daily and every day, all during the threat period, which lasted for over a month. I was happy when the case was finally closed, to our relief. Grace was not a happy person during those grueling days.

What happened did not change my attitude, and I did not reverse my decision. I knew the six individuals involved, and I had not realized that they were members of the Brotherhood. Meantime, I phoned some friends in other companies and secured each of the individuals I had fired a job.

When the cabinet decided to set up a committee to investigate the incident again, I met with the prime minister. I told him there was no point in forming another committee, since other companies already employed those whose work I terminated. He was amused. With the case finally closed, Grace and I were ready for some rest. It had been the worst and the tensest period of our life in Jordan.

Under these sensitive conditions, I had not recruited anyone for any senior position still vacant. As soon as this cloud passed, I started eagerly to identify and recruit managers, and after all the openings were staffed, the company's management normalized. Work got back to normal, properly run and managed, and I felt gratified. The company's board of directors and the relevant government circles thought I did a good job, and they were satisfied with the progress achieved. However, my happiness did not last long; it would soon be time for me to lose that job and start looking for a new source of income and a new home outside Jordan.

On Monday, March 25, 1958, Grace gave birth to our first daughter, Rania, at the Italian Hospital in Amman. Rania was a beautiful baby, and she brought tremendous happiness and a change to our life. She became the center of our attention and the focus of our life.

I became the general manager of JPMC in February of 1956. I lost my job in October 1958. During this short spell I offered my resignation several times, and on every occasion the board of directors turned it down. The board was very cautious about progress, which frustrated my efforts. In the end, I became more confident in my position, and the board of directors always went along with my points of view.

Another note regarding army and activists' use of the mines: in 1956, the feda'yeen, Palestinian fighters, crossing from Egypt through occupied lands to Jordan needed a safe base from which to operate. I accommodated them by allowing them to use two tunnels in the Rusaifa mines. At the time, Palestinian feda'yeen received popular and official support throughout the Arab world. The JPMC board of directors did not approve and said the company should not be associated with political or military activities lest we had to pay a price we could not predetermine.

I also gave the Jordanian Army two tunnels to use, each about one kilometer long, as a place to store their weapons and equipment, as they were always expecting an Israeli attack. This did not sit well with my board either, but they couldn't be openly vocal about their opposition.

IDEOLOGICAL ISLAMIC GROUPS

The Muslim Brotherhood was established by Hassan al-Banna, an Egyptian cleric and political activist, and it has been part of the political scene in Egypt since 1928. With time, it spread all over the Arab world. Al-Banna and his followers were initially united by a desire to oust the British from Egypt and rid their country of the "corrupting" western influences. Their original slogan was "Islam is the Solution." In its early years, the group concentrated on religion, education, and social services, but as its membership grew, it moved into the political arena, organizing protests against the Egyptian government. In the 1940s, the armed wing of the Brotherhood was blamed for a string of violent acts, including the assassination in 1948 of Mahmud Fahmi al-Nuqrashi, the Egyptian prime minister, shortly after he ordered the dissolution of the Brotherhood. The assassination of al-Banna convinced his supporters to claim he had been killed by "the government's wishes." In 1950, Sayyid Qutub, a member of the Muslim Brotherhood, took over the organization.

In 1945 the Association of the Muslim Brotherhood was officially registered in Jordan. Abu Qura, who became its first general supervisor, originally brought the Brotherhood to Jordan from Egypt after extensive study and spread of the teachings of Imam Hassan al-Banna. While most political parties and movements were banned for a long time in Jordan, the Brotherhood was exempted and allowed by the Jordanian monarchy to operate. In 1948, Egypt, Syria, and Transjordan offered "volunteers" to help Palestine in its war against Israel. Due to the defeat and weakening of Palestine, the Jordanian Brotherhood and Palestinian Brotherhood merged.

The newly merged Muslim Brotherhood in Jordan was primarily concerned with providing social services and charitable work as well as with politics and its role in the parliament. It was seen as compatible with the political system and supported democracy without the forced implementation of Sharia law which was part of its doctrine. However, under internal pressures from younger members of the Brotherhood who called for more militant actions, as well as his failing health, Abu Qura resigned as the leader of the Jordanian Muslim Brotherhood.

In 1953, Muhammad 'Abd al-Rahman Khalifa was elected by the movement's administrative committee as the new leader of the Jordanian Brotherhood, and he retained this position until 1994. Khalifa was different from his predecessor and older members of the organization because he had not been educated in Cairo; he was educated in Syria and Palestine. He established close ties with Palestinian Islamists during his educational life, which led him to be jailed for several months in Jordan for criticizing Arab armies performance in the war.

Now, branches of the Muslim Brotherhood are spread to all countries across the Middle East and North and East Africa, including Sudan, Jordan, Syria, and Saudi Arabia. In addition, the Brotherhood started branches outside the region. One branch that was established in the USA adopts markedly more conservative views and tries to keep its deeds and preaching acceptable to the host country. For example, the Kuwaiti branch openly opposes the right of women to vote; in fact, their beliefs exclude the rights of women wherever and whenever possible. In the 1960s, it developed the doctrine of jihad, and the radical group Hamas adopted it. Hamas is an offshoot of the Palestinian Muslim Brotherhood. The Brotherhood expanded over the decades. Now, it operates in every Arab country, and its political weight is felt by one and all.

Political strife based on religious sects is the manner of life in the Middle East. Other Muslim countries entered the fray, including Iran. There is an open war of dogma and firmly held beliefs and opinions covering futile and extreme ideologies: to mention a few, al-Qaeda, ISIS, and at least eighty other organizations that operate across a large swath of land from Afghanistan to Egypt, and even in Nigeria, where Boku Haram is one well-known name. All have the same extreme dogma generated in the far past by many scholars, including Ibn Taymiyyah (AD 1263–1328). His teachings were adopted by the Sunni extremists, including followers of Wahhabism, Salafism, and Jihadism. aspects of his teachings profoundly influenced Muhammad ibn Abd al-Wahhab, the founder of the Wahhabi movement as practiced in Saudi Arabia, where it is part of the establishment of that country. Ibn Taymiyyah's controversial fatwa, which allowed jihad against other religions and sects, was put into practice by al-Qaeda, ISIS, al-Nusra in Syria, and other jihadi groups; the differences between groups depended on their needs to achieve their goals.

On the other hand, Hezbollah in Lebanon, the mostly Shi'a People's Mobilization Forces (al-Hashd al-Sha'abi) in Iraq, the al-Huthi movement (Ansar Allah) in Yemen, and a few more are adherents of the Ayatollah Khomeini's Shi'a doctrines, adopted after the successful overthrow of the \Shah of Iran in 1979. Ayatollah Ruhollah Khomeini was the architect of the Iranian Revolution and the first leader of the Islamic republic established in 1979. He articulated the concept of vilayet-e faqih ("guardianship of the jurist") on a historical theological basis, which underlaid Iran's Islamic republic.

Back to Amman

MY LAST OFFCIAL TRIP TO EUROPE

I spent the last month of my work with JPMC in Europe with Grace, partly as the manager of JPMC and partly to conduct some Jordan government work. While traveling, I did not know of the termination of my job, and nobody cared to let me know. I carried on with my business plan, including visits to Greece, Czechoslovakia, Yugoslavia, Switzerland, and England. I negotiated and, in some cases, signed agreements representing Jordan or JPMC and conducted all the business I was expected to perform, reporting briefly by cable to the authorities concerned in Jordan. I got, in reply, advice or questions to which I responded, and everything sounded normal.

Grace and I had interesting experiences in Prague, though we were surprised by the level of poverty in the newly communist country six or seven years after the end of World War II. We saw queues of people waiting at the doors of government-run soup kitchens. On one occasion Grace and I were entertained in a fancy restaurant across the street from a soup kitchen. Grace entered into an argument with the minister of foreign trade, our host at this lunch, about the inadequacies of the Czech system. He was very tolerant, I was embarrassed, and Grace, as usual, had her day. This minister accompanied us to other events while we were in Prague, and he did not seem unhappy about what had happened at lunch earlier. We were assigned a woman guide to show us the historic landmarks and were told that she was a police officer. Walking with her through the streets of Prague, we noticed that people were staring at us. The reason for this was the high-heeled shoes Grace wore; we learned that high heels were a luxury not available in Prague, and they attracted the attention of both women and men.

JPMC had an agent in Zurich. He met us at the train station when we arrived from our trip in Yugoslavia and drove us to our hotel, and he said he would come back to take us to dinner in an hour. He came as promised, and we went to a restaurant for dinner. In Zurich at that time, restaurants did not serve after 9 p.m. Our host, Mr. Schmidlin, was a connoisseur. He ordered oysters as an appetizer, but we had to wait for the fresh oysters to arrive by plane from southern France. We were new to oysters, and when served, Grace added Tabasco to hers. Schmidlin was distraught that the oysters were being "seasoned" and said that one should not kill the oysters by adding flavoring and that they were best eaten fresh, in their own liquor. This experience and gentle reprimand came in handy later in life when our degree of sophistication improved. Mr. Schmidlin was a generous and likable host, and we enjoyed spending time with him.

Finally, we stopped in England, and the business purpose of the visit was to meet with the Coal Board, whose offices were in the City of London. After my meetings, I started my trip home. Grace stayed on in London with her brother Dr. Thomas L. Saaty, who was on assignment with the US Office of Naval Research.

At the Rome airport, where I awaited a flight to Amman via Beirut, I met by chance a United Nations officer who I knew from Amman, who was on his way back to the United States. He asked me about my problem in Jordan, and I surprised him when I said that I was not aware of any problem. He told me that my job had been terminated and an order had been issued for my arrest upon arrival in Amman. This bad news resulted from information that alleged that I participated in a coup d'état against the king. He suggested that it would be better if I remained in Beirut for a few days to contact people in Amman and find out what was going on. But, of course, going to prison on a political issue was expected of me; those imprisoned were treated as national heroes when they were freed.

When I understood my Jordan situation, I remained in Beirut and delayed my return to Jordan. I was surprised when the board of directors of JPMC instituted a lawsuit in the courts of Amman, charging me with mismanagement, but I understood the political background of all these maneuvers. I could not return to Jordan to defend myself because of the political accusations and the order to apprehend and jail me. Some of the staff I had hired cooperated with police to make whatever charges against me stick. I was a very young boss, and that did not sit well with many I employed who were older and with family roots in Jordan. My premature exit provided an opportunity for managers to move a level up the ladder.

I found myself stranded in Beirut with no work, no money, and a lot of debt in Jordan, which everybody suddenly wanted to collect. It took me three months short of a year to adjust to the fact that I had been dumped and that the political structure in the area would not facilitate my many attempts to find a job. News of my termination and the accusations spread way beyond the borders of Jordan. Grace was expecting again, and my family was still in need of financial support.

As it transpired, JPMC were pursuing legal action under political pressure from the government. I was accused of participating in a coup d'état against the king of Jordan, a grave accusation. The company was told to terminate my services and was induced to raise cases in court accusing me of the misuse of company funds and general mismanagement. They raised three different lawsuits, one accusing me of using air force planes for my personal transport and paying for this service from company funds. I cannot remember the other two lawsuits, as they were just as ridiculous.

In reply to this lawsuit, the total misappropriation of funds amounted to two flights from Amman to Aqaba and back and cost eighteen Jordan dinars. One flight was to take the IBRD committee from Amman to Aqaba to investigate the company's financial needs. I used the second flight to transport some board members and some engineers to participate in a study of the phosphate-loading problems in the not-yet-functioning Port of Aqaba.

In the end, I was never notified of the lawsuit or a decision by the court, and I did not return to Amman until almost a year later. The lawsuits were withdrawn when circumstances changed and my return to Amman was expected. I learned a lot from this intense early exposure to "friendly fire." I learned how to manage people and how and when to make decisions on the spot. I learned how to ask for information, evaluate information, and act without delay. It was a valuable education.

As I said earlier, I left Grace in London and proceeded to Beirut. My first two weeks there were tense. I did not get to know much about my new dilemma. The JPMC agent in Beirut could not fill me in on what had happened, and he said he was as puzzled as I was. Unfortunately, I had no money to meet my new obligations, and this added to my stressful situation. Grace naturally got disturbed when I repeatedly suggested she remain in London and enjoy the city and her brother's company. But she decided to come back, and I told her to stop in Beirut, where we met, and proceed to Amman together.

We met in Beirut and stayed there and decided to start a new chapter in our lives. That was easy to say, not easy to implement, but our lives took a different route which improved our lot in no vague way. We never lived as a family in Jordan again.

Grace, Rania, and I stayed for a few days with my parents in Beirut. Grace's brother John, who was living in Beirut, offered us the use of his apartment while he was away. We were glad to move into John's residence, and we stayed there for a quite a while. We then rented a small apartment in Rue Leon, just off Hamra Street, until my work situation improved. Then, we moved to a larger apartment in Raouché overlooking the Mediterranean.

While in Rue Leon, our life took another turn for the better. Early one day in September 1959, Grace gave birth to our second and charming daughter Leila, whose birth ushered a new and more challenging, exciting, and happy period in our life. She was born Friday, September 11. With both Rania and Leila, our lives became even more fulfilling.

Our focus and aspirations demanded more, and we took the cue and responded well and with enthusiasm.

The year following our departure from Amman was a testing year. My nerves were continually on edge. But we turned over a new leaf and started a new, challenging, and productive phase in our vacillating but most satisfactory life.

Just about the time I started work with Associated Management Consultants in Beirut (about which I write later), a change in the political scene in Jordan provided a new opportunity—one which I had expected, but not so soon.

RETURN TO AMMAN BY OFFICIAL INVITATION

Hazza' al-Majali, the newly appointed prime minister of Jordan, contacted me by telephone and invited me to meet him in Amman. I traveled there the following day. We had a pleasant and friendly meeting in his office, and he discussed the termination of my work in the phosphate company but, more importantly, my arrest order. He had a thick file stamped "Confidential" with my name written on its cover. In it was my work history in Jordan, the names of my contacts, and the alleged political parties to which I belonged. It covered quite a list of parties, starting with the Communists, the Ba'ath, the Arab Nationalist Movement, and a host of others, some of which I had no knowledge of their existence. He gave me the file to keep, but I said it would not be of any use to me because the authorities certainly had a copy or more in storage. He agreed, threw the file into his wastebasket, suggested we forget this episode and discuss issues that concerned me and my plans, and offered me the opportunity to return to the management of JPMC; he said JPMC needed my services. I declined, so he offered that I choose a position in the country that I would like to occupy. I laughed and told him that I had decided not to seek work as an employee anymore. Wasfi el-Tell, the chief of information in the prime minister's office and a close friend of mine, joined in this meeting. I enjoyed this meeting, and the main benefit I derived from it was its public relations value.

Both Hazza' and Wasfi were eager to have me work with them and implied that they wanted me to be involved and take the opportunity to help make substantial changes and improvements in the country's state of affairs. They said they wanted to get all the "good people" to participate in this effort. I was flattered, but I told them I had promised to concentrate on my new job, work with my new partners (one of whom was a Jordanian) and focus on Jordan. In addition, I promised that we would do our best to get investments for Jordan from the Arab countries in the Gulf. I also offered pro bono assistance for him and Wasfi whenever they needed it. Hazza' and Wasfi were happy with this suggestion and later with the work done.

The local press reported my arrival in Amman; the phosphate company dropped its lawsuits, and the small merchants who had been eager to collect suddenly became friendly. I received many invitations to lunches and dinners, and everyone I met was keen to know my needs. It was a splendid morale-boosting episode.

Hazza' was assassinated later in the year. An explosive device blew up the prime ministry's building, and most of the staff and visitors were killed or maimed; we knew many of the victims. When he died, Hazza' was only forty-four years old. Thankfully, Wasfi was not in his office when the explosion destroyed the first floor of the building.

My immediate political problems with Jordan were officially over. I could travel more or less freely in and out of Jordan. I spent time in Jordan trying to get business for our new consulting company, and I succeeded in securing several exciting and lucrative jobs. My services were also in demand, and I became an adviser to various ministries of the government. The primary and most lucrative consultancy work I got was with the Ministry of Information, and I kept getting jobs for over two decades.

EMPEROR HAILE SELASSIE

While traveling into and out of Jordan, I had a few unique experiences. On a summer day in the late 1960s, I was staying in the Jordan

Intercontinental Hotel in Amman. One day at around noontime, I left my room for a lunch appointment at a friend's home. While depositing my room key at the reception desk, I noticed a long line of dignitaries on both sides of the stairs leading to the dining room on the floor below. I looked closer and saw that one dignitary was at the head of the stairs leading to a reception room, and other dignitaries and cabinet members stood in two rows.

I learned that Emperor Haile Selassie of Ethiopia was waiting for King Hussein to arrive to attend a lunch the emperor gave in his honor after his state visit to the country. My old friend Wasfi el-Tell, who was then the prime minister, saw me and encouraged me to join him at the head of the line. He said King Hussein was delayed and then introduced me to the emperor, under whatever guise I do not remember. Wasfi asked me to strike up some conversation with the emperor. That was a request that I could not refuse, nor did I have time to decline the invitation.

I was embarrassed simply because I did not know how to start a conversation with an emperor! However, I began by commenting on how much the Jordanians loved His Imperial Majesty, manifested by the large crowds who lined the streets to welcome him on arrival. Though I was still in awe of addressing the emperor, I felt he did not mind me talking about Jordanians and their admiration of him, and so I carried on with talk about the weather. I followed that with a monologue on sundry topics, and then I apologized for the delay of the arrival of King Hussein.

The waiting time felt like an eternity. I was relieved when the king's procession sounded close to us, but before the emperor let me go, he told me not to worry about the king's late arrival at all and that kings and emperors liked to arrive late. I decided not to comment on his statement and left His Imperial Majesty to talk to the other majesty newly arrived, so I said goodbye to the emperor and hello to His Majesty and left before my services were needed again. It was an interesting statement, coming "from the horse's mouth," that royals keep royals waiting. I admit, the event now provides good material for small talk, but those minutes felt like hours, and the relief I felt after I separated from the group was like a gift of God.

THOUGHTS ON JORDAN

The end of my employment in Jordan was the end of my career involving working for others. Though exciting jobs came up, I decided I would try my hand at something else, something I would establish and operate. I would live my successes and suffer my failures—and there were many of both. This was the beginning of my life as an independent businessman, with challenges, opportunities, and dreams galore.

I am lucky to have had an upbringing in an atmosphere of love and care. I virtually forgot the difficult times in Haifa and Nazareth, and the education I was fortunate to have been outstanding. All this gave me the foundation to face the world under conditions that were never normal. My success in Jordan was due to a lot of luck and the courage to undertake risks and jobs that appeared at the time to be impossible tasks. I always had the full support and love of my wife, Grace.

I suppose I have said so much about our life in Jordan because the country played a significant role in our lives. It shaped within its borders my character, our young family, and my early career. I learned the value of adherence to local customs. The Bedouin culture is straightforward, honest, reliable, and down to earth. It left its marks on our personalities, of course, on our way of life, and on the principles we adhere to. It chiseled my personality in the process, which started in Haifa on February 22, 1931, and ended in Amman in October of 1958. Whatever I am, I am the product of the events of those twenty-seven years.

I knew many Jordanians in government and business, prime ministers, high officials, and influential individuals. Some affected my performance positively and lent me unlimited support. Each one of them was good in what he did; most, if not all of them, passed away some years back. When they come to my mind, and they do often, and whenever I think of them, I feel that I was lucky to have known every one of them.

My education and preparation for life completed, I was twenty-seven and Grace was twenty-six. We stood on firm foundations and set ourselves to start a life whose focus and scope was subject to no outside influence. We expected to face challenges, but we were determined, and we started our life with a full understanding of the difficulties we might encounter pursuing the options of our choice. The excellent reputation I enjoyed as an independent consultant enhanced the demand for my services in many countries and on many levels. I like to believe that my personality was a deciding factor in my success.

Before I close this chapter, I must say that I still have a soft spot for Amman and Jordan. Grace and I had friends and acquaintances who afforded us the luxury of opening their homes and their lives to us and allowing us to move in the inner circles of the respected Jordanians homes.

Grace and I and a few friends visited some of the landmarks of Jordan before their names became familiar to the wider world. We visited Petra in 1956 with Hamad el-Farhan and Mohammad Touqan. They spent the night in a tent, while Grace and I rested in one of the tombs carved out of the rock, and we were, after that, jokingly called "tomb mates." The route to Petra was a desert road, and it took some twelve hours to get there by car from Amman. Petra then was pristine, with no tourists and no government policy to encourage or enhance tourism. Though we visited Petra many times later, that first visit was always vivid in our minds, and we probably saw it every time we visited as we had seen it that first time.

I mentioned jobs in which I was involved; they were particularly educational for me and essential for the young country of Jordan. Again, for this, I thank my friends in both the public and the private sectors.

A Summary of My Consulting Jobs in Jordan

At the start of my work in Jordan, I signed contracts for jobs when my expertise was still green, if not lacking. Below, I list five of those jobs and describe what I did. All these I did successfully before I moved into the full-time job as general manager of the Jordan Phosphate Mines Company PLC.

THE LIQUIDATION OF THE COPPER MINING COMPANY

My first job was a straightforward, simple liquidation of a copper mining company. The reason for liquidation was that no copper was found in that location. The company had good accounting records, a clean set of books, and a simple balance sheet. The assets were adequate to pay off the liabilities and distribute about 10 percent of the initially paid capital to shareholders. It took three weeks to sell the assets, make the distribution, and write the relevant liquidation report. The company had independent auditors who also signed the financial statements and the liquidation report.

In 2021, the Jordanian government put in place plans to carve out almost a third of the Dana Biosphere Reserve to allow mining for copper. This is the same location where, some many decades earlier, no copper was extracted, though it was suspected to be present.

THE MARBLE MINING COMPANY (MMC)

My second job was more challenging. Marble rock was available in many parts of Jordan and the West Bank. Each area provided a different quality of marble, with different colors and color combinations and specific gravities. MMC had a central workshop just outside the city of Amman. It received the raw and uncut rock in its workshop and cut it into different sizes, shapes, and thicknesses through a lengthy process. Rock was sorted and stored by size, color, and quality. The most common colors were green and off-white. Reddish and rose colors were also available but in limited quantities.

It was not difficult to devise and implement a cost-accounting system for the marble by color, types of cuts, and for decorative objects such as tabletops or side lamps that were made in the workshop and sold as individual items. I stayed with MMC until I became a full-time employee of JPMC, but by request of the board of directors, I continued to attend MMC board meetings for more than one year. The owners were good people and paid well for my services. Here again, I met many businessmen and further widened my circle of acquaintances and friends. A gift of a green and white marble side lamp is still on a table beside my bed.

WATER DISTRIBUTION IN AMMAN

I was assigned to study the water network and distribution system for Amman. I was to evaluate and determine the sources of water available to Amman, the total supply, and its distribution in residential areas and industrial parks to business entities, government, and public users.

On starting the survey, I tried to find governmental, municipal, and private sources of information. It was easy to identify water sources, and it was not difficult to determine the total quantity available and pumped to Amman. A team worked on the water sources, one by one, checking the methods of assessing the contribution of each to the total supply, with seasonal variations. Some sources had measuring tools like water meters, and some did not. We did correct the situation by adding meters as needed.

The time of the year for the study did not reflect the yearly norm of supply. Since the seasonal flow of water in Jordan varied substantially, we decided to limit the present and urgent investigation of both supply and consumption to a short-term, three-month period, to get enough information to help solve the short-term problem. Then, a long-term study that considered seasonal and periodic changes in the supply was conceived, presented to the relevant authorities, and approved. Rainfall in Jordan (in the 1950s) had a five-year cycle.

The study of water usage was another ball game. We needed a lot of information, including the original distribution network maps and plans—a list of the city's central water meters and the usage quantities recorded by each meter. We studied locations where water was supplied but no water meters had been installed, such as places of worship, some army camps, and public areas. These sites did not have legal justification to use water for free and without control from the water authority. The water commission argued that security or historical rights secured by old customs and laws continued to apply but said they would take the necessary steps to repeal the historic rights. The work planned for the short-term study continued apace.

The lists of the Amman's central water meters were compiled, and networks of some water pipes were located. We had a long, routine job, measuring the daily supply and consumption by collecting meter-by-meter numbers in lists and adding up the daily totals. In three months of work, we concluded that water billed represented about 55 percent of water supplied and that the aging water pipes were deteriorating and needed replacement. In addition, some lines leaked more than others did. With the information we collected, we could pinpoint those areas where the loss was at its highest and include them in the list of locations prioritized for repair or replacement.

A rather major problem was that we did not know where all the pipes were, and so we planned to replace the ones known to us and hoping that the other water lines would be continuations of the pipes to be replaced. We could tell approximately the location of some leaking pipes in some of the areas, which was good enough to start their replacement.

We shut off the supply at the intake location of some pipelines, waited to see how this affected the collection, and for which areas and locations. We acted accordingly. At best, the process was a combination of knowledge and guessing; however, we solved the water distribution puzzle in just about a year. Overall, we did a good job. When the leaking pipes were finally replaced, more water became available for consumption in Amman by all users.

The long-term study recommended that the authorities dig tunnels and run water and wastewater pipes and cables and telephone lines through underground conduits. This eliminated the need to dig out streets to install, maintain, or replace works necessary for the entire city's underground infrastructural needs. The population of Amman at that time was just over a hundred thousand. The tunnels were made for the areas then populated and then expanded by about one kilometer in every direction. Now, Amman houses over 40 percent of the total population of Jordan, probably four million residents, and I am sure those underground conduits grew to satisfy the growing city's needs.

THE MUNICIPALITY OF AMMAN, 1956–1957

I first got involved with the municipality of Amman when Mohammad Touqan was the acting mayor. He invited me to attend a meeting over the following two weeks with all the senior departmental officers to discuss the municipality's problems in performing its duties. I was pleasantly surprised at the staff and the mayor's willingness to involve themselves in the tedious process of reviewing procedures and practices that were outdated and partially a continuation of the Ottoman methods in municipal management. They were the ones who decided at the end of the review that all procedures employed needed upgrading. It was determined that the primary lines of communication, internally and with other governmental departments, were not adequately structured and, in most cases, nonexistent.

We discovered no accounting system to speak of, no budget, and no plan of work. The financial needs of the municipality were, at best, a guess. The budget was challenging to prepare because the incomes from taxes, fees, and expenditures on salaries, wages, and ordinary services to the public were in dire need of proper recording. The municipality collected some of its taxes, while other government departments, like the Ministry of Finance, collected others. The municipality did not know who collected fees and taxes on its behalf. The gap needed to be bridged, and I included suggestions to solve this issue in my report.

We all agreed that the entire structure of the municipality needed to be reviewed in order to define, improve, and modernize it. To that end, the municipality retained me to lead an in-depth study of the organizational structure and the financial systems required and to recommend a methodology of implementation of the suggested solutions, the time frame for both the study and the actual performance, the training of personnel in the newly agreed-upon structure, and systems to be installed and used. Being a public body, the municipality was subject to some state laws that made any substantial change in its methods of operation subject to cabinet approval and some particular aspects subject to royal approvals. I needed to meet with the relevant authorities while writing my recommendations; it was necessary to secure a priori permissions by the government department with jurisdiction to accept or reject the new organizational structure and methods.

First, I devised comprehensive but straightforward bookkeeping and accounting systems sufficient for the initial period, until the staff of the municipality become competent in bookkeeping or new staff was found and employed. In addition, I investigated and devised a filing system for easy reference and a method of communication with other government departments, including paper flow.

The report was completed in about six months and then stenciled, the only method then available for duplicating documents, producing ten copies, which I submitted to the relevant users, including the prime minister, the minister of finance, and the mayor of Amman. It was good that my report got into the hands of high authority and gave me an excuse to meet and engage with those who received copies, especially the prime minister.

In the meantime, and just when I started circulating my report, a new mayor was appointed, Omar Pasha Matar, replacing the acting mayor, Mohammad Touqan. I presented the report to the new mayor along with my invoice for 500 Jordanian dinars (equivalent to 500 sterling pounds). A week later, I received a letter from him saying that the municipality did not need my report or advice. He also returned to me the message I had submitted to the municipality. I was surprised and became quite angry, especially because I needed the money. I also refused to believe that an incoming mayor could repeal a formal municipal council's approval of a contract.

Deciding to bring the matter to higher authorities, I went directly to the prime minister's office and asked to see him. The prime minister at the time was Tewfik Abul Huda Pasha. Unfortunately, I had no appointment, but he received me graciously. He did not seem surprised by my story, nor did he try to convince me otherwise, and he said he would be in touch with me soon. That done, I went around town telling my friends that I had met with Tewfik Pasha, and everyone was surprised that I went directly to him and that he received me.

Another week later, I was contacted by Mayor Omar Pasha, who said that I should not have gone to the prime minister to discuss such an unimportant issue but that we should have discussed it and indeed, we would have resolved it ourselves. I was double-angry with what he suggested, and I retorted by saying it would have been nice if he added a sentence in his letter to me to say that he rejected the report. However, there was still an opportunity to negotiate. He said he could not pay 500 dinars, as there was no budget to make this payment possible. He offered to settle for 300 dinars, and I accepted. The municipality later implemented most of what I had recommended, especially when Mohammad Touqan was reappointed as mayor, replacing Omar Pasha.

THE JORDAN ELECTRICITY COMPANY

The electricity company operated under a franchise to produce and distribute electricity for Amman and its suburbs, with a clause that gave it priority rights to cover larger areas in the Balka Directorate of the

Hashemite Kingdom of Jordan. It operated well and was adequately staffed, closely supervised, and controlled by a board of directors from the private sector and by public accountants.

Through the Ministry of Economy, the government asked me to study and report on the adopted pricing policy and whether it was fair to the consumer and rewarding to investors. So I went through the company, section by section, and found the management to be sufficient and all the functions listed in the franchise correctly performed and its terms abided by.

The study was not difficult, but the options available were minimal. The government wanted a reduced price per kilowatt of electricity, but the investors, the board of directors, enjoyed a free hand in pricing. I cannot say that they were unfair to consumers, and I did not want investors to have negative ideas about the security of their investments in the country. In its developmental infancy, Jordan was a marginal country in a desert area with no resources to speak of. Money for investment was not yet in plenty; moreover, oil royalties in the Gulf had not yet started to make a difference regionally— oil money started to make some difference in the late 1950s. Caution was the order of the day, and I made it a point, in all proposals touching investments, not to discourage or scare it out of the country.

I devised a simple formula to achieve my objectives, which I cleared with the board of directors and various government departments before presenting it: the company would have a free hand in pricing but would hold that price steady for five years. It would distribute profits to its shareholders, but not above 12 percent per year. It would use funds and surpluses to pay for the best equipment and best maintenance facilities. Further funds could be, by the company's own decision, used to expand the area of the franchise and keep the service quality at its best, and the company would be free to invest, in Jordan, whatever funds remained. We encouraged the company to invest its surpluses in other commercial or industrial startup projects then being promoted or set up in the country, especially those supported by the government. In doing this, we created a well-informed local entity that became a pioneer working side by side with the government encouraging local investments.

As time passed and money accumulated, with no use to the shareholders in investment or higher dividends, the company, with a bit of prodding, found the reduction of price to the customers a reasonable solution. The company's improved image and the benefits accrued to it and to the individuals on the board of directors were welcomed. They were no longer viewed by the consumers as exploiters. Prices went down, and the investors were encouraged to participate in other similarly run companies. As a result, other electricity companies in Palestine, aka the West Bank, adopted the same solution.

PART TWO

Preamble

The drift of the middle east into graver times started in the early days of the First World War, continued through the 1920s, and never relented through wars and uprisings. In the 1940s and '50s, many states created by the Sykes-Picot Agreement gained independence from the English and French mandates. Every state chose a path by fiat for its political future. These decisions were fundamental in formulating the region's political future and its resounding failure.

In the 1950s, I started my career in management consulting, and I retired just about half a century later under the unchanging insecurities as time moved forward. I cannot but remind the reader that the evolution of the Arab countries depended on decisions made by the major European powers of the time. Most, if not all, agreements arrived at during and immediately after World War I divided the Ottoman Empire into many smaller entities. The colonial powers sowed seeds of discord, controversy, and causes for disagreement in each new entity. The instability of the Middle East emanated from one act: the redrawing of the eastern Ottoman Empire into many nation-states.

One of these states, Lebanon, is where I lived and from where I watched what the future brought in surprises. Despite the precarious nature of the region, I had outstanding successes and serious failings, but overall, I did well both financially and socially.

On returning to Beirut from a very satisfactory visit to Amman and establishing myself again in Lebanon, I felt at ease. I overcame my disappointments and fears from my dismissal from JPMC and the political accusations. Hazza' al-Majali's invitation and the ensuing public relations added many positive value effects. It did not take long to get news of my "reinstatement" to travel from Jordan to Lebanon and the Gulf, and soon, as mentioned earlier, I was able to start my own business.

Management Consulting

ASSOCIATED MANAGEMENT CONSULTANTS, SAL (AMC)

In 1959, Dr. Nazih Taleb and Dr. Kamal al-Sha'ir, the two owners of Dar al-Handassah, created AMC as a partnership between them and me in equal shares. Initially, we did not register the company with the state, though this bureaucratic lapse came in handy later while we were resolving a sensitive internal issue. For the first few months, we used the premises of Dar al-Handassah Consultants as our temporary offices until we rented a new space. In the meantime, business kept coming, some of which were new to us and required skills we did not yet possess.

Skilled staff came from western Europe and the USA to fill the gaps. The necessary labor mix covered all kinds of workers in the construction industry, and contractors managed their new work from their workforces.

AMC provided me with many challenges in the field and with one of the partners. He and I differed on many issues, especially regarding business methods and integrity. During the partners' annual meeting and review of the final accounts, we had a significant disagreement about introducing a fourth partner, an influential government employee from Kuwait who would broker work for us. I refused to invite another person to be a partner, especially not a government official, as that meant he could use his influence to procure business for Dar al-Handassah.

AMC didn't need further procurement for work, as we were already fully occupied. After a long but not fruitful discussion, I decided to leave Dar al-Handassah and the partnership and start independently. The fact that AMC was not yet on the Commercial Register in Lebanon made my departure easy, as there was no need to go through bureaucratic paperwork. I gave up my (verbal) shares, entitlements, and shares of profit for the last fiscal year which we were reviewing, and left the meeting.

ASSOCIATED BUSINESS CONSULTANTS, SAL (ABC)

On my way home from a meeting with Dar al-Handasah, I saw an advertisement for an office rental on Hamra Street. I looked over the premises and rented sufficient space to house my company. Associated Business Consultants, SAL, was established in 1961 and successfully operated for over 42 years. There were other times when we were balancing on the edge of one financial or security problem or another. The decades to come were always challenging.

The concept of management consulting was new to the Middle East, and in the absence of competition, I broke through some Arab countries early. I was happy with what the present yielded and the future promised, and I spent long hours working to make up for insufficient staffing and meager funds. My wife, Grace, helped plan and supervise market research projects during this initial period.

Computers and similar machines were not available to us yet. As a result, we manually compiled figures to analyze our market research data, an arduous and lengthy process that did not guarantee accuracy. It took a long time before we equipped the research department with the rudimentary technology: tabulators, punching and sorting machines. These removed the burden of manual calculations and compilations into less time-consuming and more accurate methods and reports.

Within a few weeks of establishing myself as a sole proprietor, my own clients at AMC moved their accounts from AMC to ABC. One of the partners in AMC tried his best to truncate my quick progress and even wrote letters to clients to suggest that I had no right to work in the management-consulting field as I was previously in charge of that specialty at AMC. According to him, it was unfair competition. In my absence from Lebanon, he also tried to threaten my wife by phone, but to no avail.

I ventured into every field of consulting and reaped more than I expected. My portfolio included market research, television program ratings, consumer product promotions, advertising testing, and budgeting, in many Arab countries and East Africa.

In 1959 and for several years, I worked in Kuwait and Saudi Arabia for General Motors and its agents to reorganize management, enabling it to achieve its "fair share of the market," to quote a GM vice president. Oil had been discovered in Kuwait and before that in Saudi and was gushing, and for GM, selling more of their cars and trucks was a marketing necessity.

My work history started with no partners and continued throughout without partners. My only partner all through my working life was Grace.

Kuwait: Jobs in the 1960s

My first meeting for work in Kuwait in 1960 was with a vice president of General Motors, who approached me to discuss the strategy for marketing GM's many products in the Gulf area. Oil money and the quick spread of wealth in a segment of Gulf society showed us the need to market more efficiently in these countries. GM decided to start with the Kuwait market as it was relatively smaller and easy to manage and move later to Saudi Arabia. GM wanted to stay informed on what was going on in the region and how their agents were handling their franchises. Together we devised a plan of action.

Kuwait in the 1960s suddenly had great financial resources from the sale of oil, and the decision-makers, as well as the population at large, were in the mood to spend in amounts they never dreamed of possessing. The sudden economic growth created a unique situation characterized by a rapid accumulation of wealth in the government vaults and in the private sectors. As a result, the government resorted to investment in the country's infrastructure whether it was needed or not at the time, and to spend money to speed up the country's development. In many cases, the infrastructural works were bizarre; roads, for example, were built from north to south and east to west with no identifiable purpose. Such roads connected Kuwait City to the borders of the neighboring countries and stopped there.

The government also spent money buying land in the desert from its citizens at incredibly high prices. In many cases, the government "gave"

Kuwaitis plots of land in the desert and then bought them back, thus making cash more and more available to everyone—one commendable way to distribute wealth.

The speedy rise in income and consequently in consumption and industrial development induced many international corporations to look closely at the Gulf with hopes of benefiting from this extraordinary situation and the business opportunities created. The qualified and the unskilled equally found opportunities in Kuwait. They came by the thousands from countries around the region and the world. Unfortunately, many of those who came were not qualified on technical or ethical grounds. There was no way to screen arrivals, and so many came and used their skills to rob their employers dry.

I use the term "Gulf States" to include all the sheikhdoms, emirates, and sultanates of the Arabian Gulf in this story. In the late 1950s and early 1960s, theses were an unremarkable collection of tribal communities, such as the United Arab Emirates, and Qatar. The Sultanate of Oman was a closed country with little exposure to the rest of the world. Only Britain had business interests and access to the ruler, as the Sultanate was a British colony.

Neighboring countries also experienced indirect but substantial benefits through investments from the oil-producing states. With a lot of money on hand and limited investment opportunities in their own countries, Gulf investors turned to neighboring Arab countries they were familiar with. They invested primarily in real estate: land, hotels, apartments, villas. Until investment opportunities became more obvious to the unsophisticated investor, banks held a lot of currency, so businesspeople found easy credit in banks, and their businesses grew locally and regionally. Construction and contracting firms were hastily established and got major contracts in Kuwait, Saudi Arabia, and Iraq. They hired staff to operate infrastructural projects (roads, sewage, oil refineries, etc.) in their countries of origin as well as in other countries thus contributing substantially to development regionally. Service firms, including insurance companies, banks, accountants, auditors, and others, again found a rich market in the oil states.

A significant outcome in the home countries of the service firms of all these endeavors was the continued penetration of qualified and well-educated people, especially Lebanese, Syrians, and Jordanians. Consequently, expats and the educated Gulf nationals made gains in the political and social life of the country and in all phases of economic development: oil, industry, hospitality. While working in the fields in which they were employed, they naturally participated in the political and social fields and, in time, their influence on all Kuwaiti matters left its mark. Many rose the social strata to become part of the establishment and part of the decision-making process, which helped Kuwait efficiently plan its future.

In 1951, the Kuwaiti government invested in a major forward-thinking project: a water desalination plant. This supplied all the freshwater required for the population, and its capacity expanded continually to meet increasing demand. In addition, Kuwait planted trees along the main streets and used the expensive desalinated water to irrigate them. Each tree thus planted grew at the cost equivalent of one child's education from the start and through university. The greening of Kuwait was remarkable.

ABC contributed to the flow of personnel to Kuwait and Saudi Arabia and later to Dubai. I must have relocated many highly qualified managers to positions in government and the private sectors, others in service positions like sales or public relations, and some in engineering or the newly introduced Critical Path Method (CPM) positions in Kuwait's Ministry of Public Works. CPM is a technique in which you identify tasks that are necessary for project completion and determine scheduling flexibilities. A critical path in project management is the longest sequence of activities that must be finished on time for the entire project to be complete.

Other than looking for different fields of work in which I could be involved or financing a project for which we did not have sufficient funds, I concentrated on searching for firms in the service industries to acquire. I hoped that such expansions through acquisitions would help create a stable, multi-skill, geographically well-spread organization that could weather the many political and economic uncertainties we expected. But unfortunately, my hopes were dashed. I did not plan for the worst and faced significant problems in many geographic areas and practically all at the same time.

ADVISER TO GENERAL MOTORS AND AL GHANEM, 1960–1964

My work for GM related only to the local Gulf markets. Foremost on the agenda was to list and find answers to the fundamental issues at the heart of Kuwaiti society and not to breach any traditions or norms. Important functions included:

- Understanding customs and accepted procedures
- Interfacing with agents and distributors
- Setting the priorities and sequence of work
- Staffing the various divisions
- Setting the time scale necessary to achieve the objectives

GM's "fair" market share as perceived by GM and approved by the agent was the basis for the organizational work. The cost of the work being planned was to be less than the benefits accrued. The costs and benefits go parallel with a measured increase in productivity. The costs are known, while the benefits are unknown and will be measured. The job was a tall order, but in time and with cooperation by all parties, the work went well.

From the commencement of my work, I was very well received: an office was ready for my use in Al Ghanem head offices in Safat Square, a serviced villa in the Al Ghanem family residence compound provided, and a car and driver.

I had my first look at the facilities, toured the offices, met many senior staff members, discussed my views with Abdullah Al Ghanem, the CEO of Ahmad Mohammad Al Ghanem and Sons. I also met Abdullah's father, Yusuf, a highly respected person in the community who was still active in the family's business. In effect, within two weeks, I had some idea of how to proceed with my mission.

Initially, we agreed on a one-year plan to focus on the urgent and obvious needs, including but not limited to the introduction of an accounting system, which did not yet exist there. We made a quick assessment of the actual market size for car ownership in Kuwait so we will have a better basis for the number of vehicles needed to satisfy the demand in the market. First, we needed to evaluate the vehicle servicing requirements, build service garages, and staff them. A garage was built in the city, completed on time, and as planned, and staffed; the company's administration was also in progress. Then, we took stock of the vehicles in showrooms (basically in lots in open space) and ordered what we estimated would be needed until the ordering cycle for the following year's marketing plan was prepared and approved.

We planned to introduce new methods, procedures, staffing policy and goals. The local and foreign staff already being reviewed with some hired could modernize the organization in a reasonable and acceptable timeframe. The new goals in the changing market were agreed to when we started our work. Al Ghanem was the first company in the Gulf to raise the standard as a local trading organization with sales targets set and met. It was quite a challenge for me to do the work and succeed.

The experience of the vice president of GM benefited me greatly. His advice was good and well-considered and covered even some of the details of the plan I presented.

GM management and I agreed in a general way about the methodology and procedures. My work in Jordan prepared me to find temporary solutions to foreseen and possible conflicting views. and approaches between the client and the consultant. The client cannot always appreciate the quality of change that management and procedures can precipitate, and that may even affect the appearance of the daily norms of work. This "misunderstanding" may impede or slow down the work process and sometimes lead to severe conflicts.

Before I accepted the Kuwait job and met the client, I asked GM to allow me, in case of need, to make decisions on its behalf while working with their distributors in Kuwait and elsewhere. GM distributors everywhere were and still are wealthy and influential. Having misunderstandings with them or even with any family member may prejudice work progress. GM agreed with no reservations to tell the client that I had the authority to act on their behalf and, therefore, that my recommendations and suggestions are what GM recommended. Work started, and I found the client was knowledgeable, experienced, and cooperative. It was a pleasure and a precious experience that added a lot to the clarity and perception of my skills by being exposed to new social and cultural conditions.

During the initial meeting between the GM franchise owner, Abdullah Al Ghanem, and myself, I reiterated GM's position that I "represented" GM in this reorganizational job. In effect, I implied that I had the authority to decide on behalf of the principals. The franchise owners Ahmad Mohammad Al Ghanem & Co., represented by the general manager Abdullah Yusuf Al Ghanem, welcomed the arrangement with no reservation. I must say that Al Ghanem never tried to withdraw their support all through the period when I was executing my many organizational plans. I also can say the same about General Motors, which was happy with my work and supported me throughout the contract. When I was offered this job, I was thirty years old.

The job entailed the reorganization of the distribution networks and the reorganization of the agent's facilities, the procurement of personnel, the training of same, the establishment of physical plant and facilities for the marketing, maintenance, and repair of vehicles and equipment, the design and implementation of marketing strategies, and the establishment of marketing goals. I may be repeating myself, but what I did in Kuwait reflected my good presence in other countries. For example, in procuring staff for Al Ghanem, I also found personnel for other businesses. The usual sources were Jordan, Lebanon, Syria, and Iraq; I did not have contacts in Egypt, the main source for semi-skilled labor. On occasion and for more sophisticated or specialized jobs, we hired from western Europe. Thus, I became a source for job-seeking individuals from all these countries, though I worked on pro bono basis for this service. In recruiting, I became a known employer of qualified personnel in the area. My decision in recruitment was always acceptable to the clients and in most cases final, so were the salary scales that I approved—another asset for me back home in Lebanon, Jordan, and other countries where managerial skills came from. As a result, I was always able to find employment for qualified individuals without a suitable job in their own countries or in neighboring countries.

A point of contention with the Al Ghanem administration regarded hiring first class salesmen. Al Ghanem's idea was that the number of vehicles to sell depended more on the income generated by the new national source of revenue, oil, rather than added promotional efforts. However, in anticipation of a more efficient and competitive market, I insisted and got approval to hire personnel for promotional activities.

Overall, I built a good and efficient, well-defined organization for Al Ghanem companies. Departmental functions, control systems, paper flow, job descriptions, and performance measurement procedures were instituted and implemented. This approach was new in the Arab region, but it worked, and it encouraged me to apply the same standards for similar jobs. We encouraged others to follow suit. Sales teams and showrooms, maintenance facilities, organized parts stores, and accounting procedures were correctly set up. The process took a good three years. My work for Al Ghanem constituted a learning process in a subject that I knew little about. Still, the support of the GM management and Abdullah's cooperation contributed to my education in the tricky business of advising people.

Abdullah Al Ghanem became a friend, and I was to discover that his support took the form of leaving me with a total, all-inclusive power of attorney to act on his and his company's behalf. It surprised me to no end. In two years or less, GM sales increased substantially. If I remember correctly, sales increased by as much as four-fold. Of course, the market's growth accounted for most of the increase, but I was already there and known in the Gulf; my reputation was enhanced, and my client list grew again. GM was to become an important client. Working with the company's agents, the area's wealthy and powerful, I was introduced to the merchant classes both in Saudi Arabia and Kuwait and through them to the political and ruling classes. I found myself employed in demanding jobs in other countries because of my elevated contacts in these wealthy states and the reputation I enjoyed.

To go back to Abdullah Al Ghanem, I was surprised with a telephone call from him late one night in Beirut, asking me to return immediately to Kuwait to discuss a significant development. I thought we had covered everything relating to the business and did not see any change requiring a trip back to Kuwait. The surprise had nothing to do with the project at all, but a surprise it was.

I took the first available flight from Beirut and found Abdullah Al Ghanem waiting for me at the Kuwait airport. It is not something Kuwaitis did except on exceptional occasions. When we met, he told me, with no introduction, that he was going on his honeymoon and that he wanted me to take over the company's management for the month while he was away.

Running the company was not a worry for me, but I also had obligations to other clients, and my Beirut staff was not yet prepared to work independently. ABC had grown too quickly, and our staff, though good and experienced, were not yet ready to run the projects independently. I decided to spend four days in Kuwait and three days in Beirut and hoped that I would handle both ends well.

Abdullah left me an envelope on his desk in his office, which I used during his absence. When I opened the envelope, I found it contained a power of attorney giving me full authority over company business, its assets, and bank accounts, hiring and firing. In brief, it covered every aspect of his work. When he returned from his honeymoon, I returned the power of attorney. I cautioned him not to trust anybody with such a power of attorney, no matter how trustworthy he may be. I never mentioned this fact to anybody except to Grace and now in these pages. It was a rare honor.

THE CONCLUSION OF GM WORK IN KUWAIT

My description of the work might make it sound as if Al Ghanem had no facilities whatsoever, but in fact, it had enough administration to handle the sale of about one thousand vehicles a year, so we did not start from scratch. GM's and my sales estimates were closer to 3,000 units in the first year, increasing after that in the following years. The plan, when completed, foresaw an organization capable of servicing the cumulative sale of over 6,000 vehicles a year and with a maintenance and repair capacity sufficient for the total units in use in Kuwait.

What I have detailed here applies to most of my work in organization and reorganization in the oil countries at the time, because the social, technical, environmental, and educational conditions and the efficiency, or lack of it, in terms of infrastructure and government services, was practically the same. Jordan, Iran, Sudan, Ethiopia, Kenya, and East Africa generally had their own social and political conditions, making the job easier or more difficult. I hate to generalize, but this is the closest I can come to a convenient and realistic area description.

THE CHRYSLER CORPORATION

Through Abdullah al Ghanem, I met Bader Al Mulla. He was in his mid-twenties. His father, Abdullah Saleh Al Mulla, who had been foreign minister of Kuwait, started a business trading in electrical appliances in downtown Kuwait City; his keen business acumen enabled him to forge strong partnerships and utilize opportunities to create a network with reputed international brands. When he passed away, Bader replaced him in his two jobs in government and business. He was well-educated, a gentleman, good-looking, and sociable. We were about the same age, and we took to each other and became friends. I often visited him in his office in Kuwait City and at his beautiful seaside house. His wife, Badriah, a lovely person, was Abdullah Al Ghanem's sister, so the social circle was informal and pleasant.

In Bader's house in Kuwait City in the 1960s, I had my first encounter with a sensory faucet, the kind where you place your hands under it and the water comes on. I was impressed because I had never seen this before. Though Kuwait was as strongly Bedouin then as it is today, it still had something to show in advance of other places. Grace and I became friends with Bader and Badriah. They visited us in Beirut, and we attended many functions together, including the Baalbek International Festival, the Middle East's first annual cultural event, set within the Roman Temple.

I got a contract with Bader to organize his company, which represented Chrysler Corporation and other international corporations. The job was a duplicate of the GM Al Ghanem contract, and I proceeded with it and completed it in about two years. I hired an experienced, well-educated man to be the general manager. This was Abdul Ghani al-Dalli, who was secretary to the Regent, Prince Abdul Ilah of Iraq, and then minister of agriculture, head of the Industrial Bank of Iraq, and, later, ambassador to Morocco.

When the coup d'état against the Hashemite dynasty in Iraq took place, Abdul Ghani left Iraq for Morocco, where he taught economics at the University of Rabat. That was when I met him; our good relationship allowed me to evaluate his capabilities. I thought he was ideal for this job. He accepted the position of general manager of the Al Mulla organization, and he was a great help for me, especially in the implementation of my recommendations. His background and reputation made for immediate acceptance within the Kuwaiti circles. He stayed with the Al Mulla organization for over ten years and left only after the premature death of Bader. Our friendship continued until he passed away in Morocco in 2011.

THE CONSOLIDATED CONTRACTORS COMPANY (CCC)

I had several other clients. Most of my jobs were a repeat of all or part of the work done for GM and Chrysler. One job that differed substantially from the first two was the new Al Ghanem contracting business (CCC) in a joint venture with Hasib Sabbagh and Sa'id Khoury, no relation, the latter partner in charge in the Gulf area. Al-Ghanem suggested I organize the company, and both Sa'id Khoury and Hasib Sabbagh agreed promptly. Both Sa'id and Hasib were Palestinian.

I had to learn a lot before embarking on this study. Still, Sa'id, who had a lot of construction experience, was willing to help, and that provided me with sufficient support to work out the systems to cost and control construction jobs. I learned about the construction business with Sa'id in al-Ahmadi, a town south of Kuwait City. The study and the implementation of the various operational systems were successful. Later and through the years, the partners invited me to their head offices in Beirut to participate in policy decisions relating to regional expansion, reorganization, and finance. These meetings were the pro bono type. Hasib, the senior partner, and I became friends, and we met socially frequently.

Middle East markets were growing, and some international and regional contractors needed the participation of CCC to build major governmental projects in the Arab region. Some multinational firms were happy to subcontract to CCC, which became a giant construction company. The partners often advised me of what they were doing, and on occasion they sought my advice. Their reputation was great, their finances good, and their references excellent. My association with CCC and its partners was another flag I waved to support my proposals to prospective clients.

CCC became one of the largest contracting companies in the region. In the 1970s, Kamel Abdul Rahman sold his 50 percent share in CCC to his partners for US$74 million. Today, CCC is so big that it has over 200,000 workers employed in sundry and various construction jobs and has work spanning the globe. Sa'id Khoury, the last surviving partner (who passed away in 2014), brought his sons into the company, and in time, they took charge.

KUWAIT TRANSITION AND DEVELOPMENT

I was working in Kuwait in the late 1950s and '60s, when Kuwait was a small city-state with a population of barely 150,000. A vice consul of Her Majesty's government residing in Bahrain controlled all the Gulf States. He commanded governance policies, the inter-Gulf-States relations, and the salaries the various rulers were getting at the end of each month. The British had complete control. As the American influence started to grow, British power suffered slowly but surely.

In those years, very few Kuwaitis attended higher education. Those who belonged to the ruling family were groomed to occupy government positions, and the merchant families who were already well-established had trade relationships in Britain, India, Pakistan, Indonesia, and East Africa. In other words, there were no Kuwaitis available to fill managerial and technical positions, which the rapid development of the country made available and were offered by both the public and the private sectors.

On rare occasions when there was a particular reason to accept, individuals from the merchant class became available for managerial jobs. Otherwise, qualified people from Lebanon, Jordan, Syria, and Egypt filled most positions. Because of their availability, Palestinians took many of the jobs, and in time, they were to exert great influence in running both the government and the private sectors. This situation continued until the occupation of Kuwait by Iraq's Saddam Hussein. The PLO support of the Iraqi regime resulted in the deportation of most of the Palestinians working in Kuwait. It was a catastrophic event for those deported and the locals who lost personnel they trusted.

Wealth came suddenly to the area, and business flooded Kuwait and those in business there. The future looked rosy. With unbelievable gains and unimaginable wealth and promise of much more to come, Kuwait's dreams grew more ambitious. I did not realize what was happening until years later when I had the time and interest to look back, and I remember what I first saw when I was first introduced to Kuwait and how matters had changed. People I met in the late 1950s and early '60s, other than members of the trading families, suddenly became very wealthy. Many did not understand the meaning of money in such abundance and carried on with their lives as if nothing had happened. Others spent fortunes in London, Paris, Cairo, and Beirut, renting whole floors of rooms and suites in five-star hotels and entertaining all kinds of people, especially those who catered to their whims. The old, established families spent money on educating their children, further organizing their business to reap more of the benefits of oil income and exploring opportunities. They did well for themselves, their families, and the country that gave them this unprecedented abundance.

Ruling family members, in general, had more and more cash from oil revenue, and many went crazy trying to find ways to spend it.

This wealth came simultaneously to Kuwait, Bahrain, Saudi Arabia, and Iraq, the latter which did not use oil money for uncontrolled spending because of its long history with oil and the wealth it produces.

A Kuwaiti member of a merchant family who accepted a government job in the mid-1950s is well illustrated by the example of a person who was appointed director general of one of the ministries. He kept two sets of letterheads in his government office: the ministry's and that of his family's company. He did on occasion write an offer to the ministry on his company's paper and accepted or refused it using the ministry's letterheads. I witnessed this during my recurrent visits to his office. This odd behavior was not the exception, but I hasten to say that eventually, as other merchant families disapproved, the director general decided it was not worth his while to continue in his "awkward" position. Moreover, most families had more business than they could handle and did not need salaried government jobs.

During its negotiations for the Kuwait oil concession, Ahmad Al Ghanem, the acknowledged founder of the family's business, became an agent for the Anglo-Persian Oil Company (APOC). The family did business with APOC and the Kuwait Oil Company concessionaire. The short section below summarizes the Al Ghanem tribal history. I take the liberty of using their story, as I learned about it "from the horse's mouth" and witnessed part of its historical development, to illustrate how the major businesses in the area were born or created. There are similarities among tribal lineages since their cultures are based on the same fundamental beliefs and traditions and, most importantly, the desert lands with poor resources in which they lived.

THE AL GHANEM FAMILY

The Al Ghanem family, together with Al Sabah, were among the original Unaiza tribe's settlers in Kuwait during the eighteenth century. The family first made money in shipping and trade, but a disaster at sea in 1925 (the details of which I do not know) encouraged them to diversify in their interests and investments. Tribal lineage is very important to Arabs and a source of pride, which the passage of time does not diminish. In fact, every Arab I know takes lineage seriously, and belonging to Unaiza is one of the highest sources of pride. The tribe originated in the Fertile Crescent and, like many prominent tribes, predates the rise of Islam.

During the 1930s, the Al Ghanem family's income provided the government of Kuwait with two-thirds of its revenues. Ahmad's son Yusuf, along with other family members, fled Kuwait after the failure of the 1938 Majlis movement (an act considered by the ruler to be equal to a revolt) ; they returned in 1944 under a general amnesty. By the end of World War II, the Al Ghanem businesses employed 7,000 persons, forming about half the workforce of Kuwait. The family became the top labor and supply contractor for the Kuwait Oil Company, and Feisal Al Ghanem served as one of its managing directors. The family also acquired agencies and distributorships, including a lucrative arrangement with General Motors. Thunayan Feisal Al Ghanem served with the small contingent of Kuwaiti troops among the forces liberating Kuwait from Iraqi occupation in 1991. At the time, the family's Al Ghanem Industries, a holding company, ranked among the top companies in the world.

The Al Ghanem were wealthy and influential even before they attained oil wealth. My work for them gave me access to high-ranking businessmen and gave me local and regional recognition. Their support was fundamental to my success in Kuwait in a society usually closed to non-Kuwaitis. It did not take much to convince other international and regional entities to follow suit.

NEW KUWAITI CURRENCY REPLACES THE RUPEE

During this period, my work with Al Ghanem was proceeding well, with no intervention from the owners or staff. Then, a complication surfaced when the Kuwaiti government, when granted its independence from Great Britain in 1961, decided to replace the Indian rupee, which was the country's currency, with a local one and chose the dinar as its new unit.

In 1960, the Kuwaiti Currency Board was created, and the dinar was introduced to replace the rupee. The Kuwaiti and the Indian governments signed an accord agreeing that Kuwait would issue its national currency. The first Kuwaiti banknotes featured the image of the late Sheikh Abdullah bin Sabah bin Jaber Al Sabah. After one year of dealing with this currency, around Independence Day, the term "Emirate of Kuwait" was replaced by "Kuwait." The dinar coins' appearance remains essentially unchanged since their first minting in 1961. The obverse side of all Kuwaiti dinar coins features a representation of a ship, inspired by the country's rich history as a shipbuilding center in the Persian Gulf region.

When the dinar was issued in April 1961, rupee banknotes and coins were withdrawn from the markets and sent back to India. The Kuwaiti banks and post offices replaced the rupee with the dinar and pegged the dinar's value at 13.33 rupees during the following two months. Thus, the 342,000,000 Indian rupees, worth 25,646,110 Kuwaiti dinars, were replaced, agreed to, and put in circulation.

This seemingly neutral act provided those of us who were working in Kuwait and expected to deal with this supposedly simple change with problems that we regarded as monumental and impossible to sort out in a short time frame. All warehouse stocks had to be re-priced, using the new dinar currency that replaced the Indian rupee. Every spare part in stock had to be re-priced. The information cards did not usually have enough information to help the process of pricing and replenishing by ordering from the supplier. The price of every article had to be manually calculated and later verified. In some cases, we had to resort to the original invoices sent by exporters to price the individual items; this added to the time frame needed to conclude this once-in-a-lifetime occurrence.

Accounts receivable and payable presented the same problem and became more complicated due to the personal elements involved. Company clients accustomed to one type of figure, the Indian rupee, were faced with a new figure carrying a different name and different values. In many cases, debtors did not know that a new currency had been introduced to replace the old currency and had to be informed about the currency replacement. Not an easy task—it entailed explaining to the client about the change of currency in the country, what new currency would be used, and what the counter values were. It took time to explain and work out. The company later presented their bills to clients in the old currency as well as in the new one, and the debtor could pay with either currency.

New invoices in the new currency were a puzzle to the recipients as well as to the issuers, who were also new to the new currency. It is noteworthy that many Kuwaitis and residents of Kuwait were Bedouins who came to the city infrequently. The change gave them a lot to think about—paying debts or collecting dues needed recalculation and a lot of explanation. As the government was willing to extend the time for the complete replacement of the currency, I left a standing instruction to employees involved to allow clients, in case of need, to choose between two invoices in dinars or rupees, since we could use both currencies interchangeably. For us, it was simple: we collected accounts receivable in one of the two currencies and paid, in case of need, only in rupees. The bank that held the accounts made the calculations and transfers from one currency account to the other. We had to check the bank's statements carefully, at the start. One needs to remember that all calculations were manual. Technology was not a term in use. The pressures on management to move on and solve this problem required new staff, and I temporarily employed a few fresh university graduates from outside Kuwait. When they completed their tasks, I kept most of them doing other work that evolved from the widened business activities. Most stayed with the company or found other jobs in different companies and remained in Kuwait for a long time.

Al-Ra'ed al-Arabi

While going about my work with enthusiasm and devotion, I found myself entangled in journalism. In the early 1960s, printed media was not allowed in Kuwait. The government-owned radio station did not carry advertising. We needed a medium to advertise GM's products and other businesses represented or managed by our client. I came up with the idea of producing a monthly magazine in Beirut, with the Kuwait market as our target audience. Al Ghanem accepted the proposal, and I named the journal al-Ra'ed al-Arabi, meaning "the Arab Pioneer." The journal was prepared and published in Beirut. In its two years, it became a prestigious publication covering economic and commercial news of Kuwait, Lebanon, and other Arab countries of the Middle East.

I engaged a team of professionals, many of whom were political refugees from neighboring Arab states who had many friends and contacts in the Arab world. Our al-Ra'ed offices became a meeting place for politicians from Lebanon, Jordan, Syria, Iraq, Kuwait, Bahrain, and the Trucial States, some of them political refugees. I was responsible for running al-Ra'ed and did not require permission to publish whatever I deemed of value. When Kuwait relaxed its print media laws, the owners, the Al Ghanem family, took al-Ra'ed to Kuwait to be managed and published locally. It did not survive the move, and my contribution to the magazine ended.

I successfully got enough advertising income to cover the costs of al-Ra'ed, so I did not ask Al Ghanem to finance it at any stage of its publication out of Beirut. The local Al Ghanem chap, Jassem Mohammad Al Ghanem, appointed by the family to run the periodical, did not have the necessary background, nor did the journal make enough money to induce him to stay. Hence, it became peripheral to his interests. During the life of al-Ra'ed, we interviewed prominent people in many fields. I managed the journal as if it were my own and Al Ghanem's public relations tool.

Iraq-Kuwait Political Turmoil, 1961

A short-lived crisis developed in 1961 as Abdul-Karim Qassem, then the president of Iraq, threatened to invade Kuwait. Qassem first announced the annexation of Kuwait and appointed as its ruler the Emir as qa'im maqam (district manager) of Kuwait, at a monthly salary of 30 Iraqi dinars. Qassem threatened to occupy Kuwait but did not because of the international and regional rallies that took place in support of the country.

Iraq is a product of the Sykes-Picot Agreement. It included the Ottoman wilayat al-Basra but fell short of encompassing the sheikhdom of Kuwait. Iraq was founded on August 23, 1921, as the Kingdom of Iraq and Faisal was declared its first Hashemite king on that date. The omission of Kuwait in the Sykes-Picot Agreement as part of Iraq did not sit well with the Hashemites who were overthrown in a coup d'état in 1958. It did not sit well thereafter with any regime that followed.

Kuwait was part of wilayat al-Basra and was ruled according to tribal conventions of kinship. Iraq also ruled the Ahwaz in present-day southwestern Iran. In 1963, Abdul Karim Qassim seized power, and his later assassination was followed by a sequence of several unstable governments. In 1972, Saddam Hussein came to power as a strongman and remained president of Iraq until the United States occupied the country in 2003 through a devastating war—dismantling the civil administration, disbanding the army, and opening the Arab Middle East to Iranian control. Iraq still suffers from the war disaster, making one wonder if there is a future for Iraq.

A KUWAITI DELEGATION TO SOUTH AMERICA

Kuwait resorted to many measures to counter Abdul-Karim Qassim's declaration of annexation. One was to send delegations abroad to explain to the international community that Kuwait was an independent emirate, and that the Iraqi decision was aggressive and unacceptable. The Kuwaiti government formed commissions and sent delegates to the United States, western Europe, the USSR, China, Japan, and South America. They sent as many commissions as they could find people to staff.

I heard many stories and learned a lot about these commissions, as I was asked to write the report to the ruler of Kuwait, Sheikh Sabah Al-Salim Al Sabah regarding the delegation sent to countries in South America. This delegation was headed by my client Abdullah Al Ghanem, owner of Ahmed Mohammad Al Ghanem & Sons Company. All delegates were important members of the wealthy Kuwaiti merchant class.

When the delegation began its mission in South America, my business relations with Abdullah were not at their best. We occasionally had our differences, but this time the relationship was worse. When working to streamline his company, Ahmed Mohammad Al Ghanem & Sons Company, I did not consider any internal family differences and interests. I had no control over this problem, which I did not foresee, and nor did I foresee my involvement in the haggling and the internal discord and having to take sides in very sensitive family affairs.

The problem related to the interest some members of the Al Ghanem family showed in participating in the company's management, which was against Abdullah's declared stand. He wanted me to take part in the discussions and support his position. I was not in favor of the inclusion of new family members in the company's management, as this would complicate my work and slow progress in implementing and improving plans. It also would get General Motors directly involved—and with management changes in GM, who knew what their new views would be? I was not ready to become part of family disputes. Abdullah and I still worked together but in a less than friendly and sometimes tense atmosphere. So, I was surprised when Abdullah was on the phone from Beirut one Saturday afternoon asking for an immediate and urgent meeting. I had no clue what this urgency was all about.

We met that evening at the Bristol Hotel. Abdullah briefed me on the issue related to the delegation sent by Sheikh Sabah Al-Salim Al Sabah to the countries in South America to explain Kuwait's predicament. In addition, they were to report about their delegates' activities at the end of the tour. The report to the ruler would summarize their findings and make recommendations as to the measures Kuwait should take in the countries the delegation had visited.

I listened carefully and suggested that we meet the following day again so I would have time to mull ideas over and consider whether I could assist. Abdullah insisted I meet all the South America delegates before I left, to review their concerns. We met in a hotel suite, and they repeated what Abdullah had told me and said they needed to present their report to the ruler in two weeks. Listening to them gave me the feeling that they were desperate, for reasons I could not understand. They needed help writing the report and openly asked me to write it. I could not glean any more information from them, but seeing how desperate they were, and I decided to help.

Under normal circumstances, meeting with this group of influential men would have given me thoughts about business opportunities. Still, in this case, I became in my mind part of the delegation and wanted to help.

I spent over two hours with the delegation to review and agree on a methodology and procedure for writing the report. I needed information on their activities and meetings in South America. I suggested that they meet and remember among themselves details that would help my team better understand the extent to which the countries visited were positive in their discussions. I thought I might as well write a report to efficiently plan for the future of Kuwait's international policies and relations. I was happy that this. delegation had sought my help; otherwise, their report would have been a disaster.

This meeting was almost devoid of information. The delegates' draft report did not cover their meetings with government functionaries, ministers, and heads of states. One unpleasant surprise, I quickly realized, was that they did not take any notes all through their trip about their appointments, discussions, or activities.

The sequence of topics for the report was to be based on the dates and locations of meetings, and with whom they met: heads of states, government ministers, and others. I gave my staff instructions on how to interview the delegates, beginning with obtaining details of meetings, names, and positions of functionaries with whom they had met, the points discussed, and the attitude of the individuals with whom the delegates had met. The willingness to support Kuwait in whatever the delegation suggested was also examined. This section of the report would set out the facts, providing the base for introducing the report's background material before going into recommendations and plans of action for Kuwait. The facts were not available, and the report's writing became an impossibility. If we managed the accomplishment, it would be a feat. I thought seriously of getting out of this dilemma and refusing to be involved, but again, right, or wrong, I decided that if the outcome was a poorly written report, the recommendations might unnecessarily or unintentionally hurt Kuwait's relations with the countries visited. I went ahead to do what I could. I felt I owed Kuwait something, and therefore, this job became time consuming, worrying, and challenging.

The problem I foresaw was related to when the Emir received the report and circulated it to his inner circle and senior staff. The possibility of one of them checking names or, worse, checking on whether the delegation met with persons named in the report or finding inaccuracies made me very careful in the data collection.

To tackle the job required a lot of creativity. I made my plans and started attending to this exceptional job with apprehension. I called some enterprising chaps who worked for al-Ra'ed al-Arabi, formed a team of four, and met the Kuwaiti team the following day. I explained the situation, and all of us put our heads together and worked out a strategy to collect and collate information from the delegates and write the report.

My staff was eager to meet the delegation. As I had told my staff, the delegates had no recollection of what had happened during their trip, who they saw, what they discussed, and what conclusions they could draw. We divided the delegation into groups and then compared notes to ensure we got some sensible information leading to a plausible story.

I assigned one staff member to three delegates, each to prod his group to remember what happened. Then, as far as we could, we tried to verify facts by comparing various groups' stories, writing each segment relating to a country visited, and writing a summary that was passed on to me as soon as it was written.

Two of the four who worked on this report were Raji Sahyoun and Abdul Mohsen Abu Meizar. The first was a retired official spokesman for the Palestine Liberation Organization, whom I hired as editor of al-Ra'ed al-Arabi. The second became the spokesman for the PLO in the mid-1970s after the assassination by an Israeli commando team headed by Ehud Barak of the then-spokesman Kamal Nasser. Kamal was a well-known poet and novelist, and he had been my good friend.

As the delegates did not remember the names of the officials they met, we opted to use visiting cards they had in their possession as guidelines. We also inquired at the Ministry of Foreign Affairs in Beirut about the names of foreign secretaries and other likely officials they could have met to verify as much information as possible. We also checked with South American embassies in Beirut as part of our verification process.

It took us about two weeks to prepare the summaries and start writing the first draft. I passed it on to my committee of four, who made suggestions. At the end, we satisfied ourselves as to the accuracy level of the "facts" we decided we needed to maintain, and the content was unanimously approved. Even the delegates. agreed that the report described the experience and performance and did not need further checking. The information also included recommendations to the ruler concerning the course of action Kuwait was best advised to take.

Then, I started writing the final report, and I passed it on again to my committee. Some sections were rewritten many times to enhance the quality of the recommendations. The Arabic language allows for interpretations that may, if not worded properly, create unnecessary differences in evaluating the meaning of a recommendation. We made sure that the language was unambiguous.

I wrote the Kuwait diplomatic strategy for the Americas, which remained unchanged for many years. It was implemented as submitted. It covered every country separately, pointing out where embassies or consulates should be located. We advised about the various senior positions in the diplomatic and consular corps, the qualifications of staff, and the need to cement relations with these countries by inviting foreign ministers and others to visit Kuwait and sending higher level diplomats to South America. The report detailed the policy that best served Kuwait with the governments of South America.

I kept the delegation in Beirut for a further week to ensure they read the report and understood its content. Of course, I did not submit an invoice for the effort exerted, nor was I paid for it, but I was pleased at the time to predict Kuwait's diplomatic activities in South America. After all, I wrote the policy.

The report, as far as I was concerned, was a state secret. I kept one copy for six months to answer questions if the Emir needed or wanted an explanation or a detail, then I gave that copy to Abdullah Al Ghanem to deal with as he saw fit.

Interlude

THOUGHTS AND MISCELLANEOUS

My trips to Kuwait became less frequent, and I bought a project management company in the USA. I introduced it in Kuwait and signed an agreement with the Ministry of Works to introduce the then-new concept in project management, the Critical Path Method, which I mentioned earlier. The work lasted for several years, and the focus was on projects in progress operated by the Ministry of Public Works, highlighting problems which needed the attention of the higher echelons in the ministry. In agreement with the minister, we provided a red alert for projects that needed his attention and other types of signals indicating the person in the ministry to whom the alerts should be sent, so that follow-up would be secure. The individual concerned attended to the highlighted problem.

We also had the duty of documenting the good performance of contractors so that they would be placed on a list of preferred contractors for future work. This method became popular in the ministry, and those who did commendable work were sure to get future contracts. Other jobs emanating from this project were to train employees in CPM to replace the hired consultant; in this case the consultant was me.

Overall, my work and life in Kuwait were satisfactory. Sometimes it was quite enjoyable, and on other occasions it was a pain in the neck, but my curiosity was satisfied, and my understanding of the area and its people deepened.

It did strike me that people's roots in the Gulf and Saudi were more important than in the Levant, and tribal ties sometimes dictated courses of action that were alien to me. It took me time to recognize and understand the value of these background issues for people in a rooted Bedouin society. They lived by different codes and different values and had different concepts of priorities. While businesspeople benefiting from work in the Gulf and Saudi needed to understand their clients' ways, principles, traditions, and values, the locals had to learn foreign ways. Otherwise, many problems would be created that might not have arisen.

Some stories may emphasize the issues of mutual respect and understanding, which makes working together pleasant and productive. For example, some "foreign" businesspersons working in the Gulf used disparaging words about their clients or associates, reflecting poor judgment on the part of those who used that language or held those attitudes. Showing disdain of one's counterpart for whom one works and from where one's income derives shows abysmal judgment; foolishness often led some foreigners to be quickly relieved of their commitments and ousted from Kuwait.

I witnessed poor behavior on several occasions in Kuwait, the Gulf, and Saudi Arabia. Sometimes it was so embarrassing, especially when the Kuwaiti understood the language.

Through my long and close exposure to various backgrounds in various places, I learned that what is good for one may or may not be good for another. The preacher in me says that this must be recognized and accepted. Please do not underestimate your counterpart, whether that person is a client or an acquaintance.

JORDAN NATIONAL BANK LOOKING FOR INVESTMENTS

While in Kuwait working for Al Ghanem, the chairman of the Board of Jordan National Bank, Suleiman Pasha Sukkar, called me one day and said that the bank had decided to increase its capital to grow the banking sector in Jordan, Syria, and Lebanon. Furthermore, he said that he would appreciate my support with Kuwaiti investors.

Mohammad Touqan was the general manager of the bank, along with Suleiman Pasha. They came to Kuwait to get Kuwaitis to invest in the bank's capital. We met at my house in the Al Ghanem compound, and I introduced them to Yusuf Al Ghanem, Abdullah's father, who was present when they arrived. I explained to Yusuf Al Ghanem the purpose of the visit. He listened, asked a few questions, and agreed to handle the capital increase the bank needed.

He asked his son Abdullah to call Bader Al Mulla, his son-in-law, and the prior Kuwaiti foreign minister, to make an official announcement over Kuwait radio about this visit and its purpose. The announcement mentioned that the bankers were his guests. The capital increase sought was subscribed and fully paid within three days. What I got for this service was a verbal thanks for my help from Suleiman Pasha and Mohammad Touqan.

I returned to Beirut, and the bankers stayed in Kuwait to make the necessary arrangements about stock issues and finalize the mechanics of the deal. The thanks to Yusuf Al Ghanem for participating in the bank's capital and introducing Sukkar and Touqan to businessmen in Kuwait was to invite his son, my client Abdullah, to join the board of directors of the bank, which he did.

As usual, my pro bono reputation was well-advertised and expected, and I collected no fee and got no compensation. How-ever, when I visited Amman, lunch and dinner invitations became more frequent.

IRAN, 1969

I established contacts in Iran, arranged for my staff to visit and work with local personnel, and offered a Teheran University professor of social sciences an opportunity to work with us. We started work there as soon as our market research clients extended their interest into the Gulf, Saudi, and Iran. We did not get much work in Iran, but it was sufficient for me to understand the market and culture and add Iran to my company's list of areas served.

ALGERIA, 1976

We worked for SONATRAC, an Algerian public company with a monopoly over production and sale of gas. We established a company in Algiers to handle the work we expected to have; we got a first job, and I sent my brother of mine to operate the project. With Lebanon drifting into civil war, he and his family left Beirut for Algeria and, later, moved to Nice, France, from where he managed the work in Algeria.

Saba & Company

Saba & co. was a respected regional audit firm. Fuad Saba, an outstanding Palestinian nationalist and highly regarded personality, established his firm in Palestine in 1926. He was the first Arab to become a Fellow of the Institute of Certified Accountants in England and Wales. Over time, he developed an impressive list of clients, including most larger companies in the Arab world, including Kuwait and the Gulf States. I tell this story because Saba & Co. were my auditors, and I was involved for over six months in the company's survival problem.

As the first Arab to establish an accounting firm, Fuad Saba was welcome in Palestine and elsewhere in the Arab countries. When Britain became the mandate power in Palestine, Jordan, and Iraq, it introduced laws requiring tax payments. This was new to businesses in the area. Before the mandate, the government collected the tax revenue on a basis other than income and profits. The new requirements encouraged and helped audit firms get more business in Palestine and in other areas that were under British or French mandates. As a result, Saba & Co. opened branches in Palestine, Lebanon, Jordan, Syria, Iraq, Yemen, and the Gulf States and were the prime audit firm in the oil-rich states of Saudi Arabia, Bahrain, and Kuwait. With this growth, the firm needed more qualified staff and thus started creating teams of professionals. Egyptian audit firms served Egypt and North Africa.

Other companies in fields such as banking, insurance, transport, contracting, and trading also grew in the same fashion and in the same locations as Saba & Co., in anticipation of, or in tandem with, business growth. Thus, Saba & Co. was there to service them. Prime clients, including the Arab Bank, the Arabia Insurance Company, the Contracting & Trading Co. (CAT), and many more branches and associates of such companies automatically became Saba's clients.

An AUB graduate in business joined Saba & Co.'s Kuwait office as an employee. He was given every chance to do well in his job. Over the years, he climbed the ladder of this internationally recognized company to the top positions relatively quickly. He became a partner and remained in charge of the Kuwait operation. He was presentable, intelligent, and a fair public relations man. Fuad Saba continued to be actively involved and remained a senior partner for a long time. However, when he grew older, his attention shifted to overseeing the company's performance, leaving the daily work to some sound professionals.

This Kuwait office partner and manager's ambitions made him seek the number one job as the senior partner. Rightly so, Fuad Saba, the senior partner, as well as others did not approve this request. The long and short of it is that this person resigned as Kuwait branch manager, set up his own audit firm in Kuwait, in direct competition with Saba & Co., and managed to secure many of the clients to his newly established business. He must have planned this well and arranged to move clients from Saba & Co to his new outfit. This, of course, hurt Saba's reputation and overnight substantially decreased its revenue. This person who had been trusted and given all the chances to grow and achieve, used his position and relationship with the clients to move them to his newly established company.

Fuad Saba and his son Suheil, a partner, came one day to see me at home in Beirut, told me the story, and asked me to intervene. They suggested that they leave it to me to negotiate and resolve this barely ethical situation. It was a tall order, especially because it was rather late in the story, and many had already tried their hand and failed. I knew the manager who had usurped Fuad's business, and I was sure this man would not give up the newly won position which had fulfilled his business and social dreams, forgot ethics and accepted practice. He prospered at the cost of those who trusted him and paid dearly for their trust.

Fuad Saba offered me a twenty percent stake in Saba & Co. in payment for my services, whether my intervention in Kuwait succeeded or not. I declined the very generous offer and promised to do whatever I could to help him find a way out of this dilemma.

I tried, but this competitor was adamant in his demands. He promised to fold his new company if offered the senior partnership position at Saba & Co. This condition was not in the cards, and Fuad was afraid the man would use more tricks as an insider to take over the company. The level of confidence between Fuad Saba and this man was close to naught.

I thought it would be best to replace the competitor at Saba & Co. with a qualified Kuwaiti who could correct the situation and get back some, if not all, the lost accounts. I offered the position to Faisal Mazidi, a well-respected Kuwaiti with suitable qualifications and local contacts, and Faisal accepted my offer. Fuad Saba found this a satisfactory solution, so the deal was concluded.

It hurts to write my opinion on this behavior by a Palestinian who started his life as a refugee and was partially helped by Fuad Saba to pay his school fees, and on graduation applied for a job at Saba & Co, where he was hired. He worked there for many years and was promoted to regional partner. He then betrayed Fuad Saba, a Palestinian who spent his life working for his mother country. Rumors have it that the issue was sectarian; he claimed he was a devout Muslim, and Saba was a Christian.

In the 1970s, Saba & Co. hoped to continue associating with major international accounting firms while also keeping its local identity. At the same time, Touche Ross International wanted to increase its Middle East presence, and the two joined forces in 1978. After Touche Ross and Deloitte merged in 1989, Saba & Co. became Deloitte Middle East.

Saudi Arabia, 1965–1970

GENERAL MOTORS

Life and work in Saudi Arabia, in general, were similar to what I had experienced in Kuwait. I spent a lot of time commuting between Jeddah in Hejaz, Riyadh in Najd, and Khobar in al-Ahsa', thus covering most of the country's commercial and well-populated regions.

I had the opportunity to watch Saudi's economic growth and social development up close, from its inception. Early on, Saudi's financial situation was not as good as Kuwait's, so the increase in consumer spending was less noticeable and distribution of wealth to individuals was not as perceptible. Though both countries depended on oil as the primary export commodity, they differed in size and population. In fact, there was (and still is in Saudi Arabia) substantial poverty and an underprivileged class.

My experience in Kuwait helped a lot in my Saudi job for GM, as the sales problems were the same, and the management problems were almost the same except that Saudi was 120 times larger in area and needed regional offices and regional service centers. In Kuwait, distances between the head office and the sales points and service facilities were short, and owners always felt in control. In Saudi, the distances between head office and branches were a concern. It was not easy for the owners to relinquish some of their authority to regional managers, travel from between locations was time consuming, and communication facilities were inadequate. For example, traveling by plane between Jeddah and Riyadh for non-Saudis entailed delivering the passport a day in advance to the police department to get permission to travel, with a visa-like stamp on the airline ticket. This piece of bureaucracy stalled business growth in the field I was directing, as the visa on the ticket sometimes was not stamped or the decision to allow the travel was delayed, resulting in travel changes and travelers even missing government appointments.

However, both my clients together representing all GM products were excellent and generous in their hospitality. Each represented a product sector. Salah Abdul Jawad represented the cars and trucks while Yusuf al-Zahid represented all the other products including heavy machinery. They were not in competition because of the different products they managed but also because Salah's wife was the sister of Yusuf al-Zahid's. Also, their villas in Jeddah were adjacent.

Through Salah, I met Mohammad Omar Tewfik, the minister of public works. His main office was in Riyadh, but his visits to Jeddah were frequent and in time, we became friends. He was a valuable contact, and I got involved in the infrastructural plans. As a result, the minister and I talked a lot about the country's needs and the ministry's role in in the implementation of such plans. I spent most afternoons when in Jeddah at Salah's house where, he and I played backgammon, and Salah and occasionally Yusuf talked about the plans to satisfy General Motors.

Salah Abdul Jawad and Yusuf Al Zahid and Mohammad Omar Tewfik were frequent visitors to Beirut and Amman, and I entertained them in both countries. All three became good friends, and they welcomed me in their homes in Jeddah. On occasion I visited the minister in Riyad, usually early in the morning, before sunrise.

They introduced me to friends of theirs, all in business or government, and I got a better understanding of the social, tribal, and business networks. The tribal structures in both countries were similar; the powerful tribes lived in areas covering thousands of kilometers. The same tribes moved or lived in every Gulf country and north in Iraq, Jordan, and Syria. The blood relationship of people in all those areas is close and intermingled.

Salah lived in India at its partition in the late 1940s. He was close to Mohammad Ali Jenna and his movement, seeking to secede from India to form a separate Muslim country, Pakistan. The latter split into two nations years after the separation from India: Pakistan in the east and Bangladesh in the west. Salah liked to talk about that period. Because I showed interest, he went into many details of events, and indeed, I learned a lot about the Muslim perspective of the secession from India. It's good to note that at the time of this writing, India's Muslim population is larger than the total population of Pakistan and Bangladesh combined.

In Jeddah, I met Prince Sultan bin Abdul Aziz, the minister of defense, and through him I got a contract as a consultant to Saudi Arabian Airlines, a job I held for two years. This job later produced three airline clients: Sudan Airways, Libyan Airlines, and Yemenia. I turned down the offer for the Yemeni airline, which was still on the planning board and not yet operational.

I was already thinly spread in a field that was new to me. I did not need to present a proposal to the Libyan or Sudan airlines; the mere fact that I consulted for Saudi Arabian Airlines was reference enough. I lived to regret the job in Libya. I worked, produced the report, and drew in detail the plans for implementing the recommendations, but no payment was forthcoming. I submitted the final report ten days after the agreed-upon date, but that was because the airport in Beirut had closed, and we had to find other routes to send the report. After over eight months of work, including visits to Libya and discussions with management, to pay our fees of US$180,000. There is no recourse to courts in Libya, and we lost this money at a time when our cash flow was not at its best.

I decided not to pursue the payment, as visiting Libya could result in severe punishment, especially if one disagreed with an arm of the government. However, my report was already in the hands of Libyan Airlines, and I do not know whether they used it or not.

The only job I got for which I was paid a commission was a road-construction project in the north of Saudi. I recommended CAT Contracting and Trading, a prime Lebanese contracting company, in partnership with Paul Hardeman, a friend, whose company was one of the 500 constituting Standard & Poor's Index, to the Ministry of Public Works. They were awarded the contract, and I charged a commission, which they willingly paid. It was a unique contract, as signing an agreement with no tender and no competition was not common practice. This was the only time in my business career that I charged a commission for a job I produced for a client or a friend.

A DIGRESSION

The emerging oil sources in the late 1950s and '60's brought in a lot of wealth to Saudi Arabia. Senior members of the merchant families, who were accustomed to wealth knew how to continue business as usual and kept good relations with the foreigners with whom they had previous contact or business dealings.

Those with a sudden abundance of money, spent it crazily all over the Middle East and Europe, creating the image of the Arab world which lingered in the minds and beliefs of businesspersons and ordinary people in the West. This image was never wholly forgotten. Some newly affluent became less friendly and sometimes less polite to outsiders. One should remember that they had been taken advantage of by foreigners who came to work in the oil business and who, in the far past, profited greatly at the expense of the locals. I cannot say that there was no exception to this rule. Still, outsiders like me became wary of the lifestyle and values of the newly wealthy and avoided contact with the local population as much as possible.

SAUDI ARABIAN AIRLINES, 1960S

Saudi Arabia presented itself as a promising market for ABC's services. Initially, we got a contract to study the organization and staffing of Saudi Arabian Airlines (SAA), the country's flag carrier. Unfortunately, the job was more difficult than expected, especially since Trans World

Airlines (TWA) had a management agreement over SAA and did not look favorably on my presence.

While studying the airline's organization, I found that TWA had established a parallel operation. They were using TWA staff and new staff employed to do the work supposedly conducted by SAA staff, who had been "archived" in offices with nearly nothing to do. In addition, TWA used SAA as a feeder for its international network.

Many Saudi nationals employed by SAA were marginalized and could not participate in any work but were kept on the payroll. SAA paid the cost for labor imported by TWA, which manned most of the middle management; the higher echelons were entirely TWA personnel, with a few Saudis employed to please the owners of the airlines.

Saudis did not appreciate how TWA was governing SAA and managing it as if they owned it. Through dissatisfied local personnel, I became privy to much information, some helpful and some aimed to use me and ABC as allies against TWA. I got a lot of positive feedback from all the ranks in the SAA.

I brought this matter to the attention of the board of directors of Saudi Airlines, then chaired by H.R.H. Prince Sultan bin Abdul Aziz, the minister of defense. At the board meeting I attended, there was no mention relating to my views on staffing and the control of TWA over SAA. Later, Prince Sultan took me aside and told me he would address this subject—which he said was very sensitive and went beyond a business transaction to Saudi American relations—in a more appropriate setting. He did not want to share the information I had brought him with the public or the board. I let the subject drop, leaving it to politicians to find a solution. I could not have done otherwise.

Jordan Radio and Television

EARLY 1960S AND ON

The Jordan market offered plenty of market research and consulting opportunities, starting with government radio. The scope of the job we were hired to do was broad, but first, we needed to find ways to generate income by encouraging advertisers to buy time on the airwaves.

Special media surveys were needed, and ABC conducted the fieldwork to gather information on media signal reach, audience, and products and then analyze the results. We sent the findings to advertisers in the countries exporting to Jordan, initially free of charge. Advertisers started ordering ad hoc market research when the investigation proved to be well conducted and the results properly analyzed. At the time, ABC had no competitors in this field, nor was there any reluctance by our clients to buy our media reports. Jordan Radio also benefited from advertising income, which contributed to its operational costs.

Soon, I started hearing rumblings that advertising should be discouraged because it brought ideas that were not compatible with local social norms, such as scantily dressed young women. We assured the public that the government, and the laws being prepared concerning advertising, would manage the messaging. Once written and published, the rules would address all inappropriate advertising messages. A committee was formed to draft what was called an Advertising Code of Ethics, applicable to radio and later to television in Jordan.

Sharif Abdul Hamid Sharaf, the minister of information, accepted the approach. We met a few times, agreed on the content and wording, and completed the final copy. The Code of Ethics was designed to respond to all questions relating to what was acceptable and what was not welcome to be broadcast. It laid down the rules regarding language and content that advertisers had to follow when addressing the public. Lawyers reviewed the text, and when the document was officially approved, it was passed on to the Radio and TV Commercial Department. On radio, and again, later, on TV, video content was reviewed by the Commercial Department of the media. The Code of Ethics was adopted by many commercial television and radio stations throughout the Middle East, and it ensured that advertising messages did not upend social mores or offend members of the public.

The Commercial Department built over time to manage and sell advertising for both radio and TV, locally and internationally, became very capable. Local knowledge of how to sell an intangible on media, especially on radio, succeeded. In addition, we gained considerable experience relating to advertisements in printed media.

Most of ABC's initial experience came from our work for Time Life in Beirut; they managed a newly established television station known as Canal 9, a French language channel owned by the Lebanese government. Time- Life managers invited ABC to participate in media research, which was a new field to us. The guidance we received from them over the long period of work together was sufficient to make us the best-informed and best-known media research outfit in the region. As a result, media research in all its aspects became a significant specialty that we offered our clients. Many international retailers of consumer products increased their demands for media spots in the region.

Jordan Radio (and, later, Television) was a valuable client. With the field staff and personnel that we hired in Amman, it became necessary to set up a center to administer the growing business and liaison with the Ministry of Information, the oversight agency. This office managed the budgets and accounts and kept in touch with personnel in the field. In addition, we hired representatives, on a salary basis, to plan and to supervise agents in Beirut and London and other staff in vital locations, such as Paris.

In Beirut and London, these agents were tasked with soliciting advertisements for Jordan Radio. First, the agents promoted the media they represented, the Jordan Radio, and later the Jordan TV and, later, television stations in Lebanon. The combined effort produced satisfactory results for the clients and for the commercial center in Amman; ABC conducted the surveys for all the media in the area.

The next stage was to establish a television station. The Jordanian government helped build it partially with money contributed by television equipment producers and investors. In this process, we assisted—without payment—in all the functions. Both radio and TV were and still are government owned, and both served the government politically. As mentioned earlier, the added advertising income also helped improve the services the radio and TV provided for their clients.

We recruited Mohammad Kamal, a Palestinian from Lebanon, to be general manager. He was responsible for overseeing the building of a modern studio facility. The space had offices for management and staff, meeting rooms, and a beautiful garden. Employees and visitors found it an excellent place to work outside the four walls of an office. Jordan Television was successful. It had the advantage of using the established Commercial Department serving the Jordan Radio station. The two-year span between inception and operation of the TV station was spent in planning the future of activities in public relations and advertising, time well used. As a pro bono consultant, I participated and was happy to be there when needed.

The government's interest in the project was overwhelming. The king, the prime minister, the minister of information, and the general Jordanian public showed great enthusiasm for a local TV provider.

Many official guests to Jordan were invited to tour the facilities, which had become a point of pride for the country. The visits also gave those who invited the guests a break from having to keep them entertained. ABC continued the work relationship with Jordan Radio and TV for close to two decades, during which time the organizations became efficient enough not to need external advice.

Our advertisers were happy with their marketing performance, and the demand for radio and television time was stable at near-total capacity. In addition, ABC found further benefit for our business from advertisers who signed up for studies in product promotion and strategies to further their marketing goals. Among the clients were PepsiCo, Johnson & Johnson, Nestle, Unilever, Procter & Gamble, Beecham's, and many others. These international corporations became long-term clients of ABC's market research division throughout the Middle East and East Africa.

ABC East Africa, 1967

KENYA

Soon after the Arab Israeli war of June 1967, I went to Nairobi, Kenya, armed with a letter of introduction from the vice president of the Chase Manhattan Bank in Beirut to the manager of the Standard Bank in Nairobi. At that time, I did not have a network of associates or reliable contacts to help me assess the business climate and, I hoped, establish a branch office. However, I was encouraged by some prospective clients who were already located in East Africa and needed the services of ABC, especially in market research. Chase Manhattan's letter made the difference, and Standard Bank's manager provided me with full support; Dolf Knul was very friendly and gave me all the advice I called for or needed. He suggested I base the office in Nairobi under the name Associated Business Consultants (East Africa) Ltd. We rented space, hired staff, and started planning for work in Kenya, Uganda, Sudan, and Ethiopia.

ABC East Africa widened our customer base. One client was Karim Khan, the Agha Khan of Ismaili Muslims. His organization requested a study of the circulation of their newspaper, Ta'ifa, in Kenya and neighboring countries. This newspaper was published by and distributed to members of the Isma'ili sect, the head of which is the Agha Khan. Ismailism is the third of the three sects of the Shi'a in Islam. Prince Shah Karim al-Husayni, known by the religious title Mawlana Hazar Imam within Ismaili Muslim circles and as Aga Khan IV elsewhere, is the 49th and current Imam of Nizari Ismailism.

The East Africa office proved to be not profitable, but it introduced us to new markets and new clients whose needs were unique to them; the ABC East Africa office remained in Nairobi until the late 1970s, at which time we sold it to the American accounting firm Touche Ross & Co.

I relate a story about a Kenyan lunch hosted by the country's president in honor of the president of Uganda. One day, Dolf Knul and I were having lunch at the New Stanley Hotel, the most elegant and prestigious hotel in Nairobi. Dolf and I were having a drink and waiting for our order for lunch when President Jomo Kenyatta of Kenya came in, together with President Idi Amin of Uganda, followed by their entourage. A buffet table was set up and reserved for a large group. The two presidents and higher functionaries were seated by the maître d; the entourage was directed to the buffet.

Almost everyone in the entourage started to fill their plates with food. Meats were mixed with rice, cakes, fruits, seafood, salads, and whatever else on the buffet table, jumping from one end and finishing at the other end. The entourage had never seen a table laden with so much food that anyone could serve themselves in as much quantity as they wanted.

SIGHTS AND SAFARIS

On arrival to Nairobi and the registration of ABC East Africa, I hired the last of the White Hunters who indeed knew the country very well. White Hunters were professional big game hunters and safari guides. Ours came highly recommended, and he helped us move in areas where market research jobs were sought. He did a good job for our company when we started East Africa operations.

Whenever he was free from company work, he took me on safaris and visits around the country. The most interesting and unique places I remember seeing were Nairobi National Park, the rhinoceros spring, the Treetops Hotel, Mombasa city, the Stanley Hotel, and Lake Nakuru in Kenya's Great Rift Valley. These were and are landmark destinations for anyone visiting Kenya.

About Beirut in the 1960s

The American University of Beirut was the university of choice for men and women from across the region and beyond: people from Arab countries, India, Sudan, the USA, and Europe came to study there. Many went into professions such as medicine or engineering. It was a highly regarded institution with high educational standards. AUB had a relatively small student body in the 1940s and '50s, so the students got to know each other and thus had a network of friends and acquaintances who were professionals or in public service across the region.

Beirut in the 1960s was a destination for Arab intelligentsia, a city where freedom of speech, freedom of expression, and freedom of the press allowed journalists, radicals, and reformers from neighboring countries to meet openly, away from their dictatorial regimes. Many Syrians, Iraqis, and Jordanians who were citizens non grata in their countries found freedom in Beirut. Some citizens of the Gulf States, whose leaders had signed protective treaties with Britain between 1820 and 1892, headed to Beirut to escape the restrictive attitude of the British vice consul. Sidewalk cafés in the downtown area or on Hamra Street were their meeting places, and new ideas and new political parties grew out of these meetings.

In 1960–1961, we published al-Ra'ed al-Arabi, a monthly magazine specializing in economic and commercial news. The office which housed al-Ra'ed became a place for Arab expatriates and Lebanese politicians to meet. There, I met men who would influence the trajectory of their nation's political development and who in time returned to their countries as political leaders. Later, it was easy for me to reach out to decision-makers in countries where I had work, as they were some of the same men who had contributed to al-Ra'ed al-Arabi.

AMAZING DR. DAHESH

In addition to the endless political stories, there came to our attention a rather remarkable individual by the pseudonym of Dr. Dahesh. He was born in 1906 in Jerusalem as Salim Mousa el-Achi, and his family traveled the area in search of a home where freedom was accepted and so landed in Beirut. He had a charismatic personality endowed with special powers that made him, to some, a prophet. Yet, except for one year in an orphanage, he had no formal education.

A TALE BY VISITORS TO DR. DAHESH

One very early morning, there was a knock at our apartment door. I opened the door to find three of our friends, and before I could utter a word, they said they were there to have coffee with us. It sounded strange, as many cafés were open around the clock and served coffee. It was very early, maybe 3 a.m., too early for even family to visit unless there was some catastrophe.

The individuals who knocked on our door had earlier decided to go to Dr. Dahesh's house in Beirut. They had gone there to prove to one and all that he was nothing but a fad, a novelty, or a craze, something that people propagate to pass the time and create stories.

To make a long story short, earlier in the day, while this threesome were in a café, one asked the other two if they had heard the stories about Dr. Dahesh. The abbreviated answers showed an attempt to change the subject, proving that there was more to tell. So, to show that there was nothing to tell about, they decided to visit Dahesh, dismissing that his reputation alone indicated the need for better planning. Fearlessly, they started their journey and later, with psychological panicky fright, ended their ill-planned excursion.

So, here they were at our house at 3 a.m. and told us this tale:

They had just returned from a visit to the house of Dr. Dahesh. They knocked at the door of his house and the door opened, but nobody was there to welcome them. They heard some words spoken, which they took to mean you are welcome or come in, so they went in and sat on some chairs in the entrance hall, waiting.

In the hall were many paintings and pictures hanging on the wall in front of them. No one spoke, nor did they break the awe-inspiring silence (to borrow their words). They continued to wait for another half an hour, and still nobody showed up or talked to them. Suddenly, the tiger in one of the paintings stirred. He climbed out of the frame, onto the floor, and started creeping in their direction. In a terrifying instant, they ran out of the house like madmen. They were gripped with terror upon seeing a tiger emerge from a picture on the wall. They acted as one and ran with the fullest speed God bestowed on them. Each went home to safety to weather his nightmare, still shaken by the experience and speechless.

At home, one of them changed into his pajamas, took a sleeping pill, and went to bed. Suddenly, he felt that a hand was clasping his. He tried to dismiss this feeling, but the touch became more pronounced. He tried to convince himself that it was just fear that made him feel a hand touching his, but when it continued and became more persistent and moved up toward his neck, he got up and ran out of his apartment, carrying his trousers, and hoped that he was no longer in danger. He walked to the café he and his friends had been before visiting Dr. Dahesh's home to find his two companions already there.

I will not name these three friends because they were somewhat embarrassed by their story. These were men highly regarded in their communities, holding responsible positions in their countries, and not given to flights of fancy.

Their stories were similar, and what each experienced urged him to leave his home in fear. One felt as if he had been physically carried from the street to the entrance of his apartment, and when he tried to open the door, the key did not work. Wholly perplexed, he felt compelled to head to the café. I cannot remember the story of the third companion, a political refugee whom I knew. That morning, they came to our door because my wife and I lived conveniently across the street from the café where their story began. They asked that we not share their story with anyone, which we promised. I did not divulge this secret until the turn of the century, when two of the participants had passed away and the third was not in a mental state to remember what had happened.

Another story of Dr. Dahesh was well-known in Beirut; many claimed they witnessed what happened, and many claimed they heard about it: Dr. Dahesh took a taxi from his summer house in the town of Sofar up in the mountains of Lebanon to travel to Beirut. As he needed a haircut, he passed by his barber, who happened to be busy, and Dr. Dahesh could not wait his turn. He told the barber not to worry; he removed his own head, gave it to the barber, and told him to give it a good haircut and said that he would collect it in the evening upon his return from Beirut.

THE BEAUTIFUL YOUNG GIRL

Those stories are no exception to the many that were in circulation, and some sounded so real that one cannot for sure deny that they happened: One evening in 1943, Messrs. Edward Noon, George Haddad, Dr. Khabsa, and Mrs. Haddad, another group of well-educated individuals also not given to flights of fancy, were gathered around a table with Dr. Dahesh during a spiritual session. Suddenly, a beautiful young girl appeared in front of them. They were astonished and thought they were imagining the vision.

The girl told them that they were not dreaming, that her name was Nada and that she came from another world other than theirs. They could not believe their eyes or ears and hastened to touch her to ascertain whether she was, in fact, of flesh and blood. She was wearing a dress and carrying a sack, which was not of the fashion of that year, 1943. The girl said that nineteen years earlier, she had visited Dr. Dahesh. She said that she wore the same dress; and explained that this miracle confirmed the continuity and renewal of life and the soul's reincarnation, a transition from one stage to another on earth or from one planet to another, depending on the soul's merit.

DR. DAHESH, ART COLLECTOR

The Dahesh Museum of art's permanent collection originated with Dr. Dahesh (1909–1984), the Lebanese writer, philosopher, and connoisseur. He was a collector of paintings, sculptures, drawings, prints, photographs, and books by academically trained nineteenth- and twentieth-century artists. His goal was to open a premier art gallery. Friends brought Dr. Dahesh's collection from Beirut to America in 1976 and chartered the Dahesh Museum in New York City in 1987.

BEIRUT OPTIMISM

Let's now return to where we were before I told Dr. Dahesh's stories. My work and my company's various jobs all interrelated, providing a glance into the cultural, social, and accepted practices of living in different countries. They reflected attitudes toward accepting change individually or through an outsider—a consultant or adviser who digs deep into the organizational and operational history of the entities they run before giving advice. It was a unique and thrilling period in my life, always full and challenging. Grace was always by my side, she helped me when times were hard, and I had to put in long hours of work and long periods of absence away from home. She managed our very busy social life, as it was an essential element of my business and our family's needs.

My business flourished, our home was open, and Grace and I entertained often. We hosted large groups of people from many parts of the world. In a sense, I represented many companies in the region out of my Beirut operation, mainly when the company's senior officers found that

Beirut provided what they needed and interfaced with me to keep in the know about their operations in the area. They saw me as a person who could manage their business in the Middle East. The arrangement was good and profitable for me and less demanding for them.

Outside our home, we entertained at Le Casino du Liban, which had one of the best floor shows in the world. For several years, probably until late 1974, we were frequent patrons at the Casino, where we invited clients and associates from the Arab Middle East, England, Scotland, Sweden, and Japan. Guests were thrilled to have dinner, enjoy the show, and visit the clubs and gambling rooms. Celebrities and international businesspeople gambled heavily at the Casino.

Grace enjoyed traveling with our daughters Rania and Leila. She took the girls to Europe—Sweden, Denmark, Lapland, Switzerland—and the USA, usually for the whole summer. They visited England many times, and when the war of 1975 broke out in Lebanon, we rented an apartment near Regent's Park, where Grace and Leila lived for some years. I was a regular visitor from Dubai, Beirut, or wherever I was working.

Beirut was the center of business and pleasure for the Arab world, Europeans, Americans, and Asians, especially Japanese who eyed business opportunities in the region and wanted to get a share of the newfound oil wealth. Many used Beirut as the staging ground to study the best marketing approaches. Developing strategies for entering markets and choosing local agents or representatives, which in some countries was mandatory, were best done in Beirut. The city was modern, open, and trilingual and offered services like healthcare, banking, and entertainment. Beirut's geographical proximity to all points of interest in the region was a bonus. Lebanese communities living outside of Lebanon had their own contacts in many countries. Banks generally recommended to their foreign clients local people with good reputations and business experience. I had my fair share of referrals. The atmosphere of optimism and new opportunities invited competition from a variety of people. Even university professors and CIA agents tried to get in on business opportunities.

Beirut was a center also for those whose profession was to spy for their countries or clients. One spy was Miles Copeland, a CIA agent whom I knew. Years later he wrote and published the book A Game of Nations: The Amorality of Power Politics, in which he described how the game of espionage was played, with reference to Egypt in the Nasser era.

One Saturday in the summertime, I chanced upon Miles Copeland on Hamra Street; he suggested we meet on Monday morning in his office across the street from mine. He said that we needed some privacy in this meeting. On Monday morning I stopped by his office but found it closed, and through the glass door, I could see that the front room was empty. I called the concierge and asked him about Mr. Copeland, and he told me that he had come on Saturday afternoon and Sunday with some workers, packed his belongings, and left. It looked fishy, and when I tried to locate him, which was usually an easy thing to do, I failed to find him or learn about his whereabouts. It was the last time I heard of him until his book came out in 1970.

The June War of 1967 and After

On Monday, June 5, 1967, Israel attacked Egypt by air, quickly destroying its entire fleet of warplanes. Syria and Jordan joined to help Egypt, but the net result was the loss to Israel of the Sinai, the West Bank, the Gaza Strip, and the Golan Heights. The war was short and decisive. The reaction all over the Arab world was total disbelief and dismay. People in the Arab and some Islamic worlds could not fathom what had happened. A puzzled gloom reigned over everybody's head, a loss of confidence in aspirations for the future.

The ramifications of the 1967 war never left the Arab world and are still present and growing. The West Bank of Palestine was occupied, and the Golan Heights were also occupied and later officially annexed to Israel. Sinai was returned to Egypt as part of the Camp David Agreement, but Egyptian sovereignty was in doubt and anyway limited, and the Gaza Strip became a 365-square-kilometer prison for two million residents. Even Iran claims that its nuclear program is part of the Palestine problem. Unending conflicts with Israel are what the 1967 war accomplished. The increase in the number of settlements in the West Bank and the three wars between Gaza and Israel are examples of how decisively the 1967 war entrenched the status quo.

News of the 1967 war came as an anticlimax with the very-well-touted Egyptian military might and Syria's declared preparations; it was more of a mental earthquake than bad news. The ensuing sense of loss was spectacular; I am not exaggerating. Everything that happened after this debacle in the Arab world was manifested by a new concept and revelation that Israel was "unbeatable" and that the Arabs were not up to the challenge, nor would they ever be. It took every person I knew years to sort out the puzzle and understand the real facts. From that point on, the attitude of Arabs became much more hostile to both Israel and the West. The enmity created by the June war was equal to, if not more serious than, the 1948 wars and the United Nations Resolutions to create Israel.

Just one day before this 1967 war started, my brother-in-law Ben, his wife, and their two children were involved in an automobile accident in Beirut. Each one was taken to a different hospital. We searched for quite a while before we found out where each was. They suffered from broken bones and other injuries. Claude, his wife, had serious injuries in her face, which left deep marks on her forehead and near her left eye. Thankfully, they all left their hospitals with scars but none with a fatal injury.

ABC, my company, lost all its business local and regional, including works already in progress. By June 15, I realized that I could not pay end-of-month salaries, wages, and business expenses. I borrowed heavily from "friendly" banks, hoping that all the business reactions to the June war would soon fade. I did not terminate the services of any of my then-sizable staff and continued to pay costs out of bank borrowings.

I waited for a month or two and then started planning to restructure to reduce costs; staff reduction was the only solution available. In small companies like mine, where personal relations grew over time, it was difficult to tell somebody you knew very well that they were no longer employed. Before implementing these cost-reducing cuts, I decided to take a trip to the Gulf and Saudi to contact my clients. I thought they might have already terminated their contracts with consultants. I needed to check, in the hope of a renewal of what I thought were lost jobs.

I made my first trip to Jeddah late in June or early in July, when flights had to circle the north of Syria, then north of Iraq and south to the Arabian Gulf, and then east to Jeddah; all the regular airway routes had been declared "military areas." To get to my destination, the flight that was normally two hours took eight hours, nonstop. I met one client who was eager to continue our work within his organization, but he preferred, he said, to restart when "things settle down." I visited other clients in Saudi and the Gulf, and though each of them used different terminologies, the decision was always "wait and see."

Lebanon, 1965–1970s

MARKET RESEARCH

In Beirut, where ABC obtained jobs in the marketing and media fields, Grace helped me both with the creation of teams of interviewers as well as with questionnaire design. A statistician handled testing and supervision of the work in the field and worked on the numbers side of the market research reports. For market research data analysis, we bought bulky and clumsy adding machines and progressed to tabulators, punching and sorting machines, before buying our first central processor in 1965, the IBM 1131. Output from the console was via a modified IBM Selectric typewriter at 15.5 characters a second, and the price was $52,000. Core memory was 8 kilobytes to 64 kilobytes.

The IBM 1131 was the first mainframe computer introduced in Lebanon. We discovered that this expensive machine did not solve any of our problems, however, so we continued to rely mainly on manual work and mechanical aids. Occasionally, we used the machine as an excellent public relations tool to prove to ourselves that we had not blundered with our purchase. I was interviewed on television and showed how a statistical report on the IBM 1131 machine was printed by its high-speed printer, which impressed every onlooker. It was a novelty, and the computer became the talk of the town. We received many visitors from the government and the private sector to look at this beautiful machine.

IMAGE STUDIES

We learned about image studies from our American friends in the Saint Georges Hotel Bar, where they generally spent time; I did visit with them occasionally because they were rumored to be CIA personnel manning the Middle East area through this location. In fact, John Fistear, who helped us get jobs with American companies, encouraged visits to the bar to meet the CIA agents. I went, and I learned a lot from them about political goings-on but also that they were interested in individual politicians and mentioned the importance of their image, how they were perceived by the public they served.

I considered the idea and read about this possible line of business, and John Fistear helped me by calling me one day to say he would like me to meet with Mr. George Abou Adal, who was eyeing the presidency of Lebanon as a candidate. I welcomed the visit. It was a friendly and relaxed meeting, and we chatted about the political situation in Lebanon.

Lebanon's President Charles Helou's term (1964–1970) was about to conclude, and the hopes of many were raised for a chance in the presidency. Many ran for the office, but George Abou Adal was one who thought he needed to prepare for his upcoming efforts and included an image study, probably recommended to him by the team at the Saint Georges Hotel Bar.

John Fistear started the discussion about George's image and how could it be tested, how we could improve the faulty characteristics which were disliked by people, and how to minimize the effects of negative characteristics on voters. We agreed to start the study and progressed for a while but had to discontinue. At the time, presidential elections were held under Syrian government supervision, and no image could overrule a Syrian choice. Later, Abou Adal, a major merchant in Lebanon, engaged ABC for market research studies. We continued the effort and did well with others. The work was both interesting and financially rewarding.

PARTNER CONSULTING COMPANIES

We had an association with Babtie, Shaw, and Morton, a consulting engineering company established in 1906 and based in Glasgow.

In 1979, I formed a partnership with Scandiaconsult AB, an engineering consulting group based in Stockholm, Sweden, which we called Scandiaconsult ME AB. This company had two main offices, one within the premises of the mother company in Stockholm and another in the ABC offices in Beirut.

From 1971 to 1976, I entered into an association with several companies in New York. In time, I bought some of them through a holding company and became a majority owner of the holding company's stock. The holding company, International Management Company, was established and registered in New York to own the entities bought in the fields of construction management, radio, and television, such as McKee, Burger, Mansuetto (MBM) and Mauchly Construction. In addition, RTV Int'l was a television and radio consulting and management company based in New York that had branches in East Africa and Jordan. These acquisitions extended my horizon and took ABC from a Middle Eastern management-consulting company to an international multi-skill entity with an impressive work history.

TRAFFIC STUDY, 1968

I returned to Beirut to reduce my costs and plan my work anew. I was pleasantly surprised when I was contacted by a French consulting company that Lebanon's government had retained to design the country's road network. They were to conduct a transportation study to define travel patterns, traffic flows, and density of cars by hours of day and days of the week. It entailed setting up checkpoints at measured distances and time intervals and interviewing individuals about the points of departures and arrival of their trips and the number of travelers per car. The resulting numbers were necessary to define the number of lanes needed on the highways, the speed limits for each road sector, and the exits from and entries to the route from other geographic locations. In addition, counts for entrances and exits were collected and added to the information we agreed to collect. All counts were deemed necessary in the implementation process.

The traffic engineers used the figures compiled in a specific format to decide the number of lanes on each highway by selected checkpoint distances, the number of exits, the location each lead to, and the entry points and locations feeding the highway. We hoped the future refinements in the design of primary and secondary roads or connecting roads would benefit from this study.

It took two months to negotiate the contract's detailed technical terms so that nothing happened to truncate the study while implementation was in progress. We also needed to determine the workforce required to conduct the field study, which was designed to be completed within the short period of forty-five days. After that, I started hiring specialists to perform the study. We used four hundred and seventy-five temporary field workers and about twenty statisticians and engineers and signed the contract for work to proceed on November 1 and be completed by December 15, 1968. We did just that and submitted our final report on time.

The project was profitable, and it helped cover the debts ABC had incurred during the previous period. The other clients, locally and in the region, started to come back slowly but surely, and business returned to normal by the end of 1968.

In 1970, business grew well enough to justify the move to a luxurious location in the most modern office building in Beirut, the Gefinor Center; we leased an area of one thousand square meters, equal to about eleven thousand square feet. We kept the old office in Hamra Street for the BATC, Business Automation Training Center, a school I set up for teaching and training in computer sciences. As was the case for all educational institutions in Lebanon, it was established by presidential decree. This entity was a success, with an excellent cash flow.

At that same time, Grace and I moved our home to a newly leased apartment down the street from our Gefinor office. The apartment was large, beautifully finished, and in a great residential area. The lease was costly by the rents of the day, but we enjoyed living there. We moved there in part to be close to AUB so that our daughters, Rania and Leila, would have a short walk to campus when they enrolled in university.

However, we were not to be lucky enough to see them go to AUB. Rania did not live to college age, and the civil war of 1975 saw us move Leila to another country and another school.

HOTEL MANAGEMENT

Soon, we embarked on hotel management. We started with hotels in Beirut, Le Cavalier, and in Riyadh, al-Yamama. We also signed a contract with Jordan to manage the government's many rest houses and small hotels between the city of Ramtha, bordering Syria in the north, and Aqaba in the south. For this purpose, I created a company under the title Arab Hotel Management Company, SAL, with head office in Beirut to manage operations in the hospitality field.

Later, I appointed Richard Storm, an RTV executive who was also my assistant, as manager of the hotel company, to promote the business and locate other areas where hotel management prospects were good. In time, he found one in Mali and another in Rome. So we sent a team to evaluate the prospects and started talking with banks to secure finance. We started putting the elements together and were disappointed when the local government classified the Rome hotel as a historic site; the renovation was subject to red tape and restrictions. We also learned that the government approval was not forthcoming, so the funds planned and consisting of the capital and credit lines secured for the project would also not be forthcoming. We dropped this project and started looking again elsewhere. The Mali hotel was okay, but financiers were not enthusiastic about investing in there; we discovered that the corruption level in that country was high enough to scare our investors and us.

Working in hotel management brought me to the Oberoi family and, later, their Indian hotel chain. We met the Oberois first in Beirut, and in time we became friends. They visited us in Beirut, and we visited them by invitation once in India. We discussed setting up a joint company to cover specific areas of the Arab world, but that was not to be. We were in discussion with the owners of the al-Bustan Hotel in Beit Miri in the Lebanon Mountains to take it over and manage under

Oberoi's name. Unfortunately, by the time we were about to make the offer to the owners, the war in Lebanon had started, and eventually we abandoned the project.

Grace and I traveled together many times to countries in Europe, America, and once each to Mexico and India. Grace and I enjoyed this period very much, especially since I was making substantial money and our international contacts were impressive. We moved in very desirable international social circles.

THE OBEROI FAMILY

The Oberoi family invited my wife and me in 1973 to India to attend the inauguration of their Oberoi Sheraton Hotel in Bombay. We had developed a friendly relationship with Biki Oberoi, the CEO of the Oberoi Hotel Company, when he came to visit Beirut. The visit gave me a better understanding of the hospitality business, and later, it provided a prospect for cooperating in the field of hotel management.

Visiting India gave us an insight into the wealth of some people and the misery and poverty of others living side by side in Bombay and other cities and locations we visited during our stay in India. We did enjoy the luxury of Indian wealth and met maharajas, cabinet ministers, army and air force generals, ambassadors to India, many a Hollywood star, and renowned American and European journalists. We visited famous places and stayed in beautiful hotel accommodations, especially in Srinagar in Kashmir. Our hosts were very generous and took exceptional care of us. We met Raj Bahadur Oberoi, father of Biki and founder of the hotel business; we also met Biki's mother, a friendly and intelligent person who passed her time managing the Oberoi hotels in New Delhi.

That visit of ten days was interrupted by a pre-dawn assassination in Beirut by Israeli commandos. Then the defense minister of Israel assassinated three Palestinian leaders. Kamal Nasser, a close friend, was one of the three. We cut our trip short and returned to Beirut. Ehud Barak became Israel's prime minister, like all other "peace-loving" Israeli leaders. Barak himself gunned Kamal Nasser in the chest vertically and horizontally in the form of a cross to emphasize the fact that Kamal was a Christian.

Due to my globetrotting, I spent a lot of time in hotels, and so the idea of setting up a management company in the hotel industry was a natural outcome. As mentioned earlier, I registered a company in Beirut under the name Arab Hotel Management Company, SAL. In a month or so I sought and got a contract to manage al-Yamama hotel in Riyadh. It was a profitable contract which induced me to establish a hotel in Beirut. I leased a building on Hamra Street and got architects with hotel backgrounds to design Le Cavalier hotel's structure. It was a boutique hotel with sixty-four rooms and two suites. The hotel bar and restaurant became a popular meeting place for businesspersons, and the project proved to be feasible and profitable.

By the time this effort gathered speed, my problem with the Bahrain government had started to surface, thus making financing the new projects more difficult. Early in 1975, just before the civil war began in Lebanon, I sold the hotel management company and forgot this line of business. Then, finally, the cash that I needed to face this new type of disruption became available.

The Bahrain Franchise, 1972–1975

In 1972, I signed a twenty-year exclusive franchise agreement with the Sheikh of Bahrain, Isa bin Salman Al Khalifa, to build and operate a radio and television station in Manama. My company would own 80 percent and the ruler would own 20 percent. We gifted him the 20 percent share.

I was eager to bring Shaikh Isa bin Salman into the fold by making him a partner in what I thought was a profitable venture. I felt that having him on my side was the best guarantee for the safety of the investment. What I bet on did not work. Problems between Bahrain and Iran erupted, making the future of the kingdom shaky, or at least that is how decision-makers and their British advisers interpreted it. I was aware of the discussions carried on in public about the future of the television franchise with the minister of information, English lawyers and bankers, and members of the British Embassy. Those meetings did not respect the confidentiality of the subject. Ethical conduct was ignored and the law the English swear by was shelved for the moment, and they informed the public that they were nationalizing RTVB before I was informed.

I financed the project with my own money and with loans from Chase Manhattan Bank; Arthur Lipper of New York, a friend and financier; Credit Suisse; and the Bank of Bahrain. The total equity and loans amounted to some three and a half million dollars.

I appointed a board of directors composed of a chairman, the project manager, and George Hamilton, a public relations person. In addition, the board included Richard Storm, who was still working for the hotel management company; Sir Edwin Chapman-Andrews, a British ex-junior minister, former and retired ambassador of Great Britain in Lebanon; and Najib Azzouz, an Iraqi investor in this project to oversee finances. George and Richard came from RTV International with a lot of experience in the field.

We built the station, the first color station in the Gulf, called RTV Bahrain, and started the operation. We spent months testing the technical issues and regions in the planned coverage area. We discovered that there was a problem in range. The station's signal was perfect in some areas while poor in others. The terrain had never crossed our minds as a possible problem, as it was uniformly level, consisting of either the waters of the Gulf or the Arabian Desert. It took us time to discover that we needed to use other available technologies and coaxial cable to achieve uniform coverage, at a high cost and a delay not anticipated.

Otherwise, everything looked good and rosy, and I was happy with progress in this and all the other ventures. Then, suddenly, and unexpectedly, things took a different and much less rosy direction. By the time I understood what was happening, I realized I was in deep waters. My survival as a businessman was at stake, and so was my home life.

Our work in Bahrain, trying to establish new media at a great effort and high cost, did not prevent the government of Bahrain from taking it over, in effect confiscating our works and the radio and television stations. Tariq al-Mu'ayyid, Bahrain's minister of information, was the liaison on behalf of the government. He called me one day while I was in Beirut and suggested we meet immediately. I said I could not leave Beirut, and he said that he would come to meet with me to discuss an urgent issue. He arrived the following day. Unfortunately, on the day he arrived, my sister-in-law passed away, and I had to split my time between attending a funeral and meeting a Bahraini minister.

A week before this request to meet, the ruler of Bahrain had dissolved Parliament, declared a provisional state of martial law, banned media, nationalized the radio and television stations, and otherwise made his opponent's ability to express an opinion very limited. Apparently, as

Tariq relayed it to me, the problem arose from a political threat from Iran to the ruler of Bahrain.

To ensure that no opposing "propaganda" would be broadcast, the ruler carried on with his plan, wiping my investment out of existence. His promise of protection for holding a 20 percent share in the company must have been less critical than the threat of Iran to him on that bleak today. He never even suggested that we meet to discuss and maybe agree on government supervision of news; he may have been scared by the threat of Iran or, alternatively, eager to take over the station. Tariq al-Mu'ayyid made me an offer for Bahrain to buy the station at a price to be determined and sign a management contract with RTV to operate the station, sell advertising, and recoup our investment (or the cost to be determined for the takeover) from the station's income.

After consultation with the investors and banks, my board of directors declined the offer, and in turn, I advised Tariq of this decision. I knew he could not honor his offer to buy or sign a management agreement because the ruler's political decision was final and the board of directors of RTV's decision would make no difference whatsoever.

My meetings with Tariq continued in Bahrain, and I tried to reason with him about the long-term benefits to Bahrain. Confiscating businesses such as RTV Bahrain would not be reassuring to prospective investors. Our relationship, developed over the two years preceding this debacle, allowed me to express my thoughts openly. In addition, I tried to apply regional political pressure, which was meant to be passed on to the ruler.

The pressures applied were polite, and the sheikh did not budge. He was adamant, and I understood the reasons for his determination, but anybody in my shoes would probably have tried to make a dent in the decision, and I did and failed. I could do nothing but wait and see. I did not meet the sheikh after Tariq's first visit to Beirut. I had been cheated and hurt by Bahrain, its ruler, and their British advisers. If rulers do not keep their word, whom should one believe? I asked myself this question, but my later experiences answered my question. The word of a ruler in this part of the world and under the political systems they rule is of no value.

One of the options that presented itself was highly political. I could have sold my stock to Iran, gotten my money, and left Bahrain, even if this would have created a messy situation. The harm I would have left Bahrain in would have been complicated for me. Anyway, I had no direct contact with Iran, though "friends" softly approached me. After thinking it over, I decided not to pursue this option. It was too political, and the consequences could have been dire. I decided to foot the bill and face the bleak future when and as it came.

I will use this opportunity to give a short history lesson. The British were still influential in the Gulf when I experienced the takeover of RTV Bahrain. Before the virtual independence of the Gulf States, a British consul resided in Bahrain and ruled all the Gulf sheikhdoms, from Kuwait in the north through Oman in the south. A vice consul traveled around the sheikhdoms to carry out his governance duties. The sheikhdoms constituting the United Emirates of today were then known as the Trucial States.

When my negotiations with the government of Bahrain were on, I did not meet any Bahraini official, either socially or for business; all were British. The negotiators, including lawyers, bankers, accountants, and government representatives, were aggressive Englishmen who occasionally made fun of the extended negotiations. The Bahraini ministers I knew well made themselves scarce and somehow became very busy or were not in Bahrain. They were AUB graduates whom Grace and I knew when we were students and who held the same political beliefs.

On November 29, 1974, Bahrain called me to meet the committee in charge of implementing the stations' takeover—three days after the passing of my daughter Rania. (I will say much more about Rania in a later part of this story.) I did not ask for a delay, left for Bahrain, and met with the committee of maybe a dozen men in the offices of the minister of finance with all the British lawyers, accountants, and advisers to the government of Bahrain; the only Bahraini in the meeting was Tariq al-Mu'ayyid.

Members of this committee presented their case, and I listened. When asked about my views, I got up from my chair and spoke. I said that I now understood better why people in the area hated the English but had to put up with them; that their empire would disappear one of these days and they would pay the price for their rude, offensive, and demeaning treatment of others. I also said that Bahrain did not respect the signature appended to an agreement, and the advisers had found something to show their fragile importance; they could confiscate the station, and they could do that with some dignity, but that was not to be. I had come from Beirut three days after my daughter's death because I respected and honored my commitments and made no excuses to delay the agony of meeting them. (This statement, I was told by Tariq much later, was unprecedented, and the chaps in the room wondered about how serious I was and whether I had the status to say what I said.)

I had said that we despised our rulers for their willingness to accept the insult of being ruled by others, but we also had no recourse but to put up with them. That was a bit rude on my side. Al-Mu'ayyid asked whether I meant the Bahraini's or the British rulers, and I retorted that he could guess or choose and that it made no difference to me, as this would be my last visit to Bahrain. That was how I felt at the time, and I never felt differently after that. On Sunday, February 9, 1975, I had to go to Bahrain by invitation; I signed the confiscation agreement and never visited the sheikhdom, later the kingdom, again. After this last meeting, I refused to see Tariq again. He died shortly after that.

During these negotiations, the Bank of Bahrain, whose manager was British, called me one day and demanded repayment of the financial facilities extended to RTVB, just like that and through a phone call. At the time, my facilities were 600,000 Bahraini dinars, which was equal to 600,000 British pounds. As per the agreement, the loan was for five years, and the demand was to settle immediately. Maybe all the above makes no sense, but this is what happened.

In the final analysis, the government of Bahrain forced me to sign an agreement to hand over the stations with the written promise to pay me 440,000 dinars, equivalent at the time to about US$2 million. If the money promised was paid, the loss would have been heavy but manageable and payment was not made, and my loss was total. I tried to sue

Bahrain but found out that it was practically useless. Issues of sovereignty did not allow the case to be presented in courts of law in Bahrain. I tried to sue in London, but my lawyers were discouraging and suggested that it would be a long-drawn court case. The legal costs were high, and I did not want to add to my Bahrain losses. I did not have the resources to sue.

What bothered me most was that even the government of Bahrain knew that I had refused to sell my majority share to Iran, something they could not have prevented.

The new situation in Bahrain was the precursor of another dip into murky business waters, as a challenging period and an impending collapse of all the business I had nurtured was to follow. Friends and family started to distance themselves from me, including brothers who had lived for many years happily under my wing, working for me and deriving from my business good incomes, good contacts, and a good living. They did not need to worry about my profits and losses and abandoned me when I needed them.

The Emir of Bahrain was feeling pressure from most of his population, who are Shi'a, and who were treated as second-class citizens, as well as from Shi'a Iran. The Sunni rulers of Bahrain relied on rulers of other Arab Sunni states for protection from both. Life and politics changed, and Bahrain found their protectors were themselves in fear of Iran's wilayat al-faqih, and therefore, a few decades later in 2022, they found a new protector, Israel. Bahrain joined former guarantors and protectors and signed an agreement with Israel without considering the future of such a relationship.

Since Bahrain signed an agreement with Israel in 2020 and now depends on Israeli protection, I sometimes wonder what would have happened if I had sold my shares in RTV to Iran,

Bahrain took steps to defend itself from its Shi'a population and from Iran; the first was to dismiss parliament, confiscate my TV and radio stations, and forced stop all printed media in the country and forgot to pay me my dues as part of the contract I signed in 1975. Another step was to forget that they are an Arab state that since 1948 were an enemy of Israel, only to become its dependent. Another cover for their problem was to elevate the title of the ruler from sheikh in 1972 to emir (prince), then in 2002, established Bahrain as a constitutional hereditary monarchy whose head of state is king.

The moral of the story is that one should take nothing for granted. People of all kinds—kings, princes, paupers, or billionaires—can be good, evil, or indifferent. Indifference, I discovered, is not a virtue; at best, it is tolerable but best avoided.

The Years 1973–1976

This period was my life's worst. Everything that could go wrong went wrong, in health and business and in every way possible. I saw a gloomy future ahead. The various circumstances were dissimilar and not equally disturbing, but all the same, they were terrible, and all came suddenly, at the same time.

The first, and the worst of all, was our daughter Rania's premature passing. Much else went wrong, but nothing else was so irreparable, irrevocable, and final.

The second was the fifteen-year civil war in Lebanon, which started in 1975 and was declared officially over in 1990. Its ramifications lingered and did not disappear, by any stretch of the imagination. As I write this almost fifty years later Lebanon skirts the fringe of in and out of war. The war destroyed the country and, not surprisingly and in a substantial way, my business. The downside for the country and its economy is still felt at large.

The third was the decision made in 1974 by the government of Bahrain to take over the radio and television stations and revoke the franchise the government of Bahrain had granted me in 1972. I was afraid the takeover would be tantamount to expropriation or confiscation, which would leave the Bahrain business in the government's hands. However, what happened was even worse. On Sunday, February 9, 1975, I signed an unfair but compulsory agreement, under political and business pressure. No compensation was ever entertained.

Fourth was the collapse in 1974 of the stock exchange markets globally, particularly in New York, where I had some investments that unfortunately lost value and substantially limited my ability to borrow. It was a frightening and intense period in my life, one which left many physical and mental scars, some that never healed.

Fifth is that I was shot by a sniper in the left knee late in 1975. The injury immobilized me for a long time, in the hospital and at home, recuperating at a time when I needed to be mobile; instead, I spent time resting in bed. My suffering lasted for a long time and left me much less mobile for a more extended period. I describe the incident in detail later in this story.

RANIA

For Grace and me, our daughter Rania's premature death took away our wits, our strength, and largely our sanity. In late June of 1969, at the age of eleven, Rania started having spells of intense headaches. She was diagnosed with an aneurysm, a knot of distended blood vessels atypically and irregularly arranged. It caused bleeding in the brain's stem. We lived in dread of the blood vessel rupturing, and we consulted with many medical specialists in the field. After an episode in 1970, we took Rania to the Maudsley Hospital in London, where this specialty's best doctors practiced. Their prognosis was not definitive; they informed us that her health might improve as time passed, but nothing was sure. Grace stayed with her at the hospital for the duration, and I stayed in a London hotel. We left Leila in Beirut with her grandmother.

One of the options for her was brain surgery, but the risks were not acceptable. One risk was that surgery might result in her death, and the other was that it might correct the situation but that her brain might not function normally again. The chief surgeon suggested surgery and set a time to operate. Unfortunately, he did not show up on time, as he had a heart attack and died before the surgery. We took that as a bad omen and decided to leave matters to nature and God.

When we returned to Beirut after spending time in the Maudsley Hospital, Rania was fine, with occasional spells of headaches. She had to be careful not to exert herself physically, and so she wasn't able to participate in any sports. She continued until November 1974, when she suddenly had another episode.

That evening, she walked home from the Goethe Institute's library at the end of Bliss Street in Beirut. She had a headache and insisted we call her doctor, our friend Dr. Adel Afifi. Adel arrived and said that Rania would be immediately taken to the American University Hospital. Rania was hospitalized at the American University Hospital, where she passed away on the afternoon of Tuesday, November 26, 1974, and a piece of our lives and all our happiness died with her.

She was laid to rest in Beirut in the Melkite Greek Catholic cemetery, which is located behind the Saint-Joseph University medical school. My father and aunts and my brother Victor are buried in the same cemetery. Grace and I visited her often. Our loss was unimaginable. Our lives felt empty. We never could forget what she went through—her pain, and her knowledge that her health was not stable and her life at risk.

The funeral took place at the Greek Catholic Church on Hamra Street. Dozens of her friends, students, and teachers from school and many of our other friends attended the service. Condolences continued at home for about two weeks. It was very tiring, but it was helpful to share our loss with friends and know that so many people had cared about her and cared about us.

While receiving condolences, I thought it was time to take off and go somewhere where Grace, Leila, and I could maybe lose ourselves in our grief and come to terms with our great loss. We decided to drive to Jordan and spend Christmas there. Our trip was helpful; we visited many places, and fortunately we did have many good friends, the Farhans, the Touqans, and the Muftis, whose presence was a comfort to us.

We returned to Beirut to resume our everyday lives. We needed to take care of Leila. Grace was grieving deeply for the loss of her firstborn, but life went on. I was probably more down to earth, especially since I had many other problems on my hands to keep me busy, worried, angry, and sad.

THE MARKET COLLAPSE, 1973–1974

The New York stock exchange bear market in 1973 and 1974 negatively affected all the major stock exchanges in the world. The crash came after the collapse of the Bretton Woods system.

(The 1944 Bretton Woods Agreement had established the rules for commercial and financial relations among the United States, Canada, western European countries, Australia, and Japan. It was intended to govern monetary relations among independent states.) The market crash was compounded by the outbreak of the 1973 oil crisis in October of that year.

In the 694 days between January 11, 1973, and December 6, 1974, the New York Stock Exchange's Dow Jones Industrial Average benchmark lost over 45 percent of its value, making it the seventh-worst bear market in the index's history. Unfortunately, I lost some money in the market crash, and together with all my problems elsewhere, my ability to borrow dwindled as the need to repay old debts and credit lines became imminent.

Life goes on. I witnessed more of the kind of a problem where one cannot have any input and is denied participation in decision-making and must be satisfied with what is handed to him; I suffered, and enjoyed, and my story adds to my life's events and becomes longer.

Murphy's Law is a popular adage that states that "things will go wrong in any given situation, if you give them a chance," or, more commonly, "whatever can go wrong, will go wrong." Maybe I gave them a chance, or perhaps I didn't, but the adage reveals the aftermath and demonstrates how I took to heart what I experienced in material and psychological loss; I faced the collapse of all that I had built in this life of mine.

The loss of the franchise in Bahrain, the untimely sale of the hotel management company, my suffering from the sniper's bullet, and its aftermath destroyed what business I had built in America and in Beirut, which operated in a war zone. The psychological, physical, and operational sides of my state of affairs created a nightmare over a period of about one year or more. Describing what happened during that period brings back painful memories, which I will not inflict on my very few and very close readers.

Both of my brothers, who were in charge of two fully staffed departments at ABC, suddenly left work and Beirut, each to find a more secure place to live. I took over one department and terminated the other by canceling all outstanding contracts and paying off the contractual penalties. Within a few weeks of leaving Beirut, one set up an office in Nicosia, Cyprus, the other in Nice, France, using ABC clients they knew, and the clients assumed they represented ABC. As a result, my brothers left me with incomplete studies for clients in Lebanon and other countries. I found myself compelled to take over all the incomplete jobs and do my best to complete them, deliver them to the clients, and collect the fees I direly needed.

The completion of some jobs required skills that I did not possess, and the pressure from clients to deliver on the promises and presentations we had made when we had signed the contracts did not help. I found it less costly to pay back fees already collected and get out of the projects that I could not complete, leaving the clients sometimes with half-completed or nearly completed jobs for free. Whenever this failed, I paid the penalties the contracts foresaw. Abandoning jobs proved to be wise. Some of the lost clients, in time, returned, offered me work on other projects, and helped keep the company's reputation intact.

With this situation becoming the norm, where my time was over-engaged, qualified staff not available, and still paying salaries and wages for employees of lower grades who presumably could not find a better deal elsewhere, I was not in an enviable position. I found myself assuming substantial financial losses and started to feel the creditor's initial pressures to settle loans. It all started softly, but I knew what would be coming and my mental preparations for the worst intensified. Although, I must be fair, most of the banks which extended me credit gave me ample time to settle and did not increase the interest rates at which these loans were first advanced.

The contracts we signed outside Lebanon were ultimately to provide more problems. ABC sent specialists to the project location for days or weeks and sent others, or the same persons, when needed. Every project had a plan of performance and work schedules drawn before work commenced and, whenever possible, before signing a contract. This gave us an advantage, especially when we could write schedules for many projects and try to have similar functions performed by workers with appropriate skills in the same geographical area, at or very close to the schedule for the largest contract. This eliminated many costs, but the main saving was on air travel and hotel accommodations.

Under the new safety concerns in Lebanon, staff members refused to travel and leave their families in Beirut, and on occasion I had to rent housing for the staff and their families to induce them to travel to job locations. Staff thus located could only work on the job closest to where they lived, an inefficient and costly way of doing business, and the oversight on these projects was in most cases poor or even nonexistent.

I managed to continue my work and find resources to finance these new operational costs; still, my workload became unbearable and reduced my abilities to the possible and not the desirable. I had nightmares about the quality of work as handled and could do nothing about it.

When the militia fighting became unbearable, I went to Amman and stayed in the Jordan Intercontinental Hotel, hoping to manage some business out of Amman. I used a friend's office facilities and felt comfortable with them. Grace and Leila were in London.

Beirut, 1975

The Lebanese civil war broke out early in 1975 and ended in 1990 and changed Beirut and all of Lebanon. Many Lebanese left the country to seek work and sign their children up for schools overseas. Some moved their businesses to Cyprus, Athens, Amman, Paris, or London, but most kept their office in Lebanon in order to stay in touch with their home and eventually return to Beirut. Jordan and Cyprus benefited appreciably from the disruption of business by providing an option that was both hospitable and close to Beirut.

As one indeed would expect, many of ABC's best educated and trained staff left Beirut and found jobs outside Lebanon. Unfortunately, those who stayed were not necessarily of the quality needed to associate with the clients or handle the business routines. I had to take a more significant role in every project, thus living my work hour by hour again. It was a burden and a considerable limitation and took time away from my family.

I also started worrying and giving more attention to our financial situation in the Middle East, Europe, and America. The market crash of 1974 affected us more than marginally. The television station in Bahrain, which I wrote about earlier in this story, was nationalized, with a consequent significant financial loss; indemnity was not paid, though the agreement we signed included a clause that mentions an indemnity of about 440,000 Bahraini dinars. It was a challenging situation and I tried to carry on, but 1975 did not end well. Late in November of 1975, as mentioned earlier, I was shot in the knee by a sniper perched on the roof of the Holiday Inn Hotel on Beirut's Green Line, and the injury took a long time to heal.

THE INTERCONTINENTAL HOTEL, JORDAN, 1976

One day in the early morning of November 1976, I got a telephone call from one of my Beirut employees, who told me that he had just arrived in Amman and that he had driven my car from Beirut for me to use in Jordan. He said he would wash it and bring it over in an hour or two. I was waiting, when suddenly shooting started in and around the Jordan Intercontinental Hotel before the car arrived. The concierge, a longtime friend, called to tell me that a group of seven Iraqi activists, now generically referred to as "terrorists," had occupied the hotel and that I should not leave my room until the police arrived. Army soldiers stormed the hotel, and General Arabiyat, an army officer I knew, telephoned, and asked me not to leave my room. He told me that the attackers were on the hotel roof and in the lounge on the ground floor. My room was on the sixth floor, two floors below the roof. Army helicopters joined the melee and started circling the hotel and shooting at whatever moved in the rooms—not a comfortable situation. The room across the corridor from mine caught fire. I could smell the fumes but could not open the door to see what was happening.

To make a very long story short, at about 3 p.m., General Arabiyat called and told me he was sending a team of Special Forces to take me down to the lobby. The takeover by the activists had failed and the hotel was liberated. I was escorted downstairs by the Special Forces. Walking down the stairs, I had a chance to observe the outcome of what happened: broken glass all over and blood still fresh on the stairs and the walls. I survived the incident but suffered added psychological scars.

I wanted to call Grace and Leila to tell them that I was safe because surely, I thought, they would have heard the news and been extremely worried. The death toll reported in this attack was thirteen, with two or three injured.

When I left the hotel, I walked through army units toward the Mufti's house less than a kilometer away. Izzedine Mufti and his daughter were waiting for my news. I was well received when I showed up. We tried again to call Grace in London, but there was no answer. Izzedine's wife, Huda, was also in London, so we tried to call her but with no success. Finally, we learned that Huda and Grace had been together, enjoying their morning, and luckily, neither had heard the news. Izzedine and I assured them that everything was under control.

I am sure I was scared all through the ordeal, but I kept control of myself, and as soon as the show was over and I had contacted Grace, I noticed that my hands were shaking, and the cup of coffee offered me was spilling over the edges. I spent the afternoon at the Muftis' home and went back to the hotel at around midnight.

The following morning, I went to the office of an insurance company run by the Majalis, of the Majali clan, and many friends and acquaintances there were eager to listen to my firsthand account about what had really happened in the hotel the day before. We talked politics and had coffee when suddenly an explosion rocked the building, and everyone jumped, including yours truly. It transpired that a gas bottle in the kitchen adjacent to the room had caught fire and exploded. I left the gathering and went back again to the Muftis' home to relax.

Lebanon: The Civil War, 1975

The civil war in Lebanon, the division of the country by religion and sect, the siege and later occupation of the city of Beirut by the Israeli Army, the skirmishes between local militias and the Israeli Army then under the wing of Ariel Sharon, the massacre committed in the Sabra and Shatila camps for Palestinian refugees, and on and on deserves more pages than I will write.

We lived those times, and they still leave their deep mark on everyone unlucky enough to have witnessed the savagery of this invasion. Of course, we did not "see" until later, on TV and in the newspapers, but the massacre was close to us, and we had some acquaintances who either witnessed or suffered from the savagery that continues to be an acceptable way of settling conflicts. Today's wars in Syria, Iraq, Yemen, and Libya tell the story again. The local leaders and the world leaders could not care less.

We experienced another occupation and the presence of an enemy whose conduct and behavior confirmed what we knew and had experienced at its hands in the 1940s. We were reminded of those days in Palestine when the same enemy created the refugee problem by terrifying Palestinians into leaving their homes, inducing them to flee and hope to have a place to live in neighboring countries. Many people had the same idea: that the Israelis were coming to Lebanon to ensure Palestinians would never return home.

We do not know the number of casualties of this invasion, but a list of names covered some thousand individuals in the first few days of the occupation. Lebanese newspapers recorded many details of those days, in photos and in text. The massacre in Sabra and Shatila, Palestinian refugee camps south of Beirut, was committed by the Lebanese Forces under the auspices and direction of the Israeli army then commanded by General Ariel Sharon, who later became prime minister of Israel. The encroachment into the camps by the perpetrators and the grisly affair started on Thursday, September 16, 1982, at approximately 6 p.m. and ended at about 8 a.m. on Saturday, September 18. Not until Saturday afternoon did the news begin to spread out from the area, and word of the heinous activity leaked into the media and by word of mouth by people who were able to escape from the camps. The total number of deaths in this massacre was never exactly known but estimates range between 1,800 and 3,000.

At the time of writing, this enemy continues to make widows out of Palestinian women and orphans out of children who are still living in the remnants of what was once upon a time a country called Palestine. Israel has the full support of the western powers, which describe it as a peace-loving country. Israelis pride themselves that their policy is to expand into Palestinian territories and not in self-defense. Balfour was bad, Sykes-Picot worse, and US policies have allowed the damage to continue.

I WAS SHOT BY A SNIPER

During the civil war in Beirut, a truce and a ceasefire were called by the warring factions. One day during the ceasefire, in late November 1975, I left home to check on my mother and my mother-in-law. I planned to return home in the early afternoon. However, the declared truce did not hold, and I needed to get back home before the fighting resumed. While I was trying to park my car in our garage, a street fighter shouted to me that I was in a fighting zone and should go back. I tried to park the car on the other side of our building, but there was sniper fire. I waited for some time, and when I thought there was a lull in the shooting, I decided to take the risk and sneak around the corner to the building's entrance, a few meters from where I was parked. The main door of the building was locked. I didn't have my key. I tried the service door, which was usually manned by the concierge and his family, but that was closed too. Nobody answered my insistent knocks or shouting calls. Going back to the corner where I had been hiding safely was not possible now, and what I feared would happen happened: I was shot by a sniper perched on the roof of the Holiday Inn Hotel. The bullet went through my left knee.

That was not a good day on Rue Kennedy. The sniper shot several passersby, killing some and wounded some. I was not the only casualty of the day.

The bullet went through my left knee, leaving me stranded in the street with nowhere to go, dodging bullets as best as I could; shots were coming in barrages, hitting the walls, and ricocheting around me, adding to my uncomfortable wait at the service door with one leg not functioning. It was quite a half-hour of hunkering down in a corner while a shooter had me in the crosshairs of a rifle.

When the concierge and his wife finally opened the gate and pulled me into their floor-level apartment, I was exhausted. My wounded leg had stopped functioning, and not having first aid expertise, I poured whiskey and arak on the wound, the two near-antiseptics available in the concierge's apartment. Two, maybe three hours elapsed before a lull in the shooting allowed some men from my office building to carry me to the nearby American University Hospital. I was lucky that the guards and service personnel at the Gefinor Center heard about my injury, came in from an entrance in the back of the building, and took me to the hospital in a small Volkswagen, with my leg already stiff and impossible to fold. I entered the car with my leg extended out of the car's window.

All told, it was a tough day for me, but I survived to tell the story. In the hospital, at least four doctor friends attended me, and the operation lasted as long as three hours, with no anesthesia administered., they gave me what was available: an epidural. The hospital was short of anesthesia that day because of the war situation. The pain I went through is difficult to describe, but the doctors present kept telling me that I was "brave" and could take the pain and relied on me to cooperate for the surgery to succeed. The surgery did succeed. This incident kept me immobilized for about five months.

Because of the wound and about a month later, I developed a pulmonary embolism in my left lung. I was admitted again to the hospital, but I was put on the "critical" list this time. My doctors suggested I tell Grace about my serious health situation, indicating her need to know. I telephoned her in Windsor, England, where Grace and Leila were, and asked her to return to Beirut. She came back to Beirut with Leila, which made me happy yet uncomfortable because of the dangerous situation there.

Many months later, as the battles raged close to our house, which was not 500 meters from the Green Line of demarcation between East Beirut and West Beirut, I wanted Grace and Leila to leave the city. Beirut was divided into two sectors, separated by the Green Line. The west of the line was controlled by Palestinian Fatah militias under the leadership of Yasser Arafat. The east side was controlled by the Christian militia, the Lebanese Forces, under a young, energetic, and charismatic Christian leader of a well-known family, Bashir Gemayel. We lived in West Beirut.

On at least one occasion, we experienced a rocket entering through the outside walls into the living room, as well as many less destructive but scary bullets. Finally, Grace and Leila did leave Beirut to England, this time to London so Leila could get back to school.

We rented a small apartment in London, and then a few months later we found a more suitable apartment on Park Road, a more desirable location because we would be neighbors to the al-Awar family. These interim arrangements added to my family's maintenance costs. Our budget deficit became bigger, causing my worries to increase.

THE LEBANESE FORCES

As I wrote earlier, for safety reasons, Grace and I rented an apartment in London late in 1975, and when the war appeared to be ending in 1979, we moved back to Beirut. Unfortunately, as soon as we settled down and started to reorganize, a new round of battles started. During this war, both Fatah and the Lebanese forces communicated, exchanged views, and negotiated. It was a busy and sensitive period for me. Conveniently, their representatives met in my Beirut offices, since both sides had trust and confidence in me. I think I succeeded in playing a role that helped keep the confrontation levels lower than they might have been. A representative of the Lebanese Forces would meet with a representative of Fatah to negotiate tactical issues. But, of course, my Palestinian nationality and my connections with the adversary were something to contend with; the PLO was not a hindrance, though. Both sides used the weekly public opinion reports ABC produced on issues of the day and possibly used them for planning purposes.

One evening at home, during a serious exchange of fire that included rockets and similar artillery, Grace answered the phone, and the voice on the other end said "a friend" wanted to talk to me. The caller was Bashir Gemayel; he did not mention his name for security reasons. He was the leader of the Lebanese Forces, which were then in control of all the Christian areas in Lebanon. We talked for the first time and agreed to meet in his office the following morning. Going to his office meant crossing the Green Line, which was always dangerous. I would have to answer many questions to armed men on both sides of the line. There was no certainty that I would get to the other side safe and unharmed. Bashir promised that he would arrange the trip, however. He did, and we met in his office in Karantina, just north of Beirut, as agreed. Apparently, there were rules of engagement which were honored, even at the height of the exchange of rockets.

The meeting went very well, and Bashir was astonishingly open. He told me in detail what he wanted me to help with. He also told me in detail about the problems he faced with his political party, the Kata'eb, and their allies. He made it clear that his trust in me was total. Later, I discovered that he made a thorough check before he decided to meet with me. It also transpired that we had some friends in common.

I attended many high-level policy meetings of the Lebanese Forces, and I contributed to the formation of some of the policies. My presence had a moderating effect on the aggressive leadership of the forces and, in a way, encouraged the adoption of less-ruthless policies. At the time, the Lebanese Forces were the single most important Christian militia in Lebanon.

Bashir founded and commanded the Lebanese Forces and succeeded in getting all the Christian leaders, including a Maronite church leader Abati Boulos Ni'man, to unite. Bashir coordinated with the Maronite Church hierarchy to get their silent approval for some of the Lebanese Forces' actions. Their enemy was the coalition of the Syrian Army, then occupying the country (initially by invitation from the Christian militias), the PLO, and the Sunni militant groups. His father, Pierre Gemayel, was a prominent Christian leader who in the 1940s had created the Kata'eb Phalangist Party. His brother Amin Gemayel, who later became president, was a continuous problem for Bashir—at least, according to Bashir.

Bashir and I agreed that Lebanon should have a much smaller government and a very active private sector. We talked a lot about the future of Lebanon and even went into details of organizing the country based on these principles.

I knew Bashir valued my advice, and later, when he became a candidate for the presidency of Lebanon, he said he would want me to be a close adviser. He was elected president of the republic by a majority vote in the country's parliament on August 23, 1982. Unfortunately, he was assassinated by the Syrian National Party on September 14, 1982, before taking the oath of office. That was two days before the Sabra and Shatila massacre. He was thirty-five years old. I was sorry and sad. I believe that if he had lived to assume the presidency of Lebanon, he would have changed the course of the country's history. Our meetings started a pleasant and productive relationship that continued until his assassination.

Dubai Municipality, 1978

In 1978, the chips were down, and again, my finances left a lot to be desired. I spent time in London with Grace and Leila, as nothing serious needed my presence in Beirut. The war in Lebanon was still on, Bahrain's business was lost, and the USA business was not at its best.

One day, I got a telephone call from an ex-employee who at the onset of war in Lebanon had resigned, gone to Dubai, and established himself in the furniture business. He was successful and, being quite a sociable person, got his contacts in the Emirates right. On the phone, he told me that the municipality of Dubai was seeking a consultant to reorganize the municipality and assured me that though many consultants had offered their services, mine would be accepted.

I sent a telex (a precursor of the fax, still in use) addressed to the mayor of Dubai, who was a member of the ruling family, expressing my interest in taking the job. I got an immediate positive reply and traveled direct to Dubai from Heathrow.

On arrival, I met the director general of the municipality, a respectable Sudanese with whom I discussed the details of the job and then met Sheikh Hamdan bin Rashid Al Maktoum, the mayor of the city. At the time, Sheikh Hamdan was also the head of the department which was later organized to become the Central Bank for the United Arab Emirates. I signed a simple contract of one page and started immediately to look into the job requirements and determine the staffing accordingly.

It was a new type of a job. There was no municipality to speak of, but separate offices dealing with a variety of functions, such as building permits, pest control, water distribution, and all normal parts of a municipal organization. I discovered there were some engineers, qualified but underemployed, and one or two administrative employees, imported and qualified. However, they operated from different locations and made decisions on their own. On occasion, when they thought it was necessary, they got approvals from the director or the mayor of Dubai Municipality. Decisions were usually made based on less than complete information. The mayor sometimes showed up and made himself available. I developed a nice relationship with Sheikh Hamdan and met quite frequently with him in his office or home. On occasion, we went together to Abu Dhabi to investigate the needs of the Finance Ministry, which he headed.

I decided to review the laws establishing the municipality and I was pleasantly surprised that there is, within the statutes and laws enacted for the emirate, a section that details the functions the municipality is supposed to perform. Listing the functions therefore was the first order of the day. That list helped guide the setting up of the organizational structure of the municipality and define its components and its role in the community. This was the only document I used as a base for my work, but I did go through the departments already functioning to better define their tasks and blend them all into the one organization designed for the entire municipality.

I called on Scandiaconsult in Stockholm, Sweden, to help and they sent me two engineers, both young but impressive and knowledgeable. I called on another firm with which ABC had in the past coordinated joint projects, an English company specializing in local government. Galmore PLC saw in this job a good introduction for work in the Gulf, and they were right. The senior partner participated and headed his team. ABC brought in the flow charts and computer expertise. I headed the operating team and worked with them for over a year.

The procedure we used for the study started with a tour of all the sections already operational. We met at length with the various managerial and engineering staff and agreed that all of us would cooperate to list all the functions the municipality was, by law, supposed to perform. Similar functions were grouped into "similar groups," and when all the lists were ready for analysis we had listed and grouped all and every function the law required. We called each group list a "department." We defined in words each department and worked to create all the sublists, with each sub-list becoming a "section," and so on, to the lower echelons. This sounds simple, and it was, but it was also time consuming.

We started recruiting staff under this organizational structure, and whenever we were lucky to find good applicants, we relisted the functions and made amendments, so the organization was upgraded while we were implementing. We also used the functions to create job descriptions, which was a new concept in the Gulf area. Therefore, whenever a senior employee was selected, his job description was ready. We continued until our job was over and submitted our report. It showed the structure and the flow of information up the organizational chart and decisions and instructions down the organization, and it described an entity that was organized to deal with the demanding needs of the Dubai ruler. He dreamed of making the city very special if not unique, a city that would attract the attention of the world. That is the way he bragged about Dubai and its future. Dubai was blessed to have a ruler who dreamed well. Today, as controversial as Dubai's development may be, its town planning and design are a miracle of architecture, futuristic design, and investment attractors.

I wrote the various and sundry interim reports, which I used to get approvals from the municipality to implement while work progressed. When the time came to submit the final report, everything was in order: a municipality well set up and operational under the new organizational chart and staff, who had been recruited to perform the functions and the routines. All the routines, including flow charts, were already defined and in place. The hierarchy established the reporting channels and even the design of the forms needed to be filled by users of the facilities of the municipality, printed and ready for use. In effect, we at least partially succeeded in turning the administration at all levels into one defined procedure. Excepted from this procedure were the first line directors, who in addition to overseeing work progress were also, in time, ready to help upgrade the systems. We provided the municipality with tools to upgrade as necessary and procedures and training manuals to help the staff cope with sophisticated systems.

It is good to remember that at that time, computers were not in common use. Communication tools like the fax were just coming up in the business world. At the municipality, we got an offer from a German firm to supply us with fax machines, but a demonstration of their capability revealed that they were not yet an efficient tool. I declined the offer and continued to use the telex, which at the time was the best tool for written communication.

The rest of the story becomes technical and will not add much to all that I said. This experience was somewhat special because of the caliber of the individuals who made decisions in this emirate.

The 1980s

LEILA, 1982

These notes will not be complete if I do not tell the story of when Leila graduated from Bryn Mawr College and returned home to Beirut. Her return gave us joy and opened a door for me to engage in activities that I thought might provide her with options to plan her immediate and long-term objectives. Her dreams two decades later became mine too, and they absorbed all Leila's energies and mine for a substantial portion of my productive life.

I had a subsidiary to ABC called Communications Consulting Group, SAL (CCG), which I set up with a well-known Lebanese journalist. CCG published a daily Arabic language newsletter distributed to subscribers in Beirut during the 1982 Israeli invasion of Lebanon and for another year.

The Lebanese Civil War began with battles between Palestinian PLO fighters, left-wing groupings, Muslim factions, and the Lebanese Forces and other right-wing militias and culminated in an Israeli war machine invasion of Lebanon, the occupation of all the south of the country, and later occupation of the capital city of Beirut. The invasion displaced over a million civilians from the south, forcing them to find refuge in Beirut and its environs and in Syria.

On the early morning of the occupation in July 1982, at about 5 a.m., Leila was already at the CCG office not far from home, where her job was associate editor of the newsletter.

Unfortunately, the Israeli Army arrived and occupied Beirut on the morning of that very day. Grace and I watched the incursion into West Beirut from the windows of our apartment in Rue Kennedy.

We tried to call Leila but could not get in touch with her. The telephone lines were already down, and we were very worried. Later, we learned that Leila and her five colleagues were able to take the stairs from the eighth floor to the basement of the building, where they waited with other residents for a break in the shooting. Happily, sometime in the midafternoon, she came home from a day to remember.

We were relieved to learn that she did not have any untoward experience, except anxiety and worry about us and how we were coping with the Israeli presence in Beirut. Our family lived in the building that housed the Embassy of Switzerland on its first floor, and their Swiss flag probably deterred Israeli soldiers from entering the building. Later that day and for many days, we spent a lot of time in the basement of our building.

The Israeli soldiers were everywhere in West Beirut, shooting toward any movement they perceived, driving their tanks and other heavy equipment on the one-lane streets of Beirut, driving right over parked cars, and squashing them. They fired their heavy artillery into residential buildings for no apparent reason. Besides Jerusalem, Beirut was the only Arab capital city to be occupied by Israel. Resistance started as soon as the next day, and within a few days, Israeli soldiers were attacked in Hamra Street and other streets in Beirut. The Israelis found it uncomfortable to try to enjoy Beirut life. The Lebanese, in general, were civil but not welcoming. Eventually, the Israeli Army withdrew to 25 kilometers from the international Israel-Lebanon border and stayed there for close to two decades.

Once the heat of war subsided, Leila designed a trilingual guide, called The Guide, Le Guide, الدليل, to cultural life in Beirut and its suburbs, Arabic, French, and English, being the common languages of the

Lebanese and also of most visitors and tourists. Getting content for the guide required outreach to various cultural venues, art galleries, foreign cultural centers, and even cinemas, which was a great way to know the cultural life and those who produced it. Unfortunately, a new battle between local factions erupted, Beirut seemed to be on the brink of conflict again, and the guide never went into production.

AL-HAKAWATI

Her next project was eager to compile in a database of information about the history and culture of the Arab region. As we had at our disposal a Univac 1100 computer system, at that time the state-of-the-art mainframe machine, we planned to use it for data storage. We hired a former teacher of Arabic and a researcher to collect stories, biographies of Arab personalities, architecture, traditions, geography, and more. The first objective was to produce a monthly Arabic language children's magazine. The result was three mock issues of al-hakawati magazine.

The work was disrupted at its inception by the 1982 Israeli war on Lebanon, but was then resumed ten years later, in 1992.

By the year 2000, the Internet had become a familiar feature in peoples' lives, and that sparked the creation of a website rather than a print magazine. al-hakawati.net was launched in 2003, coming full circle from the initial concept of a database. The project's goal was to portray to the Arab world a fresh representation and reminder of our history and cultural and scientific accomplishments and to share those with the rest of the world. We also wanted the Arabic language to have a place on the Internet, which was a stepping-stone to the future.

The effort became an educational resource, a useful online destination. The well-regarded al-hakawati website was much visited by people and institutions across the globe. Many universities in the US accessed its content. We knew from usage statistics that the Arabic department at the University of Texas at Austin used the content as teaching material in their classes.

Later in about 2015, we collaborated with the University of Pennsylvania's Arabic department on selecting Arabic heritage books to digitize as searchable text, which total around four hundred books.

I liquidated my business in 2003, waited until all the ramifications of this liquidation were over, and then started on this new and most exciting and productive job of helping plan and collect content for al-hakawati.net. I greatly enjoyed selecting the heritage books and giving my time and attention to tribes and tribal history in the Arab world, especially of Saudi Arabia, Iraq, Jordan, and Palestine. al-hakawati.net, in its initial ten years, was a rare primary resource for Arab and Islamic cultures. We published the articles of al-Ra'ed al-Arabi on al-hakawati.net, connecting the past with the present.

I write about al-hakawati in this story because I was involved in it from its beginnings and spent most of my time working to support this vision of an online library. We created a unique reference and an open access site for anyone who can read the Arabic language. As a collateral benefit for me, I retired into a phase of learning about the Arab and Islamic cultures and spent my time enjoying reading material that ended up on the website for others to enjoy and benefit from.

NICOSIA, CYPRUS, 1985–1989

In 1985 and Grace and I decided to move to Nicosia because ABC had a nucleus of an office there. As I wrote earlier, the advantage of Cyprus is its proximity to Beirut, and I carried on with my work as well as possible. Though the decision did not prove sound, we kept up the image that we were still in business.

While in Cyprus, I learned a new line of work: trade. I bought a vessel load of shrimp from Argentina, sold it in the US, bought local Cypriot Halloumi cheese, and sold it to a Beirut supermarket. After that, I wondered why I did not start my life trading rather than selling an intangible product called "consulting."

INTELLIGENCE AGENCIES

In late 1994, at a time when the Syrian Army and its intelligence branches were in tight control of the country and everybody was careful about what they said or did, two individuals who ran the two leading intelligence agencies in Lebanon found it helpful to ask for my input. One was the military intelligence director, whose wife worked for me in ABC's Computer Training Center (BATC) when he was a junior army officer. She remained in my employ throughout her husband's rise in the ranks of military intelligence.

The other was the director of national security, a lawyer by training whom I initially hired on a case relating to a Saudi contract. He later joined my company as a functionary. He was appointed by then-President Amin Gemayel as acting director of national security, but all the same, he continued working for me.

The Intelligence and Security Departments asked for my help with public opinion surveys. A national security organization was set up for sectarian reasons. Lebanon, a country of eighteen religious sects, is administratively built to satisfy the constitutional rights of those sects. The National Security Organization was established by the president of the republic, always a Maronite, who appointed a temporary chief, also a Maronite, to be confirmed or replaced by a permanent one in due course. I was asked to set up the organizational structure of this newly created outfit. It took over a year to do what I had to do, and then I made myself scarce and left it with the staff to run the newly established entity and complete the job.

The Last Decade of the Twentieth Century and After

This section attempts to present a summary and general survey of what I did with myself and how I spent my time during the last decade of the twentieth century and the first one of the twenty-first century. The writing of this section in its entirety needed a lot of time and the input of Grace and Leila. Grace shared every detail of my life with me and gave me unlimited support.

Our diaspora in Beirut was reaching an end, and though we did find occasions to go to Nicosia, we were close to home and work. I had an office in Beirut and Nicosia and with staff helping me maneuver a new work environment, and everything seemed to be moving slowly in the right direction.

At the end of 1989, we thought we were settled and comfy at home in Beirut. Suddenly, a new war erupted between Lebanese Army General Michel Aoun (later president of Lebanon) and Dr. Samir Geagea, the head of the Lebanese Forces, both Maronite Christian and militia leaders. It was an intense and cruel battle in which both sides used heavy artillery to fight it out within Beirut. In all the fifteen years of the civil war, Beirut got its most significant damage during this period of the Aoun-Geagea war.

The first night of this new war was so bad that Grace and I cowered in the corner of our bedroom, expecting to be hit by a rocket. Grad missiles and other projectiles were exchanged. The sound of every rocket when it was launched, even en route and before it hit a target, was incredible; the intensity of the explosions convinced us it was time to leave Beirut, this time for the USA. We planned to settle there and forget this part of the world—but unfortunately, we later found this was impossible.

In 1995 we moved from our lovely apartment on Rue Kennedy to an apartment we owned on Rue May Ziadeh and lived there until 2010, when we sold it and rented an apartment in the center of Hamra, where we lived until July 2019.

During these years, Sara and Nadia, separately, came to AUB for their college junior year abroad, and they were a joy. Sara witnessed the devastating 2006 war between Israel and Hezbollah, and for that war most Lebanese were supporting Hezbollah against the heavily destructive Israeli attacks. As the situation became very dangerous, Americans were being evacuated. Sara was whisked by AUB to the American Embassy compound and then via Marines helicopter onto the warship USS Whidbey Island. The vessel carried US citizens evacuating from Beirut and was heading out to an unknown port.

When Sara was on board, she contacted us briefly by phone, and that was the last we heard from her on that tense day in July. The warship's destination was secret; no information was divulged. We eventually heard that the vessel was heading to Cyprus. Luckily, the ship docked in Limassol, Cyprus, and Michael Janssen, a friend and journalist who lived in Nicosia, drove there and picked Sara up. Sara stayed at Michael's home until her bookings to the US were arranged and confirmed. One day, I will prevail on Sara to help me write about this unique and incredible experience.

Nadia had less excitement during her junior year at AUB. Still, she did live through the Nahr el-Bared battle between an extreme Muslim Group (Fatah al-Islam) and the Lebanese Army then headed by General Michel Suleiman, who later became president of Lebanon.

Lebanese Personalities

I will introduce this section by saying that my contacts in Lebanon were always good, though I did not give much of my time to Lebanon because of my work overseas. However, that did not prevent the preservation of old contacts and new ones at the highest political and social levels. Some of the major decision-makers I knew contributed much to my expanded relations in Lebanon and elsewhere in the Arab world. In fact, through the individuals mentioned in this section, I gained access to many prominent personalities.

KAMEL AL-ASSAD

Kamel al-Assad, a longtime Speaker of Parliament in Lebanon, comes from an influential Lebanese Shi'a family. He was one of my excellent contacts. While he was speaker and for several months, I provided him with a private office in our Gefinor suite of offices, where he said he wanted to work in a quiet atmosphere with no interruptions from members of Parliament and other visitors. While he was with us, I helped him in his research in writing or reviewing of draft laws to be reviewed and eventually approved by Parliament. We had many meetings and discussions, and I valued his intelligence and fluency in Lebanon's constitutional law. His privacy was assured for some months, but the information was soon leaked about his whereabouts, and visitors, literally in the dozens, started stopping by to meet him.

Many of those were distinguished Lebanese personalities, and some did ask me to intervene to secure an appointment with him. When my work suffered due to his presence and the daily crowds, I asked him in a friendly manner to hide elsewhere, but he did not, and my offices continued to house the Speaker of Parliament for a few additional months. His presence was beneficial to my life in Beirut.

His personality and political performance were subject to controversial estimations—but being such an important figure with the authority of his position and personal influence, this controversy was understandable. I think of him as a likable person endowed with good humor. I must say that I learned a lot from him, professionally and socially.

SHEIKH MAURICE GEMAYEL

Sheikh Maurice Gemayel, of the noted intelligentsia in Lebanon and an influential person through his family, also secured a room in my Hamra offices, where he met his peers. He was a member of Parliament and later assumed the office of the minister of planning. Parliament approved and enacted into law many of the development plans which he prepared with the help of my staff. Typical of the way things work in Lebanon, most of these laws were passed, but their implementation was delayed.

Maurice Gemayel conducted studies and drew up designs and plans for most of the sectors, believing that otherwise, no state could ever live up to its duties. These are his foremost milestones:

- A master plan for water distribution for Lebanon
- Plans for designing agricultural and industrial production
- Regulating banks
- Regulating commerce
- Regulating tourism and summer vacations
- Drawing up plans for transportation
- Drawing up plans for oil industry

- Designing the Beirut-Beqaa' Tunnel (to facilitate transport to Beirut from the agricultural areas)
- Drawing up the Litani River plan
- Drawing up designs for monetary, credit and borrowing sectors

I sat in on many meetings with local and foreign specialists and local officials, and through them, I learned a lot about what was planned and what was resulting, and I contributed some. Sheikh Maurice stayed with us for over two years, and we lost him when he died while addressing Parliament. He was a special person, and he is still mentioned, when issues take a bad turn, as a person who would have handled the day's problems differently.

PRESIDENT OF LEBANON

The president of Lebanon from 1998 until 2007, and I, had a standing meeting with him every Wednesday at 10:30 a.m. I advised him on various issues, some economic, some political, and also on his public image, which was a concern. He took my advice seriously, and I left nothing for unnecessary interpretation. I committed my advice to paper, which I handed to him at the beginning of every session. As a result, I was privy to many personal issues and got to know more about the influences, local and regional, that had a bearing on the political process in Lebanon. When and if I write the details of my work during this particular job, I will try to be impartial, but what I saw was not always conducive to impartiality.

I met him when he was the general of the Lebanese Army. He contacted me and asked me to meet with him at the Ministry of Defense. When I arrived at the ministry, the director of military intelligence accompanied me to the general's office, introduced me, and left. The meeting was introductory, pleasant, and ended with a personal request to prepare a draft letter in English, which he wanted to send to the ambassadors to Lebanon of the five permanent members of the UN Security Council. He gave me a document, which he or his staff had prepared in Arabic, expressing his views on various issues, and he asked me to use it as a basis for my draft. I agreed and spent a weekend writing the letter, which was lengthy, but I had accepted the task and sent the English version on a Monday. This letter started a relationship that was to continue for a long while.

Later meetings were mainly general discussions about his performance in the army, his image, and his chances for election as president of the country. I had some comments and reservations about his image and suggested some ideas for improving what God had given him in terms of his appearance and public speaking abilities. However, he became fixated on his popularity and his chances of becoming president. One day, after a lot of research relating to his popularity, he told me, "Why should I worry? Both Syria and the US endorse me for president, and therefore, I feel secure with the outcome." He was right, but we continued to conduct image and popularity studies, the outcomes of which led him and his military intelligence staff to argue with me ad nauseum.

The relationship lasted for over eighteen months, after which it was apparent to me that we were not on the same page. However, during this period, I did a lot of work. I am proud of two essential projects, which I suggested, and he and the prime minister approved:

- The Public Corporation for Housing
- The Investment Development Authority of Lebanon (IDAL)

SALIM EL-HOSS

My school friend, a veteran politician, served several terms as prime minister of Lebanon and was a longtime member of Parliament representing his hometown, Beirut. We first met at the International College in 1947 and went on to AUB at the same time. We were enrolled in the same business courses and received our undergraduate degrees the same year, 1952, he with a Bachelor of Business Administration and I with a BA.

He came from a modest family and his early life was not easy. His aunt and family members contributed to help him through college, but because he was an outstanding student, he won scholarships and took jobs in the department of business, so in time he became financially independent. Later, in 1954, we both graduated from AUB, he with an MBA and I with an MA.

Salim is honest, hardworking, and respected by all. Today, when a Lebanese mentions honesty and integrity in a politician, Salim is the example. He was prime minister five times and in-between he was appointed to many important positions. "Who is Salim el-Hoss?" is answered by his own autobiographical summary, with no exaggerations or understatement, which he wrote for us to publish on al-hakawati.

He served as prime minister when Emile Lahoud became president, and he asked me for help on issues of reconstruction resulting in the damages of the war; the need to rebuild was urgent. Though I did cooperate in many projects, I gave considerable time and thought to two projects: one was establishing a housing mortgage company, which found quick approval and quick success. The president and Salim el-Hoss, the prime minister, prevailed on me to supervise this entity until it became operational. I stayed with this organization for about a year. It was time consuming. The second was IDAL, Lebanon's Investment Development Authority. Both organizations were created as departments of the Lebanese government.

Beirut: Two Major Projects Entrusted to Me

THE PUBLIC CORPORATION FOR HOUSING

The housing mortgage company decreed by Lebanon's president and prime minister, which was placed under my management and supervision, was established in 2001 with the purpose of facilitating to all citizens the purchase of a home in the location most convenient to them, with loans at a reasonable interest rate for thirty years. This was done by using banks to provide the loans under an acceptable guarantee by the Public Corporation for Housing. The corporation itself also was able to extend loans like the individual banks. This provided the banks with a new investment opportunity and the buying citizens with a chance to live in a house they owned. Banks in Lebanon did not, as a rule, provide housing loans.

We appointed Antoine Chamoun, a career public servant, as director general of the Public Corporation for Housing. He was energetic, his hands clean and reputation good, and he was ready to take over this job. He reported to me for about a year. I recommended that Chamoun run the corporation on his own, and he accepted the recommendation. I told Hoss, the prime minister, about this decision and then passed the good news on back to Chamoun. I was pleased with my performance, and the success of this project was phenomenal.

In the first year of operation, we completed about 500 mortgage contracts. The second year the number rose to about 5,000 completed mortgages. The average Lebanese citizen finally had a path to home ownership and stability in a time of unrest and instability in the country.

I never regretted my decision to commend Antoine Chamoun to run the Corporation for Housing on his own. He was a skillful manager and led the corporation to great success: At the start of its establishment, we wrote the qualifications for loans. In time, the banks cooperated in advancing loans to qualified applicants. The Public Corporation for Housing is still operational and extending loans to prospective homebuyers, well managed with vigor and dedication.

THE INVESTMENT DEVELOPMENT AUTHORITY OF LEBANON (IDAL)

Another suggestion i made was to establish an entity to encourage investments by assessing feasibility studies of various projects suggested for approval and cutting through the red tape and the corrupt administration. The Investment Development Authority of Lebanon (IDAL) interfaces between the investor and the relevant government departments until a decision is made to approve or reject a project. No more handouts or commissions for granting permissions to start a business.

Other than working out the details of how this corporation should operate, a director was appointed who took over, except at one or two meetings where I made my suggestions clear. I made my recommendations to the prime minister and the president to approve, which they did. I had no role in IDAL's management. I contributed to both projects pro bono, and I thought enough was enough.

IDAL's functions and authority expanded as it gained experience and became a fundamental and practical entity in economic development, finance of feasible projects, and generally many business fields in Lebanon.

The Young Men's Club

Early in this century, I reconnected with a few old friends, all retired, all AUB graduates and Arab Nationalists, and all over seventy-five years of age. They met regularly on Wednesdays, and I joined them in the "Young Men's Club." All of us in the group have a history of which we are proud. Several wrote and published their experiences describing their time periods in various countries where they lived or worked.

We came from different professional backgrounds; some were in public service, mainly in the foreign office, others were government ministers, and others were medical doctors and businessmen. We come from many Arab countries, including Iraq, Palestine, Kuwait, Lebanon, and Jordan.

Every Wednesday, over a cup of Turkish coffee, espresso, Nescafé, or fruit juice, we discussed the Arab area's constantly changing state of politics, and our discussions were based on a background of information and not rumor. Each member brought with them insights, news, and information from reliable and good contacts, and maybe from the perspective of their home country. In all, our club numbered eleven members; those of us who lived in Beirut and others when they happened to be in town, as some lived abroad but visited frequently. Occasionally, we would invite a new person, a friend of a member. Some of the visitors contributed a lot to our discussions. Other times, a guest would fail to be approved.

Many in Beirut and other locations in the region knew of this Wednesday meeting and wondered if they could join. But most of the members were happy with the club and did not want to open it up to more members.

Among the regular group were the following, each man's name followed by his profession before retirement:

- Abdel Ghani Dalli Minister of agriculture in Iraq; secretary to the heir to the throne in Iraq
- Amjad Ghanma, MD Chief medical director at Aramco, personal physician to King Saud
- Shawki Hakoura, MD Pediatrician in Kuwait
- Yusuf Shedid Career diplomat; ambassador of Lebanon to Austria, inter alia
- Nadim Dimashqiya Career diplomat, ambassador of Lebanon to the United Kingdom, inter alia
- Ahmad al-Khateeb, MD Tropical diseases physician, physician to the Emir of Kuwait, member of Kuwait Parliament
- Abel Hamid Fakhoury Chairman of the board of Middle East Airlines
- Adel K. Afifi, MD Professor of neurology at AUB and the University of Iowa and myself, Maurice N. Khoury

This summarizes my and my family's main life events between 1975 and my retirement.

Reviewing this section, I feel I should spend more time filling in the blanks, and they are many. Therefore, I will need to exercise both patience and determination, and I will, God willing, try.

APPENDICES

Appendix 1

Hussein–McMahon Correspondence: 1915–1916

In July 1915, Sir Henry McMahon, British High Commissioner in Egypt, and Sharif Hussein of Mecca, engaged in a correspondence in which Britain promised to support the independence of the Arab lands in exchange for an Arab revolt against Ottoman rule. The exact territory of the future Arab state was left unclear. The Arabs believed it would include Palestine; the British later claimed that Palestine had never been part of the agreement. The letters were written in the local language and translated for the recipient.

Letter No.1, Sharif Hussein's first note to Sir Henry McMahon

Mecca, Ramadan 2, 1333 (July 14, 1915)
Compliments.

Whereas the entire Arab nation without any exception have decided in these last years to accomplish their freedom, and grasp the reins of their administration both in theory and practice; And whereas they have found and felt that it is in the interest of the Government of Great Britain to support them and aid them in the attainment of their firm and lawful intentions (which are based upon the maintenance of the honour and dignity of their life) without any ulterior motives whatsoever unconnected with this object;

And whereas it is to the Arabs' interest also to prefer the assistance of the Government of Great Britain in consideration of their geographic position and economic interests, and also of the attitude of the above-mentioned Government, which is known to both nations and therefore need not be emphasized;

For these reasons the Arab nation has decided to approach the Government of Great Britain, if it should think fit, for the approval, through her deputy or representative, of the following fundamental propositions, leaving out all things considered secondary in comparison with these, so that it may prepare all means necessary for attaining this noble purpose, until such time as it finds occasion for making the actual negotiations:-

1. Great Britain recognizes the independence of the Arab countries, bounded on the north by Mersina and Adana up to the 37th degree of latitude, on which degree fall Birijik, Urfa, Mardin, Midiat, Jezirat (Ibn 'Umar), Amadia, up to the border of Persia; on the east by the borders of Persia up to the Gulf of Basra; on the south by the Indian Ocean, with the exception of the position of Aden to remain as it is; on the west by the Red Sea, the Mediterranean Sea up to Mersina. England to approve the proclamation of an Arab Khalifate of Islam.

2. The Arab Government of the Sharif will acknowledge that England shall have the preference in all economic enterprises in the Arab countries whenever conditions of enterprises are otherwise equal.

3. For the security of this Arab independence and the certainty of such preference of economic enterprises, both high contracting parties will offer mutual assistance, to the best ability of their military and naval forces, to face any foreign Power which may attack either party. Peace not to be decided without agreement of both parties.

4. If one of the parties enters into an aggressive conflict, the other party will assume a neutral attitude, and in case of such party

wishing the other to join forces, both to meet and discuss the conditions.
5. England will acknowledge the abolition of foreign privileges in the Arab countries and will assist the Government of the Sharif in an International Convention for confirming such abolition.
6. Articles 3 and 4 of this treaty will remain in vigour for fifteen years, and, if either wishes it to be renewed, one year's notice before lapse of treaty is to be given.

Consequently, and as the whole of the Arab nation have (praise be to God) agreed and united for the attainment, at all costs and finally, of this noble object, they beg the Government of Great Britain to answer them positively or negatively in a period of thirty days after receiving this intimation; and if this period should lapse before they receive an answer, they reserve to themselves complete freedom of action. Moreover, we (the Sharif's family) will consider ourselves free in work and deed from the bonds of our previous declaration which we made through Ali Effendi.

Compliments.

Letter No. 2, Sir Henry McMahon's first note to the Sharif Hussein

Cairo, August 30, 1915
To his Highness the Sharif Hussein.
Compliments.

We have the honour to thank you for your frank expressions of the sincerity of your feeling towards England. We rejoice, moreover, that your Highness and your people are of one opinion - that Arab interests are English interests and English Arab. To this intent we confirm to you the terms of Lord Kitchener's message, which reached you by the hand of Ali Effendi, and in which was stated clearly our desire for the independence of Arabia and its inhabitants, together with our approval of the Arab Khalifate when it should be proclaimed. We declare once more that His Majesty's Government would welcome the resumption of the Khalifate by an Arab of true race. With regard to the questions of limits and boundaries, it would appear to be premature to consume our time in discussing such details in the heat of war, and while, in many portions of them, the Turk is up to now in effective occupation; especially as we have learned, with surprise and regret, that some of the Arabs in those very parts, far from assisting us, are neglecting this their supreme opportunity and are lending their arms to the German and the Turk, to the new despoiler and the old oppressor.

Nevertheless, we are ready to send your Highness for the Holy Cities and the noble Arabs the charitable offerings of Egypt so soon as your Highness shall inform us how and where they should be delivered. We are, moreover, arranging for this your messenger to be admitted and helped on any journey he may make to ourselves.

Friendly reassurances. Salutations!

Letter No. 3, Sharif Hussein's second note to Sir Henry McMahon

Mecca, Shawwal 29, 1933 (September 9, 1915)

To his Excellency the Most Exalted, the Most Eminent-the British High Commissioner in Egypt; may God grant him Success.

With great cheerfulness and delight I received your letter dated the 19th Shawal, 1333 (the 30th August, 1915), and have given it great consideration and regard, in spite of the impression I received from it of ambiguity and its tone of coldness and hesitation with regard to our essential point.

It is necessary to make clear to your Excellency our sincerity towards the illustrious British Empire and our confession of preference for it in all cases and matters and under all forms and circumstances. The real interests of the followers of our religion necessitate this.

Nevertheless, your Excellency will pardon me and permit me to say clearly that the coolness and hesitation which you have displayed in the question of the limits and boundaries by saying that the discussion of these at present is of no use and is a loss of time, and that they are still in the hands of the Government which is ruling them, &c., might be taken to infer an estrangement or something of the sort.

As the limits and boundaries demanded are not those of one person whom we should satisfy and with whom we should discuss them after the war is over, but our peoples have seen that the life of their new proposal is bound at least by these limits and their word is united on this.

Therefore, they have found it necessary first to discuss this point with the Power in whom they now have their confidence and trust as a final appeal, viz., the illustrious British Empire.

Their reason for this union and confidence is mutual interest, the necessity of regulating territorial divisions and the feelings of their inhabitants, so that they may know how to base their future and life, so not to meet her (England?) or any of her Allies in opposition to their resolution which would produce a contrary issue, which God forbid.

For the object is, honourable Minister, the truth which is established on a basis which guarantees the essential sources of life in future.

Yet within these limits they have not included places inhabited by a foreign race. It is a vain show of words and titles.

May God have mercy on the Khalifate and comfort Moslems in it.

I am confident that your Excellency will not doubt that it is not I personally who am demanding of these limits which include only our race, but that they are all proposals of the people, who, in short, believe that they are necessary for economic life.

Is this not right, your Excellency the Minister?

In a word, your high Excellency, we are firm in our sincerity and declaring our preference for loyalty towards you, whether you are satisfied with us, as has been said, or angry.

With reference to your remark in your letter above mentioned that some of our people are still doing their utmost in promoting the interests of Turkey, your goodness (lit. "perfectness") would not permit you to make this an excuse for the tone of coldness and hesitation with regard to our demands, demands which I cannot admit that you, as a man of sound opinion, will deny to be necessary for our existence; nay, they are the essential essence of our life, material and moral.

Up to the present moment I am myself with all my might carrying out in my country all things in conformity with the Islamic law, all things which tend to benefit the rest of the Kingdom, and I shall continue to do so until it pleases God to order otherwise.

In order to reassure your Excellency, I can declare that the whole country, together with those who you say are submitting themselves to Turco-German orders, are all waiting the result of these negotiations, which are dependent only on your refusal or acceptance of the question of the limits and on your declaration of safeguarding their religion first and then the rest of rights from any harm or danger.

Whatever the illustrious Government of Great Britain finds conformable to its policy on this subject, communicate it to us and specify to us the course we should follow.

In all cases it is only God's will which shall be executed, and it is God who is the real factor in everything.

With regard to our demand for grain for the natives, and the moneys ("surras") known to the Wakfs' Ministry and all other articles sent here with pilgrims' caravans, high Excellency, my intention in this matter is to confirm your proclamations to the whole world, and especially to the Moslem world, that your antagonism is confined only to the party which has usurped the rights of the Khalifate in which are included the rights of all Moslems.

Moreover, the said grain is from the special Wakfs and has nothing to do with politics.

If you think it should be, let the grain of the two years be transported in a special steamer to Jedda in an official manner, in the name of all the natives as usual, and the captain of the steamer or the special "Mamur" detailed as usual every year to hand it over on his arrival at the port will send to the Governor of Jedda asking for the Mamur of the grain at Jedda or a responsible official to take over the grain and give the necessary receipt signed by the said Ma'mur, that is the Ma'mur of the grain himself. He should make it a condition that he would (? not) accept any receipt but that signed by this Ma'mur.

Let the captain of the steamer or the "Ma'mur" (detailed with the grain) be instructed that if he finds anything contrary to this arrangement, he should warn them that he will return home with the cargo. Thereupon the Mamur and the special committee detailed with him, which is known as the committee of the grain for the natives, will take over the grain in the proper form.

Please accept my best regards and salutations.

If you choose to send a reply to this, please send it with the bearer.

Letter No. 4, Sir Henry McMahon's second note to the Sharif Hussein

Cairo, October 24, 1915

I have received your letter of the 29th Shawal, 1333, with much pleasure and your expressions of friendliness and sincerity have given me the greatest satisfaction.

I regret that you should have received from my last letter the impression that I regarded the question of the limits and boundaries with coldness and hesitation; such was not the case, but it appeared to me that the time had not yet come when that question could be discussed in a conclusive manner.

I have realised, however, from your last letter that you regard this question as one of vital and urgent importance. I have, therefore, lost no time in informing the Government of Great Britain of the contents of your letter, and it is with great pleasure that I communicate to you on their behalf the following statement, which I am confident you will receive with satisfaction: -

The two districts of Mersina and Alexandretta and portions of Syria lying to the west of the districts of Damascus, Homs, Hama and Aleppo cannot be said to be purely Arab and should be excluded from the limits demanded.

With the above modification, and without prejudice of our existing treaties with Arab chiefs, we accept those limits.

As for those regions lying within those frontiers wherein Great Britain is free to act without detriment to the interest of her ally, France,

I am empowered in the name of the Government of Great Britain to give the following assurances and make the following reply to your letter: -

1. Subject to the above modifications, Great Britain is prepared to recognize and support the independence of the Arabs in all the regions within the limits demanded by the Sharif of Mecca.
2. Great Britain will guarantee the Holy Places against all external aggression and will recognise their inviolability.
3. When the situation admits, Great Britain will give to the Arabs her advice and will assist them to establish what may appear to be the most suitable forms of government in those various territories.
4. On the other hand, it is understood that the Arabs have decided to seek the advice and guidance of Great Britain only, and that such European advisers and officials as may be required for the formation of a sound form of administration will be British.
5. With regard to the vilayets of Bagdad and Basra, the Arabs will recognise that the established position and interests of Great Britain necessitate special administrative arrangements in order to secure these territories from foreign aggression, to promote the welfare of the local populations and to safeguard our mutual economic interests.

I am convinced that this declaration will assure you beyond all possible doubt of the sympathy of Great Britain towards the aspirations of her friends the Arabs and will result in a firm and lasting alliance, the immediate results of which will be the expulsion of the Turks from the Arab countries and the freeing of the Arab peoples from the Turkish yoke, which for so many years has pressed heavily upon them.

I have confined myself in this letter to the more vital and important questions, and if there are any other matters dealt with in your letter which I have omitted to mention, we may discuss them at some convenient date in the future.

It was with very great relief and satisfaction that I heard of the safe arrival of the Holy Carpet and the accompanying offerings which, thanks to the clearness of your directions and the excellence of your arrangements, were landed without trouble or mishap in spite of the dangers and difficulties occasioned by the present sad war. May God soon bring a lasting peace and freedom to all peoples!

I am sending this letter by the hand of your trusted and excellent messenger, Sheikh Mohammed Ibn Arif Ibn Uraifan, and he will inform you of the various matters of interest, but of less vital importance, which I have not mentioned in this letter.

Compliments.

Letter No.5, Sharif Hussein's third note to Sir Henry McMahon

Mecca, Dhul Hejja 27, 1333 (November 5, 1915)
Compliments.

To his Excellency the most exalted and eminent Minister who is endowed with the highest authority and soundness of opinion.
May God guide him to do His Will.
I received with great pleasure your honoured letter, dated the 15th Zil Hijja (the 24th October, 1915), to which I beg to answer as follows:

1. In order to facilitate an agreement and to render a service to Islam, and at the same time to avoid all that may cause Islam troubles and hardships-seeing moreover that we have great consideration for the distinguished qualities and dispositions of the Government of Great Britain-we renounce our insistence on the inclusion of the vilayets of Mersina and Adana in the Arab Kingdom. But the two vilayets of Aleppo and Beirut and their sea coasts are purely Arab vilayets, and there is no difference between a Moslem and a Christian Arab: they are both descendants of one forefather.

    We Moslems will follow the footsteps of the Commander of the Faithful Omar ibn Khattab, and other Khalifs succeeding him, who ordained in the laws of the Moslem Faith that

Moslems should treat the Christians as they treat themselves. He, Omar, declared with reference to Christians: "They will have the same privileges and submit to the same duties as ourselves." They will thus enjoy their civic rights in as much as it accords with the general interests of the whole nation.

2. As the Iraqi vilayets are parts of the pure Arab Kingdom, and were in fact the seat of its Government in the time of Ali ibn Abu Talib, and in the time of all the Khalifs who succeeded him; and as in them began the civilisation of the Arabs, and as their towns were the first towns built in Islam where the Arab power became so great; therefore they are greatly valued by all Arabs far and near, and their traditions cannot be forgotten by them. Consequently, we cannot satisfy the Arab nations or make them submit to give us such a title to nobility. But in order to render an accord easy, and taking into consideration the assurances mentioned in the fifth article of your letter to keep and guard our mutual interests in that country as they are one and the same, for all these reasons we might agree to leave under the British administration for a short time those districts now occupied by the British troops without the rights of either party being prejudiced thereby (especially those of the Arab nation; which interests are to it economic and vital), and against a suitable sum paid as compensation to the Arab Kingdom for the period of occupation, in order to meet the expenses which every new kingdom is bound to support; at the same time respecting your agreements with the Sheikhs of those districts, and especially those which are essential.

3. In your desire to hasten the movement we see not only advantages, but grounds of apprehension. The first of these grounds is the fear of the blame of the Moslems of the opposite party (as has already happened in the past), who would declare that we have revolted against Islam and ruined its forces. The second is that, standing in the face of Turkey which is supported by all the forces of Germany, we do not know what Great Britain and her Allies

would do if one of the Entente Powers were weakened and obliged to make peace. We fear that the Arab nation will then be left alone in the face of Turkey together with her allies, but we would not at all mind if we were to face the Turks alone. Therefore, it is necessary to take these points into consideration in order to avoid a peace being concluded in which the parties concerned may decide the fate of our people as if we had taken part in the war without making good our claims to official consideration.

4. The Arab nation has a strong belief that after this war is over the Turks under German influence will direct their efforts to provoke the. Arabs and violate their rights, both material and moral, to wipe out their nobility and honour and reduce them to utter submission as they are determined to ruin them entirely. The reasons for the slowness shown in our action have already been stated.

5. When the Arabs know the Government of Great Britain is their ally who will not leave them to themselves at the conclusion of peace in the face of Turkey and Germany, and that she will support and will effectively defend them, then to enter the war at once will, no doubt, be in conformity with the general interest of the Arabs.

6. Our letter dated the 29th Shawal, 1333 (the 9th September, 1915), saves us the trouble of repeating our opinions as to articles 3 and 4 of your honoured last letter regarding administration, Government advisers and officials, especially as you have declared, exalted Minister, that you will not interfere with internal affairs.

7. The arrival of a clear and definite answer as soon as possible to the above proposals is expected. We have done our utmost in making concessions in order to come to an agreement satisfying both parties. We know that our lot in this war will be either a success, which will guarantee to the Arabs a life becoming their past history, or destruction in the attempt to attain their objects. Had it not been for the determination which I see in the Arabs for the attainment of their objects, I would have preferred to

seclude myself on one of the heights of a mountain, but they, the Arabs, have insisted that I should guide the movement to this end.

May God keep you safe and victorious, as we devoutly hope and desire.

Letter No. 6, Sir Henry McMahon's third note to the Sharif Hussein

Cairo, December 14, 1915
Compliments.

I am gratified to observe that you agree to the exclusion of the districts of Mersina and Adana from boundaries of the Arab territories.

I also note with great pleasure and satisfaction your assurances that the Arabs are determined to act in conformity with the precepts laid down by Omar Ibn Khattab and the early Khalifs, which secure the rights and privileges of all religions alike.

In stating that the Arabs are ready to recognise and respect all our treaties with Arab chiefs, it is, of course, understood that this will apply to all territories included in the Arab Kingdom, as the Government of Great Britain cannot repudiate engagements which already exist.

With regard to the vilayets of Aleppo and Beirut, the Government of Great Britain have fully understood and taken careful note of your observations, but, as the interests of our ally, France, are involved in them both, the question will require careful consideration and a further communication on the subject will be addressed to you in due course.

The Government of Great Britain, as I have already informed you, are ready to give all guarantees of assistance and support within their power to the Arab Kingdom, but their interests demand, as you yourself have recognised, a friendly and stable administration in the vilayet of Bagdad, and the adequate safeguarding of these interests calls for a much fuller and more detailed consideration than the present situation and the urgency of these negotiations permit.

We fully appreciate your desire for caution, and have no wish to urge you to hasty action, which might jeopardise the eventual success of your projects, but, in the meantime, it is most essential that you should spare no effort to attach all the Arab peoples to our united cause and urge them to afford no assistance to our enemies.

It is on the success of these efforts and on the more active measures which the Arabs may hereafter take in support of our cause, when the time for action comes, that the permanence and strength of our agreement must depend.

Under these circumstances I am further directed by the Government of Great Britain to inform you that you may rest assured that Great Britain has no intention of concluding any peace in terms of which the freedom of the Arab peoples from German and Turkish domination does not form an essential condition.

As an earnest of our intentions, and in order to aid you in your efforts in our joint cause, I am sending you by your trustworthy messenger a sum of twenty thousand pounds.

Compliments.

Letter No. 7, Sharif Hussein's fourth note to Sir Henry McMahon

Mecca, Safar 25, 1334 (January 1, 1916)
Compliments.

To his Excellency the eminent, energetic and magnanimous Minister.

We received from the bearer your letter, dated the 9th Safar (the 14th December, 1915), with great respect and honour, and I have understood its contents, which caused me the greatest pleasure and satisfaction, as it removed that which had made me uneasy.

Your honour will have realised, after the arrival of Mohammed (Faroki) Sharif and his interview with you, that all our procedure up to the present was of no personal inclination or the like, which would have been wholly unintelligible, but that everything was the result of the decisions and desires of our peoples, and that we are but transmitters and executants of such decisions and desires in the position they (our people) have pressed upon us.

These truths are, in my opinion, very important and deserve your honour's special attention and consideration.

With regard to what had been stated in your honoured communication concerning El Iraq as to the matter of compensation for the period of occupation, we, in order to strengthen the confidence of Great Britain in our attitude and in our words and actions, really and veritably, and in order to give her evidence of our certainty and assurance in trusting her glorious Government, leave the determination of the amount to the perception of her wisdom and justice.

As regards the northern parts and their coasts, we have already stated in our previous letter what were the utmost possible modifications, and all this was only done so to fulfill those aspirations whose attainment is desired by the will of the Blessed and Supreme God. It is this same feeling and desire which impelled us to avoid what may possibly injure the alliance of Great Britain and France and the agreement made between them during the present wars and calamities; yet we find it our duty that the eminent minister should be sure that, at the first opportunity after this war is finished, we shall ask you (what we avert our eyes from to-day) for what we now leave to France in Beirut and its coasts.

I do not find it necessary to draw your attention to the fact that our plan is of greater security to the interests and protection of the rights of Great Britain than it is to us, and will necessarily be so whatever may happen, so that Great Britain may finally see her friends in that contentment and advancement which she is endeavouring to establish for them now, especially as her Allies being neighbours to us will be the germ of difficulties and discussion with which there will be no peaceful conditions. In addition to which the citizens of Beirut will decidedly never accept such dismemberment, and they may oblige us to undertake new measures which may exercise Great Britain, certainly not less than her present troubles, because of our belief and certainty in the reciprocity and indeed the identity of our interests, which is the only cause that caused us never to care to negotiate with any other Power but you. Consequently, it is impossible to allow any derogation that gives France, or any other Power, a span of land in those regions.

I declare this, and I have a strong belief, which the living will inherit from the dead, in the declarations which you give in the conclusion of your honoured letter. Therefore, the honourable and eminent Minister should believe and be sure, together with Great Britain, that we still remain firm to our resolution which Storrs learnt from us two years ago, for which we await the opportunity suitable to our situation, especially in view of that action the time of which has now come near and which destiny drives towards us with great haste and clearness, so that we and those who are of our opinion may have reasons for such action against any criticisms or responsibilities imposed upon us in future.

Your expression "we do not want to push you to any hasty action which might jeopardise the success of your aim" does not need any more explanation except what we may ask for, when necessary, such as arms, ammunition, &c.

I deem this sufficient, as I have occupied much of your Honour's time. I beg to offer you my great veneration and respect.

Letter No. 8, Sir Henry McMahon's fourth note to the Sharif Hussein

Cairo, January 25, 1916
Compliments.

We have received with great pleasure and satisfaction your letter of the 25th Safar (the 1st January) at the hands of your trusty messenger, who has also transmitted to us your verbal messages.

We fully realise and entirely appreciate the motives which guide you in this important question, and we know well that you are acting entirely in the interests of the Arab peoples and with no thought beyond their welfare.

We take note of your remarks concerning the vilayet of Baghdad and will take the question into careful consideration when the enemy has been defeated and the time for peaceful settlement arrives.

As regards the northern parts, we note with satisfaction your desire to avoid anything which might possibly injure the alliance of Great Britain and France. It is, as you know, our fixed determination that nothing shall be permitted to interfere in the slightest degree with our united prosecution of this war to a victorious conclusion. Moreover, when the victory has been won, the friendship of Great Britain and France will become yet more firm and enduring, cemented by the blood of Englishmen and Frenchmen who have died side by side fighting for the cause of right and liberty.

In this great cause Arabia is now associated, and God grant that the result of our mutual efforts and co-operation will bind us in a lasting friendship to the mutual welfare and happiness of us all.

We are greatly pleased to hear of the action you are taking to win all the Arabs over to our joint cause, and to dissuade them from giving any assistance to our enemies, and we leave it to your discretion to seize the most favourable moment for further and more decided measures.

You will doubtless inform us by the bearer of this letter of any manner in which we can assist you and your requests will always receive our immediate consideration.

You will have heard how El Sayed Ahmed el Sharif el Senussi has been beguiled by evil advice into hostile action, and it will be a great grief to you to know that he has been so far forgetful of the interests of the Arabs as to throw in his lot with our enemies. Misfortune has now overtaken him, and we trust that this will show him his error and lead him to peace for the sake of his poor misguided followers.

We are sending this letter by the hand of your good messenger, who will also bring to you all our news.

Compliments.

Letter No. 9, Sharif Hussein's fifth note to Sir Henry McMahon

Mecca, Rabi' el thani 14, 1934 (February 18, 1916)
In the name of the Merciful, the Compassionate.

To the most noble His Excellency the High Commissioner. May God protect Him.

We received your Excellency's letter dated 25th Rabi' el awal, and its contents filled us with the utmost pleasure and satisfaction at the attainment of the required understanding and the intimacy desired. I ask God to make easy our purposes and prosper our endeavours. Your Excellency will understand the work that is being done, and the reasons for it from the following:

Firstly.—We had informed your Excellency that we had sent one of our sons to Syria to command the operations deemed necessary there. We have received a detailed report from him stating that the tyrannies of the Government there have not left of the persons upon whom they could depend, whether of the different ranks of soldiers or of others, save only a few, and those of secondary importance; and that he is awaiting the arrival of the forces announced from different places, especially from the people of the country and the surrounding Arab regions as Aleppo and the south of Mosul, whose total is calculated at not less than 100,000 by their estimate; and he intends, if the majority of the forces mentioned are Arab, to begin the movement by them; and, if otherwise, that is, of the Turks or others, he will observe their advance to the Canal, and when they begin to fight, his movements upon them will be different to what they expect.

Secondly.—We purposed sending our eldest son to Medina with sufficient forces to strengthen his brother (who is) in Syria, and with every possibility of occupying the railway line, or carrying out such operations as circumstances may admit. This is the beginning of the principal movement, and we are satisfied in its beginning with what he had levied as guards to keep the interior of the country quiet; they are of the people of Hejaz only, for many reasons, which it would take too long to set forth; chiefly the difficulties in the way of providing their necessities with secrecy and speed (although this precaution was not necessary) and to make it easy to bring reinforcements when needed; this is the summary of what you wished to understand. In my opinion it is sufficient, and it is to be taken as a foundation and a standard as to our actions in the face of all changes and unforeseen events which the sequence of events may show. It remains for us to state what we need at present:

1. The amount of £50,000 in gold for the monthly pay of the troops levied, and other things the necessity of which needs no explanation. We beg you to send it with all possible haste.

2. 20,000 sacks of rice, 15,000 sacks of flour, 3,000 sacks of barley, 150 sacks of coffee, 150 sacks of sugar, 5,000 rifles of the modern pattern and the necessary ammunition, and 100 boxes of the two sample cartridges (enclosed) and of Martini-Henry cartridges and "Aza," that is those of the rifles of the factory of St. Etienne in France, for the use of those two kinds of rifles of our tribes; it would not be amiss to send 500 boxes of both kinds.
3. We think it better that the place of deposit of all these things should be Port Sudan.
4. As the above provisions and munitions are not needed until the beginning of the movement (of which we will inform you officially), they should remain at the above place, and when we need them we will inform the Governor there of the place to which they may be conveyed, and of the intermediaries who will carry orders for receiving them.
5. The money required should be sent at once to the Governor of Port Sudan, and a confidential agent will be sent by us to receive it, either all at once, or in two installments, according as he is able, and this (§) is the (secret) sign to be recognized for accepting the man.
6. Our envoy who will receive the money will be sent to Port Sudan in three weeks' time, that is to say, he will be there on the 5th Jamad awal (9th March) with a letter from us addressed to Al Khawaga Elias Effendi, saying that he (Elias) will pay him, in accordance with the letter, the rent of our properties, and the signature will be clear in our name, but we will instruct him to ask for the Governor of the place, whom you will apprise of this person's arrival. After perusal of the letter, the money should be given to him on condition that no discussion whatever is to be made with him of any question concerning us. We beg you most emphatically not to tell him anything, keeping this affair secret, and he should be treated apparently as if he were nothing out of the way.

    Let it not be thought that our appointment of another man results from lack of confidence in the bearer; it is only to avoid waste of time, for we are appointing him to a task elsewhere. At the same time, we beg you not to embark or send him in a steamer, or officially, the means already arranged being sufficient.

7. Our representative, bearer of the present letter, has been definitely instructed to ensure the arrival of this, and I think that his mission this time is finished since the condition of things is known both in general and in detail, and there is no need for sending anyone else. In case of need for sending information, it will come from us; yet as our next representative will reach you after three weeks, you may prepare instructions for him to take back. Yet let him be treated simply in appearance.
8. Let the British Government consider this military expenditure in accordance with the books which will be furnished it, explaining how the money has been spent.

To conclude, my best and numberless salutations beyond all increase.

Letter No. 10, Sir Henry McMahon's fifth note to the Sharif Hussein

Cairo, March 10, 1916
Compliments.

We have received your letter of the 14th Rabi' el thani (the 18th February), duly delivered by your trusted messenger.

We are grateful to note the active measures which you propose to take. We consider them the most suitable in the existing circumstances, and they have the approval of His Majesty's Government. I am pleased to be able to inform you that His Majesty's Government have approved of meeting your requests, and that which you asked to be sent with all haste is being despatched with your messenger, who is also the bearer of this letter.

The remainder will be collected as quickly as possible and will be deposited at Port Sudan, where it will remain until we hear from you officially of the beginning of the movement and of the places to which they may be conveyed and the intermediaries who will carry out the orders for receiving them.

The necessary instructions, as set forth in your letter, have been issued to the Governor at Port Sudan, and he will arrange everything in accordance with your wishes.

Your representative who brought your last letter has been duly facilitated in his journey to Jeizan, and every assistance has been given him in his mission, which we trust will be crowned with good results.

We have arranged that, on completion, he will be brought to Port Sudan, whence he will proceed by the safest means to join you and report the results of his work.

We take the opportunity, in sending this letter, to explain to you a matter which might otherwise not have been clear to you, and which might have given rise to misunderstanding. There are various Turkish posts and small garrisons along the coasts of Arabia who are hostile to us, and who are said to be planning injury to our naval interests in the Red Sea. We may, therefore, find it necessary to take hostile measures against these posts and garrisons, but we have issued strict instructions that every care must be taken by our ships to differentiate between the hostile Turkish garrisons and the innocent Arab inhabitants, towards whom we entertain such friendly feelings.

We give you notice of this matter in case distorted and false reports may reach you of the reasons for any action which we may be obliged to take.

We have heard rumours that our mutual enemies are endeavouring to construct boats for the purpose of laying mines in the Red Sea, and of otherwise injuring our interests there, and we beg of you that you will give us early information should you receive any confirmation of such reports.

We have heard that Ibn Rashid has been selling large quantities of camels to the Turks, which are being sent up to Damascus.

We hope that you will be able to use influence with him in order that he may cease from this practice and, if he still persists, that you will be able to arrange for the Arabs who lie between him and Syria to seize the camels as they pass, a procedure which will be to our mutual advantage.

I am glad to be able to inform you that those misguided Arabs under Sayed Ahmed el Senussi, who have fallen victims to the wiles of Turkish and German intriguers, are now beginning to see the error of their ways, and are coming in to us in large numbers, asking for forgiveness and friendship.

We have severely defeated the forces which these intriguers had collected against us, and the eyes of the Arabs are now becoming open to the deceit which has been practiced upon them.

The capture of Erzerum, and the defeats sustained by the Turks in the Caucasus, are having a great effect in our favour, and are greatly helping the cause for which we are both working.

We ask God to prosper your endeavors and to further the work which you have taken in hand.

In conclusion, we beg you to accept our warmest salutations and expressions of friendship.

From *The Arab Awakening*, George Antonius, Capricorn Books, 1965

Appendix 2

The Sykes–Picot Agreement, 16 May 1916

The Sykes–Picot Agreement was a secret treaty between the United Kingdom and France, with assent from the Russian Empire and the Kingdom of Italy, to define their mutually agreed spheres of influence and control in an eventual partition of the Ottoman Empire. The primary negotiations leading to the agreement occurred between 23 November 1915 and 3 January 1916, on which date the British and French diplomats, Mark Sykes and François Georges-Picot, initialed an agreed memorandum. The agreement was ratified by their respective governments on 9 and 16 May 1916.

It is accordingly understood between the French and British governments:

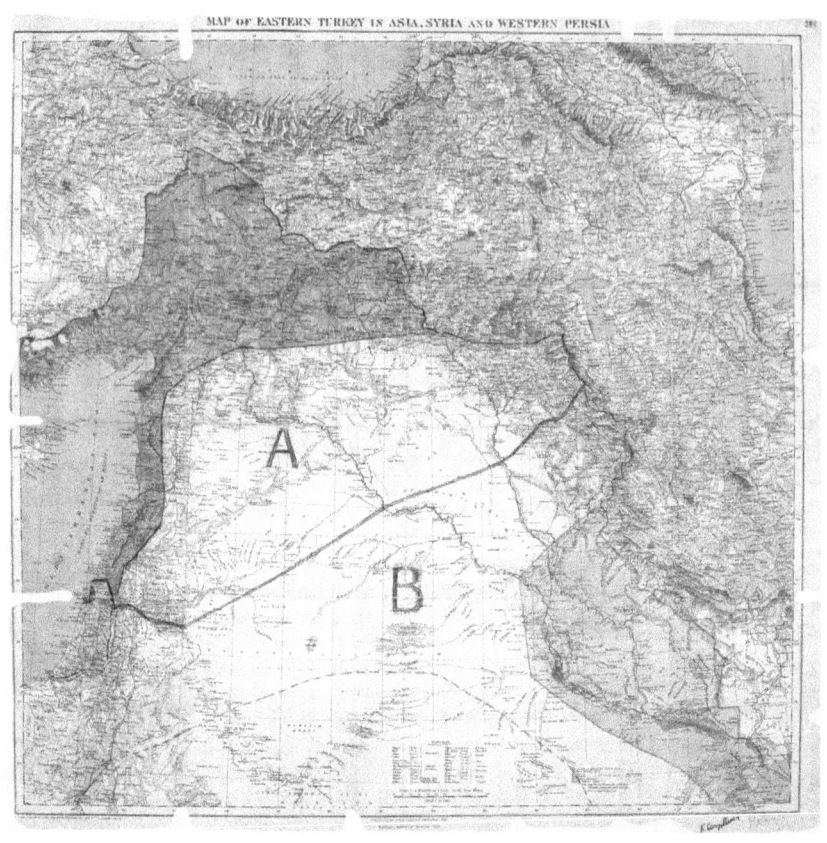

Map of Sykes-Picot Agreement

1. That France and Great Britain are prepared to recognize and protect an independent Arab state or a confederation of Arab states (A) and (B) marked on the annexed map, under the suzerainty of an Arab chief. France in area (A) and Great Britain in area (B) shall have a right of priority in enterprise and local loans. France in area (A) and Great Britain in area (B) shall alone supply advisers or foreign functionaries at the request of the Arab state or confederation of Arab states.
2. France in the Blue area, and Great Britain in the Red area, shall be at liberty to establish such direct or indirect administration or control as they desire and as they may deem fit to establish after agreement with the Arab state or confederation of Arab states.

3. That in the Brown area there shall be established an international administration, the form of which is to be decided upon after consultation with Russia, and after subsequent agreement with the other allies, and the representatives of the Sharif of Mecca.
4. There shall be accorded to Great Britain (1) the ports of Haifa and Acre, (2) guarantee of a specific supply of water from the Tigris and Euphrates in area (A) for area (B). His Majesty's government, on their part, undertake that they will at no time initiate negotiations for the concession of Cyprus to any third power without the previous consent of the French government.
5. That Alexandretta shall be a free port as regards the trade of the British empire, and that there shall be no discrimination in port charges or facilities as regards British shipping and British goods; that there shall be freedom of transit for British goods through Alexandretta and by railway through the Blue area, whether such goods are going to or coming from the Red area, area (A) or area (B); and there shall be no discrimination, direct or indirect, at the expense of British goods on any railway or of British goods and shipping at any port serving the areas in question.

    Haifa shall be a free port as regards the trade of France, her dominions and protectorates, and there shall be no discrimination in treatment or privilege with regard to port dues against French shipping and commerce. There shall be freedom of transit through Haifa and over British railways through the Brown area, whether those goods are intended for or originate in the Blue area, area (A), or area (B), and there shall be no discrimination, direct or indirect, at the expense of French goods and shipping in any port serving the areas in question.
6. In area (A) the Baghdad Railway shall not be extended southwards beyond Mosul, and in area (B) it shall not be extended northwards beyond Samarra, until a railway connecting Baghdad and Aleppo along the basin of the Euphrates will have been completed, and then only with the concurrence of the two governments.

7. That Great Britain has the right to build, administer, and be sole owner of a railway connecting Haifa with area (B), and shall have the right in perpetuity and at all times of carrying troops on that line. It is understood by both governments that this railway is intended to facilitate communication between Baghdad with Haifa by rail, and it is further understood that, in the event of technical difficulties and expenditure incurred in the maintenance of this line in the Brown area rendering the execution of the project impracticable, that the French government shall be prepared to consider plans for enabling the line in question to traverse the polygon formed by Banias-Umm Qais-Salkhad -Tall 'Osda-Mismieh before reaching area (B).
8. For a period of twenty years, the Turkish customs tariff shall remain in force throughout the Blue and Red areas, as well as in areas (A) and (B), and no increase in the rates of duties and no alteration from *ad valorem* duties to specific duties shall be made without the consent of the two Powers.

   There shall be no internal customs barriers between any of the areas mentioned above. The customs duties levied on goods destined for the interior shall be collected at the port of entry and remitted to the administration of the area of destination.
9. It is understood that the French government will at no time initiate any negotiations for the cession of their rights and will not cede their prospective rights in the Blue area to any third Power, other than the Arab state or confederation of Arab states, without the previous consent of His Majesty's Government, who, on their part, give the French government a similar undertaking in respect the Red area.
10. The British and French governments shall agree to abstain from acquiring and to withhold their consent to a third Power acquiring territorial possessions in the Arabian Peninsula; nor shall they consent to the construction by a third Power of a naval base in the islands on the eastern seaboard of the Red Sea. This, however, shall not prevent such rectification of the Aden boundary as may be necessary in view of the recent Turkish attack.

11. The negotiations with the Arabs concerning the boundaries of the Arab states or confederation of Arab states shall be pursued through the same channel as heretofore in the name of the two Powers.
12. It is understood that measures for controlling the importation of arms into the Arab territories will be considered by the two Governments.

From *The Arab Awakening*, George Antonius, Capricorn Books, 1965

Appendix 3

The Balfour Declaration, November 2, 1917

The Balfour Declaration, or, Balfour's Promise, in Arabic وعد بلفور, was a letter written by British Foreign Secretary Arthur Balfour to Lionel Walter Rothschild, in which he expressed the British government's support for a Jewish homeland in Palestine. The long-term effects of the Balfour Declaration and the British government's involvement in Palestinian affairs are still felt today.

Foreign Office
November 2nd, 1917
Dear Lord Rothschild,

    I have much pleasure in conveying to you, on behalf of His Majesty's Government, the following declaration of sympathy with Jewish Zionist aspirations which has been submitted to, and approved by, the Cabinet:

    His Majesty's Government view with favour the establishment in Palestine of a national home for the Jewish people and will use their best endeavors to facilitate the achievement of this object, it being clearly understood that nothing shall be done which may prejudice the civil and religious rights of existing non-Jewish communities in Palestine, or the rights and political status enjoyed by Jews in any other country.

    I should be grateful if you would bring this declaration to the knowledge of the Zionist Federation.

Yours sincerely, Arthur James Balfour.

Appendix 4

The British Mandate for Palestine, 1920

Britain was granted a Mandate for Palestine on 25 April 1920 at the San Remo Conference, and, on 24 July 1922, this mandate was approved by the League of Nations.

The Council of the League of Nations:

Whereas the Principal Allied Powers have agreed, for the purpose of giving effect to the provisions of Article 22 of the Covenant of the League of Nations, to entrust to a Mandatory selected by the said Powers the administration of the territory of Palestine, which formerly belonged to the Turkish Empire, within such boundaries as may be fixed by them; and

Whereas the Principal Allied Powers have also agreed that the Mandatory should be responsible for putting into effect the declaration originally made on November 2nd, 1917, by the Government of His Britannic Majesty, and adopted by the said Powers, in favor of the establishment in Palestine of a national home for the Jewish people, it being clearly understood that nothing should be done which might prejudice the civil and religious rights of existing non-Jewish communities in Palestine, or the rights and political status enjoyed by Jews in any other country; and

Whereas recognition has thereby been given to the historical connection of the Jewish people with Palestine and to the grounds for reconstituting their national home in that country; and

Whereas the Principal Allied Powers have selected His Britannic Majesty as the Mandatory for Palestine; and

Whereas the mandate in respect of Palestine has been formulated in the following terms and submitted to the Council of the League for approval; and

Whereas His Britannic Majesty has accepted the mandate in respect of Palestine and undertaken to exercise it on behalf of the League of Nations in conformity with the following provisions; and

Whereas by the afore-mentioned Article 22 (paragraph 8), it is provided that the degree of authority, control or administration to be exercised by the Mandatory, not having been previously agreed upon by the Members of the League, shall be explicitly defined by the Council of the League of Nations; confirming the said Mandate, defines its terms as follows:

ART. 1. The Mandatory shall have full powers of legislation and of administration, save as they may be limited by the terms of this mandate.

ART. 2. The Mandatory shall be responsible for placing the country under such political, administrative and economic conditions as will secure the establishment of the Jewish national home, as laid down in the preamble, and the development of self-governing institutions, and also for safeguarding the civil and religious rights of all the inhabitants of Palestine, irrespective of race and religion.

ART. 3. The Mandatory shall, so far as circumstances permit, encourage local autonomy.

ART. 4. An appropriate Jewish agency shall be recognised as a public body for the purpose of advising and co-operating with the Administration of Palestine in such economic, social and other matters as may affect the establishment of the Jewish national home and the interests of the Jewish population in Palestine, and, subject always to the control of the Administration to assist and take part in the development of the country.

The Zionist organization, so long as its organization and constitution are in the opinion of the Mandatory appropriate, shall be recognised as such agency. It shall take steps in consultation with His Britannic Majesty's Government to secure the co-operation of all Jews who are willing to assist in the establishment of the Jewish national home.

ART. 5. The Mandatory shall be responsible for seeing that no Palestine territory shall be ceded or leased to, or in any way placed under the control of the Government of any foreign Power.

ART. 6. The Administration of Palestine, while ensuring that the rights and position of other sections of the population are not prejudiced, shall facilitate Jewish immigration under suitable conditions and shall encourage, in co-operation with the Jewish agency referred to in Article 4, close settlement by Jews on the land, including State lands and waste lands not required for public purposes.

ART. 7. The Administration of Palestine shall be responsible for enacting a nationality law. There shall be included in this law provisions framed so as to facilitate the acquisition of Palestinian citizenship by Jews who take up their permanent residence in Palestine.

ART. 8. The privileges and immunities of foreigners, including the benefits of consular jurisdiction and protection as formerly enjoyed by Capitulation or usage in the Ottoman Empire, shall not be applicable in Palestine. Unless the Powers whose nationals enjoyed the afore-mentioned privileges and immunities on August 1st, 1914, shall have previously renounced the right to their re-establishment, or shall have agreed to their non-application for a specified period, these privileges and immunities shall, at the expiration of the mandate, be immediately reestablished in their entirety or with such modifications as may have been agreed upon between the Powers concerned.

ART. 9. The Mandatory shall be responsible for seeing that the judicial system established in Palestine shall assure to foreigners, as well as to natives, a complete guarantee of their rights.

Respect for the personal status of the various peoples and communities and for their religious interests shall be fully guaranteed. In particular, the control and administration of Wakfs shall be exercised in accordance with religious law and the dispositions of the founders.

ART. 10. Pending the making of special extradition agreements relating to Palestine, the extradition treaties in force between the Mandatory and other foreign Powers shall apply to Palestine.

ART. 11. The Administration of Palestine shall take all necessary measures to safeguard the interests of the community in connection with the development of the country, and, subject to any international obligations accepted by the Mandatory, shall have full power to provide for public ownership or control of any of the natural resources of the country or of the public works, services and utilities established or to be established therein. It shall introduce a land system appropriate to the needs of the country, having regard, among other things, to the desirability of promoting the close settlement and intensive cultivation of the land.

The Administration may arrange with the Jewish agency mentioned in Article 4 to construct or operate, upon fair and equitable terms, any public works, services and utilities, and to develop any of the natural resources of the country, in so far as these matters are not directly undertaken by the Administration. Any such arrangements shall provide that no profits distributed by such agency, directly or indirectly, shall exceed a reasonable rate of interest on the capital, and any further profits shall be utilized by it for the benefit of the country in a manner approved by the Administration.

ART. 12. The Mandatory shall be entrusted with the control of the foreign relations of Palestine and the right to issue exequaturs to consuls appointed by foreign Powers. He shall also be entitled to afford diplomatic and consular protection to citizens of Palestine when outside its territorial limits.

ART. 13. All responsibility in connection with the Holy Places and religious buildings or sites in Palestine, including that of preserving existing rights and of securing free access to the Holy Places, religious buildings and sites and the free exercise of worship, while ensuring the requirements of public order and decorum, is assumed by the Mandatory, who shall be responsible solely to the League of Nations in all matters connected herewith, provided that nothing in this article shall prevent the Mandatory from entering into such arrangements as he may deem reasonable with the Administration for the purpose of carrying the provisions of this article into effect; and provided also that nothing in this mandate shall be construed as conferring upon the Mandatory authority to interfere with the fabric or the management of purely Muslim sacred shrines, the immunities of which are guaranteed.

ART. 14. A special commission shall be appointed by the Mandatory to study, define and determine the rights and claims in connection with the Holy Places and the rights and claims relating to the different religious communities in Palestine. The method of nomination, the composition and the functions of this Commission shall be submitted to the Council of the League for its approval, and the Commission shall not be appointed or enter upon its functions without the approval of the Council.

ART. 15. The Mandatory shall see that complete freedom of conscience and the free exercise of all forms of worship, subject only to the maintenance of public order and morals, are ensured to all. No discrimination of any kind shall be made between the inhabitants of Palestine on the ground of race, religion or language. No person shall be excluded from Palestine on the sole ground of his religious belief. The right of each community to maintain its own schools for the education of its own members in its own language, while conforming to such educational requirements of a general nature as the Administration may impose, shall not be denied or impaired.

ART. 16. The Mandatory shall be responsible for exercising such supervision over religious or eleemosynary bodies of all faiths in Palestine as may be required for the maintenance of public order and good government. Subject to such supervision, no measures shall be taken in Palestine to obstruct or interfere with the enterprise of such bodies or to discriminate against any representative or member of them on the ground of his religion or nationality.

ART. 17. The Administration of Palestine may organise on a voluntary basis the forces necessary for the preservation of peace and order, and also for the defense of the country, subject, however, to the supervision of the Mandatory, but shall not use them for purposes other than those above specified save with the consent of the Mandatory. Except for such purposes, no military, naval or air forces shall be raised or maintained by the Administration of Palestine. Nothing in this article shall preclude the Administration of Palestine from contributing to the cost of the maintenance of the forces of the Mandatory in Palestine.

The Mandatory shall be entitled at all times to use the roads, railways and ports of Palestine for the movement of armed forces and the carriage of fuel and supplies.

ART. 18. The Mandatory shall see that there is no discrimination in Palestine against the nationals of any State Member of the League of Nations (including companies incorporated under its laws) as compared with those of the Mandatory or of any foreign State in matters concerning taxation, commerce or navigation, the exercise of industries or professions, or in the treatment of merchant vessels or civil aircraft. Similarly, there shall be no discrimination in Palestine against goods originating in or destined for any of the said States, and there shall be freedom of transit under equitable conditions across the mandated area. Subject as aforesaid and to the other provisions of this mandate, the Administration of Palestine may, on the advice of the Mandatory, impose such taxes and customs duties as it may consider necessary, and take such steps as it may think best to promote the development of the natural resources of the country and to safeguard the interests of the population. It may also, on the advice of the Mandatory, conclude a special customs agreement with any State the territory of which in 1914 was wholly included in Asiatic Turkey or Arabia.

ART. 19. The Mandatory shall adhere on behalf of the Administration of Palestine to any general international conventions already existing, or which may be concluded hereafter with the approval of the League of Nations, respecting the slave traffic, the traffic in arms and ammunition, or the traffic in drugs, or relating to commercial equality, freedom of transit and navigation, aerial navigation and postal, telegraphic and wireless communication or literary, artistic or industrial property.

ART. 20. The Mandatory shall co-operate on behalf of the Administration of Palestine, so far as religious, social and other conditions may permit, in the execution of any common policy adopted by the League of Nations for preventing and combating disease, including diseases of plants and animals.

ART. 21. The Mandatory shall secure the enactment within twelve months from this date, and shall ensure the execution of a Law of Antiquities based on the following rules. This law shall ensure equality of treatment in the matter of excavations and archaeological research to the nationals of all States Members of the League of Nations.

(1) "Antiquity" means any construction or any product of human activity earlier than the year 1700 A. D.
(2) The law for the protection of antiquities shall proceed by encouragement rather than by threat.

   Any person who, having discovered an antiquity without being furnished with the authorization referred to in paragraph 5, reports the same to an official of the competent Department, shall be rewarded according to the value of the discovery.
(3) No antiquity may be disposed of except to the competent Department, unless this Department renounces the acquisition of any such antiquity.

   No antiquity may leave the country without an export license from the said Department.
(4) Any person who maliciously or negligently destroys or damages an antiquity shall be liable to a penalty to be fixed.
(5) No clearing of ground or digging with the object of finding antiquities shall be permitted, under penalty of fine, except to persons authorized by the competent Department.
(6) Equitable terms shall be fixed for expropriation, temporary or permanent, of lands which might be of historical or archaeological interest.
(7) Authorization to excavate shall only be granted to persons who show sufficient guarantees of archaeological experience. The Administration of Palestine shall not, in granting these authorizations, act in such a way as to exclude scholars of any nation without good grounds.
(8) The proceeds of excavations may be divided between the excavator and the competent Department in a proportion fixed by that Department. If division seems impossible for scientific reasons, the excavator shall receive a fair indemnity in lieu of a part of the find.

ART. 22. English, Arabic and Hebrew shall be the official languages of Palestine. Any statement or inscription in Arabic on stamps or money in Palestine shall be repeated in Hebrew and any statement or inscription in Hebrew shall be repeated in Arabic.

ART. 23. The Administration of Palestine shall recognize the holy days of the respective communities in Palestine as legal days of rest for the members of such communities.

ART. 24. The Mandatory shall make to the Council of the League of Nations an annual report to the satisfaction of the Council as to the measures taken during the year to carry out the provisions of the mandate. Copies of all laws and regulations promulgated or issued during the year shall be communicated with the report.

ART. 25. In the territories lying between the Jordan and the eastern boundary of Palestine as ultimately determined, the Mandatory shall be entitled, with the consent of the Council of the League of Nations, to postpone or withhold application of such provisions of this mandate as he may consider inapplicable to the existing local conditions, and to make such provision for the administration of the territories as he may consider suitable to those conditions, provided that no action shall be taken which is inconsistent with the provisions of Articles 15, 16 and 18.

ART. 26. The Mandatory agrees that, if any dispute whatever should arise between the Mandatory and another member of the League of Nations relating to the interpretation or the application of the provisions of the mandate, such dispute, if it cannot be settled by negotiation, shall be submitted to the Permanent Court of International Justice provided for by Article 14 of the Covenant of the League of Nations.

ART. 27. The consent of the Council of the League of Nations is required for any modification of the terms of this mandate.

ART. 28. In the event of the termination of the mandate hereby conferred upon the Mandatory, the Council of the League of Nations shall make such arrangements as may be deemed necessary for safeguarding in perpetuity, under guarantee of the League, the rights secured by Articles 13 and 14, and shall use its influence for securing, under the guarantee of the League, that the Government of Palestine will fully honour the financial obligations legitimately incurred by the Administration of Palestine during the period of the mandate, including the rights of public servants to pensions or gratuities.

The present instrument shall be deposited in original in the archives of the League of Nations and certified copies shall be forwarded by the Secretary-General of the League of Nations to all members of the League.

Appendix 5

Israeli Absentee Property Law, 5710-1950

The Israeli Absentee Property Law is the main law that regulates the treatment of property belonging to Palestinians who left, were forced to flee, or were deported during and after the 1948 War. The Palestinians left behind a great deal of property and the Absentee Property Law has served as the legal basis for transferring such property into the possession of the State of Israel. The Absentee Property Law has become a significant obstacle, hindering Palestinians from successfully establishing rights to property or land, particularly in East Jerusalem. This has had serious effects on, amongst other things, obtaining Israeli-issued licenses to build, completing property transactions and planning procedures. Given the automatic application of the Absentee Property Law to property considered to be "absentee property," people often only find out that they have lost ownership of their property when trying to sell, transfer, build on it, etc. The Absentee Property Law has been used over the years as a tool by Israeli settler associations for the takeover of Palestinian owned properties in East Jerusalem. https://www.nrc.no/globalassets/pdf/legal-opinions/absentee_law_memo.pdf

1. In this Law -
    (a) "property" includes immovable arid movable property, moneys, a vested or contingent right in property, goodwill and any right in a body of persons or in its management;
    (b) "absentee" means –

(1) a person who, at any time during the period between the 16th Kislev, 5708 (29th November, 1947) and the day on which a declaration is published, under section 9(d) of the Law and Administration Ordinance, 5708-1948(1), that the state of emergency declared by the Provisional Council of State on the 10th Iyar, 5708 (19th May, 1948)(2) has ceased to exist, was a legal owner of any property situated in the area of Israel or enjoyed or held it, whether by himself or through another, and who, at any time during the said period –

(2) was a national or citizen of Lebanon, Egypt, Syria, Saudi Arabia, Trans-Jordan, Iraq or the Yemen, or

(ii) was in one of these countries or in any part of Palestine outside the area of Israel, or

(iii) was a Palestinian citizen and left his ordinary place of residence in Palestine
   (a) for a place outside Palestine before the 27th Av, 5708 (1st September, 1948); or
   (b) for a place in Palestine held at the time by forces which sought to prevent the establishment of the State of Israel or which fought against it after its establishment;

(3) a body of persons which, at any time during the period specified in paragraph (1), was a legal owner of any property situated in the area of Israel or enjoyed or held such property, whether by itself or through another, and all the members, partners, shareholders, directors or managers of which are absentees within the meaning of paragraph (1), or the management of the business of which is otherwise decisively controlled by such absentees, or all the capital of which is in the hands of such absentees;
   (c) "Palestinian citizen" means a person who, on the 16th Kislev, 5708 (29th November, 1947) or thereafter, was a Palestinian citizen according to the provisions of the Palestinian Citizenship Orders, 1925-1941, Consolidated (3), and includes a Palestinian resident who, on the said day or thereafter, had no nationality or citizenship or whose nationality or citizenship was undefined or unclear;

(d) "body of persons" means a body constituted in or outside Palestine, incorporated or unincorporated, registered or unregistered, and includes a company, partnership, cooperative society, society under the Law of Societies of the 29th Rajab, 1327 (3rd August 1909) and any other juridical person and any institution owning property;

(e) "absentees' property" means property the legal owner of which, at any time during the period between the 16th Kislev, 5708 (29th November, 1947) and the day on which a declaration is published, under section 9(d) of the Law and Administration Ordinance, 5708-1948, that the state of emergency by the Provisional Council of State on the 10th Iyar, 5708 (19th May 1948), has ceased to exist, was an absentee, or which, at any time as aforesaid, an absentee held or enjoyed, whether by himself or through another; but it does not include movable property held by an absentee and exempt from attachment or seizure under section 3 of the Civil Procedure Ordinance, 1938(4);

(f) "vested property" means property vested in the Custodian under this Law.

(g) "held property" means vested property actually held by the Custodian, and includes property acquired in exchange for vested property.

(h) "released property" means property released under section 28.

(i) "area of Israel" means the area in which the law of the State of Israel applies.

(j) "bill" means a bill of exchange, a cheque, a promissory note or any other negotiable instrument.

2. Custodian of Absentees' Property.

(a) The Minister of Finance shall appoint, by order published in Reshumot, a Custodianship Council for Absentees' Property, and shall designate one of its members to be the chairman of the Council. The chairman of the Council shall be called the Custodian.

(b) The Custodian may bring an action and institute any other legal proceeding against any person and be a plaintiff, defendant or otherwise a party in any legal proceeding.

(c) The Custodian is entitled to be represented in any legal proceeding by the Attorney-General or his representative.

(d) When the Custodian ceases to hold office, his functions, powers, rights, and duties shall automatically pass to the Minister of Finance; when another person is appointed Custodian, the said functions, powers, rights and duties shall automatically pass to him, and so on from Custodian to Custodian.

3. Appointment of Inspectors, agents and employees.

(a) The Custodian may, with the written approval of the Minister of Finance, appoint inspectors of absentees' property and delegate to any of them any of his powers, except the power to appoint inspectors. A notice of the appointment and scope of powers of every inspector shall be published by the Custodian in Reshumot.

(b) The Custodian may appoint agents for the management of held property on his behalf and may fix and pay their remuneration.

(c) The Custodian may appoint officials and other employees, whose status shall be the same as that of other State employees.

4. Vesting of absentees' property in Custodian.

(a) Subject to the provisions of this Law -

(1) all absentees' property is hereby vested in the Custodian as from the day of publication of his appointment or the day on which it became absentees' property, whichever is the later date;

(2) every right an absentee had in any property shall pass automatically to the Custodian at the time of the vesting of the property; and the status of the Custodian shall be the same as was that of the owner of the property.

(b) The proceeds of vested property shall be dealt with like the vested property yielding the proceeds.

(c) Vested property -

(1) shall remain vested property so long as it has not become released property under section 28 or ceased to be absentees' property under section 27;

(2) may be taken over by the Custodian wherever he may find it.

    (d) Where the Custodian has acquired any property which was not absentees' property at the time of the acquisition, in exchange for vested property, the acquired property shall become held property and shall be dealt with as was the property in exchange for which it was acquired.

5. Identity of absentee unknown.

The fact that the identity of an absentee is unknown shall not prevent his property from being absentees' property, vested property, held property or released property.

6. Handing over Property to Custodian.
   (a) A person who has in his possession any absentees' property is bound to hand it over to the Custodian.
   (b) A person who has a debt to, or any other obligation towards an absentee shall pay such debt or discharge such obligation to the Custodian.

7. Care of held property, expenses and investments.
   (a) The Custodian shall take care of held property, either himself or through others having his consent.
   (b) The Custodian may, himself or through others having his written consent, incur any expenses and make any investments necessary for the care, maintenance, repair or development of held property or for other similar purposes.

8. Absentees' businesses.
   (a) The Custodian may carry on the management of a business on behalf of an absentee, whether or not he indicates that the business is managed by the Custodian, but he shall always have the right to sell or lease the whole or a part of the business, and -

(1) if it is the business of an individual - to liquidate it;
(2) if it is the business of a partnership all the partners of which are shareholders of which are absentees, or of a cooperative society all the members of which are absentees - to wind up the partnership, company or cooperative society by order published in Reshumot.
  (b) Where the Custodian has published a winding-up order under subsection (a)(2), the winding up shall be conducted -
(1) in the case of a partnership or company - as if the winding-up order had been made by a competent court in accordance with part V of the Partnership Ordinance (5) or in accordance with part VI of the Companies Ordinance (6), as the case may be;
(2) in the case of a cooperative society - as if the winding-up order had been made by the Registrar of Cooperative Societies in accordance with section 47 of the Cooperative Societies Ordinance (7), and in every case as if the Custodian had been appointed as a liquidator not replaceable by another liquidator.

9. Payments to persons supported by absentees, and to absentees; payments for purposes of a trust.
   (a) If the Custodian is of the opinion that a particular person was a dependent of an absentee, he may grant allowances to that person out of the held property of that absentee, in such amounts as in the opinion of the Custodian is necessary for the maintenance of that person, provided that they shall not exceed 50 pounds per month in respect of any such person.
   (b) If several persons were dependents of the same absentee, and in the opinion of the Custodian there are family ties between them, the Custodian may pay the allowances to one of them for all of them.
   (c) The Custodian may grant an allowance as aforesaid also to the absentee himself if, in the opinion of the Custodian, it is necessary for the maintenance of the absentee.
   (d) Income from vested property which is a trust may be expended by the Custodian, wholly or in part, for purposes for which the trust was established.

10. Expulsion.
    (a) Where vested property of the category of immovable property is occupied by a person who, in the opinion of the Custodian, has no right to occupy it, the Custodian may confirm such fact by a certificate under his hand describing the property. The certificate shall have the effect of a judgment in favour of the Custodian for the expulsion of the occupier of the vested property.
    (b)
(1) Where the certificate has been filed in the Execution Office, such Office shall serve a copy thereof on every occupier of the property described therein, in like manner as a copy of a judgment is served on a judgment debtor and shall proceed as it would in the execution of a judgment for expulsion. The expulsion shall be considered as an urgent matter within the meaning of section 38 of the Execution Law of the 11th of May 1914, except that the time within which the occupier of the property shall be required to relinquish it shall be seven days.
(2) If a person occupying property as aforesaid contends that he has a right to occupy it, and he proves to the Chief Execution Officer that there is some substance in his contention, the Chief Execution Officer may stay the execution for such time as he may think fit, with a view to enabling that person to apply to a competent court and to establish his right.
    (c) Where an occupier has applied to a competent court and has established his right to occupy the property, the court shall annul the certificate and the execution proceedings taken thereunder.

11. Demolition of buildings and dis- continuance of building operations.
    (a) If on any vested property, being of the category of immovable property, a building has been or is being built without the written permission of the Custodian, the Custodian may order that -
(1) all building operations on such property shall be discontinued within operations the time prescribed in the order;
(2) the building shall be demolished;

(3) the expenses of implementing an order under paragraph (2) shall be paid to him by the persons responsible for the building operations or by the persons who carried them out.

  (b) An order under subsection (a)(1) shall be posted up in a conspicuous position in or as near as possible to the property to which it relates, and any person contravening the order shall be guilty of an offence and shall be dealt with as provided in section 35(a).

  (c) An order under subsection (a)(2) shall be filed in the Execution Office, and such Office shall serve a copy thereof on everyone concerned, in like manner as a copy of a judgment is served on a judgment debtor, and shall proceed as it would in the -execution of a demolition order.

  (d)

(1) Whosoever considers himself aggrieved by an order under paragraph (1) or (2) of subsection (a) may appeal within seven days from the day on which the order came to his knowledge to the District Court in whose area of jurisdiction the property is situated.

(2) The appeal shall be lodged and heard in. the form of an application by motion. The Custodian shall be respondent in the appeal.

(3) the lodging of an appeal shall not stay the implementation of the order unless a judge of the District Court so orders.

(4) The District Court may confirm the order, with or without modifications, or annul it.

(5) The decision of the District Court in an appeal under this section shall be final.

  (e) Where the Custodian has made an order as specified in paragraph (2) of subsection (a), he may remove from the property, or retain control of, any materials, tools and implements found on the property, with a view to clearing the property or to securing the reimbursement of his expenses in connection with the implementation of the order.

  (f) "Building", in this section, has the same meaning as in section 2 of the Town Planning Ordinance, 1936(8).

12. Application of Rent Restrictions (Dwelling-Houses) Ordinance, 1940, and Rent Restrictions (Business Premises) Ordinance, 19'1.

(a) In the case of property to which the provisions of the Rent Restrictions (Dwelling-Houses) Ordinance, 1940 (9), or the Rent Restrictions (Business Premises) Ordinance, 1941(10), apply, and which has been vested in the Custodian, the person who occupied it immediately before the day of its vesting - whether under an agreement made before the owner of the property became an absentee or in virtue of the protection afforded by the provisions of one of those Ordinances - or his successor shall be protected by those provisions even after the vesting of the property.

(b)

(1) Where vested property, being a house or a part of a house, has been let by the Custodian as a separate dwelling, within the meaning of section 3 of the Rent Restrictions (Dwelling-Houses) Ordinance, 1940, the provisions of that Ordinance shall apply to it subject to subsections (c), (d) and (e) and with the following modifications and adaptations:

(i) The rent fixed in the contract of lease, as reduced under subsection (d) (if so reduced), shall be regarded as the standard rent;

(ii) the words "rent at the agreed rate as modified by this Ordinance", appearing in section 8(1) of that Ordinance, shall be regarded as referring to the rent fixed in the contract of lease, as reduced under subsection (d) (if so reduced).

(2) Where vested property, being business premises within the meaning of the Rent Restrictions (Business Premises) Ordinance, 1941, situated in an area to which that Ordinance has been made applicable, has been let by the Custodian, the provisions of that Ordinance shall apply to it subject to subsections (c), (d) and (e), except that the rent fixed in the contract of lease, as reduced under subsection (d) (if so reduced), shall be regarded as the maximum rent fixed under section 6(1) of that Ordinance.

(c) The Minister of Finance may, by regulations, prescribe rules to be followed in fixing the rent.

(d)

(1) A lessee who considers himself aggrieved by the fixing of the rent in his contract of lease may appeal against it to the Magistrates' Court in whose area of jurisdiction the property is situated.

(2) The appeal shall be lodged and heard in the form of an application by motion. The Custodian shall be respondent in the appeal.

(3) The Magistrate's Court may confirm or reduce the rent fixed in the contract of lease, having, reference to the rules (if any) prescribed under subsection (c) and having regard to all the circumstances of the case.

(4) Where the Magistrate's Court has reduced the rent -

(i) it shall fix the date from which the reduction shall have effect, provided that this date shall not be earlier than the day of the lodging of the appeal;

(ii) it may order that any amount in excess of the rent as reduced which the lessee has paid in respect of a period subsequent to the date fixed under subparagraph (i) shall be refunded to him.

(5) The decision of the Magistrate's Court in an appeal under this subsection shall be final.

(e)

(1) Where vested property is occupied by a person in virtue of the protection afforded by the provisions of the Rent Restrictions (Dwelling Houses) Ordinance, 1940, or the Rent Restrictions (Business Premises) Ordinance, 1941, in accordance with subsection (b), and its vacation by the occupier is, in the opinion of the Custodian, required for the purposes of the development of the place or area in which it is situated, the Custodian may, after placing suitable alternative accommodation at the occupier's disposal, make an order of vacation in respect of the property. The order shall have the effect of a judgment in favour of the Custodian for the expulsion of the occupier of the vested property.

(2) Where the order has been submitted to the Execution Office, such Office shall serve a copy thereof on the occupier of the property, in like manner as a copy of a judgment is served on a judgment debtor and shall proceed as it would in the execution of a judgment for expulsion.

(3)

(i) An occupier of property in respect of which an order of vacation has been made under this subsection may appeal against it within fourteen days from the day on which the order came to his knowledge to the District Court in whose area of jurisdiction the property is situated, on the ground that no suitable alternative accommodation has been placed at his disposal.

(ii) The appeal shall be lodged and heard in the form of an application by motion. The Custodian shall be respondent in the appeal.

(iii) The lodging of an appeal shall stay any execution proceedings under paragraph (2).

(iv) The District Court may confirm the order, with or without modifications, or annul it.

(v) The decision of the District Court in an appeal under this paragraph shall be final.
Cultivators (Protection) Ordinance not to apply.

13. A person who occupies vested property, being a holding within the meaning of the Cultivators (Protection) Ordinance (11), shall not be protected by the provisions of that Ordinance unless immediately before the vesting of the property in the Custodian he occupied it by virtue of the protection afforded by those provisions.

14. Cultivator and his right to the produce.

Where the vested property is a citrus grove, a vineyard or any other plantation, or any other agricultural land, and the Custodian has handed it over to a person for the purpose of cultivation, that person shall be entitled to enjoy the produce in accordance with the terms stipulated between him and the Custodian, and his right shall have priority over any charge vested in another person theretofore; but any such charge shall extend also to the income due to the Custodian from that property.

15. Vested property- charge thereon and attachment thereof.
   (a) The fact that any property has become absentees' property or vested property shall not exonerate it from any mortgage, pledge or other charge, or from any right of tenure or use, legally created theretofore.
   (b) No execution proceedings shall be taken, no act under section 14 of the Land Transfer Ordinance(12) shall be done, and no recourse shall be had to sections 8, 9 or 10 of the Law Concerning the Partition of Immovable Property of the 14th Muharram, 1332, in respect of vested property, except by permission in writing from the Custodian or, if such permission, having been applied for after the 13th Nisan, 5710 (31st March, 1950), has not been given within one year from the day on which it was applied for, upon the expiration of that year.
   (c) An attachment imposed on absentees' property, whether before or after it became vested property, shall not prevent the Custodian from relinquishing control of the property in accordance with this Law; and where he has done so, the attachment shall apply, instead of to the property, to the consideration which he has received for it.

16. Extent of responsibility of Custodian and persons acting under his instructions.

   Where the Custodian or a person who acted, directly or indirectly, under his instructions has taken over, or has done any act in respect of, any property in the honest and reasonable, but mistaken, belief that the property is absentees' property, the Custodian or that person shall bear no civil responsibility therefor beyond that which he would bear if the property had at the time been absentees' property.

17. Validity of transactions

   Any transaction made in good faith between the Custodian and another person in respect of property which the Custodian considered at the time of the transaction to be vested property shall not be invalidated and shall remain in force even if it is proved that the property was not at the time vested property.

18. Extent of property erroneously considered vested property.
    (a) Where a competent court has decided that some property which the Custodian considered to be vested property is not vested property, the Custodian, shall, subject to the provisions of section 17, hand over the property or the consideration which he has received for it, as the case may be, to such person as the court has in its decision directed or, if no such direction has been given by the court, to the person from whom he received the property; and if that person is not known to him, he shall apply to a competent court for directions.
    (b) Where the Custodian has found that some property which he considered to be vested property is not vested property, he may, subject to the provisions of section 17, hand over the property or the consideration which he has received for it, as the case may be, to the person who in the opinion of the Custodian is entitled to possession of the property or of the consideration.

19. Limitation of powers of Custodian.
    (a) Where the vested property is of the category of immovable property, the Custodian shall not -
(1) sell or otherwise transfer the right of ownership thereof; provided that if a Development Authority is established under a Law of the Knesset, it shall be lawful for the Custodian to sell the property to that Development Authority at a price not less than the official value of the property;
(2) grant a lease of the property for a term exceeding six years, except -
(i) to the said Development Authority; and on leasing property to it, that Custodian shall stipulate with the Development Authority in the contract of lease that the annual rent payable by it shall not be less than an amount equal to 4.8 per cent of the official value of the property; or,

(ii) to another lessee who undertakes in the contract of lease to cultivate or develop the property to the satisfaction of the Custodian.

(b) A voluntary partition of immovable property held in musha' shall not for the purpose of subsection (a) be regarded as a transfer of the right of ownership of such immovable property.

(c) Where the Custodian has granted a lease of any property for a term exceeding three years, the provisions of the Land Transfer Ordinance shall not apply to the lease; but the Custodian may apply for registration of the lease in accordance with that Ordinance.

(d) "Official value", in this section, means -

(1) in relation to property which, in the financial year 1947-1948, was chargeable with urban property tax under the Urban Property Tax Ordinance, 1940(13) - an amount 16 2/3 times the amount of the net annual value determined for it, for the purposes of that Ordinance, in the last assessment before the 6th Iyar, 5708 (15th May 1948):

(2) in relation to property which, in the financial year 1947-1948, was chargeable with rural property tax under the Rural Property Tax Ordinance, 1942(14) -

(i) if it is an industrial building, within the meaning of that Ordinance - an amount 16 2/3 times the amount of the net annual value determined for it, for the purposes of that Ordinance, in the last assessment before the 6th Iyar, 5708 (15th May 1948);

(ii) if it belongs to category 1, 2, 3, 4 or 17 referred to in the Schedule to that Ordinance - an amount 300 times the amount of tax which was or would have been charged on it in respect of that financial year if it belonged or had belonged to category 1 referred to in the said Schedule,

(iii) if it belongs to one of the other categories referred to in the Schedule to that Ordinance - an amount 75 times the amount of tax which was charged on it in respect of that financial year;

(3) in relation to other property - an amount 16 2/3 times the amount of the net annual value which would have been determined for it in the

financial year 1947-1948 for the purposes of the Urban Property Tax Ordinance, 1940, had it been chargeable, in that financial year, with urban property tax under that Ordinance; provided at the Minister of Finance may reduce any of the rates mentioned in this subsection in the case of property the possibilities of using which are, in his opinion, limited owing to damage or neglect or for another similar reason.

(e) Where the vested property is a voidable charge, the Custodian may void it only for a consideration or in accordance with the conditions of the charge; where it is a waivable right, the Custodian may waive it only for a consideration.

(f) Nothing in this Law shall derogate from the powers of the Minister of Agriculture under the Emergency Regulations (Cultivation of Waste Lands) 5708-1948(15).

20. Debts of absentees and actions in connection therewith.

(a) The Custodian shall not pay a debt due from, or in connection with any property of an absentee, or discharge any other obligation incurred by an absentee, except -

(1) if it is a debt in respect of taxes, rates or other similar obligatory charges, or
(2) if the debt or obligation has been proved to the complete satisfaction of the Custodian, or
(3) under a judgment of a competent court, and to the extent that the held property of that absentee is sufficient for the purpose.

(b) The court which deals with a claim for a debt due from, or in connection with any property of, an absentee or a claim for the discharge of any other obligation incurred by an absentee may, notwithstanding anything contained in any other law -

(1) postpone from time to time the hearing of the claim, in order to enable the submission of evidence as complete as possible;
(2) strike out or dismiss the claim if it has not been proved beyond all reasonable doubt.

(c) The Minister of Finance may, by regulations, determine categories of vested immovable property in respect of which the

Custodian shall have the right to postpone the payment of all or any taxes, rates or other similar obligatory charges due on such immovable property, for such period and on such conditions as the Custodian, with the approval of the Minister of Finance, may determine in each case.

21. Duty to make notification of absentees' property.
    (a) A person or body of persons holding, managing or enjoying vested property shall deliver to the Custodian a written notification, containing the particulars of vested property, within thirty days from the day of publication of the Custodian's appointment or, if the property came to be held, managed or enjoyed by him or it - otherwise than with the consent of the Custodian - after the day of publication, within thirty days from the day on which it came to be so held, managed or enjoyed, or, if the property became vested property after the day of publication, within thirty days from the day of the vesting.
    (b) A company which is registered in the area of Israel or which has therein an office for the transfer of shares, or an office for the registration of shares, shall deliver to the Custodian, within thirty days from the day of publication of his appointment, a written notification containing full particulars of all securities (including shares, stocks, debentures, debenture stock and bonds) which have been issued by the company and are registered in the name or in favour of or held on behalf of or by an absentee; and where the securities relate in any such manner as aforesaid to a person who became an absentee after the day of publication of the Custodian's appointment, the company shall deliver the said notification to the Custodian within thirty days from the day on which that person became an absentee.
    (c) Where a partnership has among its partners an absentee or absentees, the partnership and each of the partners shall deliver to the Custodian, within thirty days from the day of publication of his appointment, a written notification containing full

particulars of the share in the partnership, and of the other rights in respect of the partnership and of the partners, of each absentee partner; and where a partner became an absentee after the day of publication of the Custodian's appointment, the partnership and each of the partners shall deliver the said notification within thirty days from the day on which the partner became an absentee.

(d) Anyone bound under this section to deliver to the Custodian a written notification shall also deliver to him from time to time returns, accounts or other documents, or other information, as the Custodian may from time to time require, in connection with the property in respect of which he is bound to deliver a notification.

(e) Where the Custodian has required a person to deliver to him, within the time prescribed in the notice, any returns, accounts or other documents, or any other information, as specified in subsection (d), that person shall comply with everything contained in the notice.

(f) Whosoever was bound under this section to deliver a notification before the 13th Nisan, 5710 (31st March 1950) and has not fulfilled this obligation may do so until the 13th Iyar, 5710 (30th April, 1950); and if he does so, he shall not be prosecuted for not fulfilling his obligation in time.

22. Prohibited Acts.

(a) A person shall not without the written consent of the Custodian -
(1) hold, manage, or otherwise deal with, or relinquish or transfer, vested property, or hand over vested property to any person other than the Custodian;
(2) pay to any person other than the Custodian a debt, or discharge to any person other than the Custodian any other obligation, the right of claim in respect of which has been vested in the Custodian;
(3) act under a power of attorney or other authorisation of an absentee principal, whether the principal became an absentee before the

giving of the power of attorney or other authorisation or whether he became an absentee thereafter; however, an advocate duly authorised on that behalf by an absentee who is at the time in the area of Israel may represent that absentee with regard to any legal act; if the absentee is not at the time in the area of Israel, his representation by an advocate with regard to any legal act requires the written consent of the Attorney-General.

(b) Consent under this section may be given before or after the fact.

(c) An act which has been done in contravention of this section is null and void; and if it was a transfer of a bill, then any subsequent transfer is likewise void, notwithstanding anything contained in any other law.

(d) No act in respect of vested property may be registered in the Land Register otherwise than with the written permission of the Custodian, given before the registration, or under a judgment of a competent court. If a registration has been effected in contravention of this provision the Court shall, on the application of the Custodian, order that such registration and any subsequent registration shall be deleted.

(e) Anyone who contends that an act was done in respect of any property before it became vested property or in respect of any person before he became an absentee, or that an act was done with the consent or written permission of the Custodian, shall bear the onus of proving the same.

23. ransfers to be void.

(a)

(1) A transfer or handing-over of property to an absentee or to another for the benefit of an absentee during the period between the 21st Adar Bet, 5708 (1st April, 1948) and the day of publication of the appointment of the Custodian, effected with intent to smuggle the whole or a part of the property or the whole or a part of the consideration received for it to a part of Palestine which at the time of the transfer or handing-over was outside the area of Israel, or to

the Lebanon, Egypt, Syria, Saudi-Arabia, Trans-Jordan, Iraq or the Yemen, is null and void.
(2) A transfer or handing-over of property from the hands of an absentee to another person during the period referred to in paragraph (1), effected for a fictitious or insufficient consideration or without consideration, or under unfair pressure, is null and void.
  (b) Property which has been transferred or handed over as stated in subsection (a) shall be regarded as vested property, and any person who has transferred or handed over or received the property shall be responsible to the Custodian for the property or for its value.
  (c) The Custodian may require in writing any person whom he regards as responsible under subsection (b) to hand over to him the property or its value, and that person shall comply with the requirement, but he may appeal against it to the District Court of Jerusalem within thirty days from the day of receipt of the requirement.
  (d) The appeal shall be lodged and heard in the form of an application by motion. The Custodian shall be respondent in the appeal.
  (e) Where the District Court has found that the requirement of the Custodian is not justified in law or in fact, it shall annul the requirement and declare its effects to be void.
  (f) Any party who considers himself aggrieved by a decision of the District Court under this section may appeal against it to the Supreme Court sitting as a Court of Civil Appeal, and the provisions of the Civil Procedure Rules, 1938(16), shall apply as if the decision of the District Court were a judgment of that court in a civil action in which the party who appeals against the requirement had been the plaintiff and the Custodian the defendant.
  (g) Anyone who contends that a transfer or handing-over of property to an absentee or to another for the benefit of an absentee, during the period referred to in subsection (a)(1), was effected

otherwise than with intent to smuggle the whole or a part of the property, or the whole or a part of the consideration received therefor, as specified in that subsection, or that a transfer or handing-over of property from the hands of an absentee to another person during the said period was effected for full consideration or otherwise than under unfair pressure, shall bear the onus of proving the same.

24. Provisions as to partnership in which there is an absentee partner.
    (a) Where a notification concerning an absentee partner has been delivered to the Custodian under section 21(c) and the Custodian intends to participate in the management of the business of the partnership, he shall give notice to that effect to the other partners within six months from the day on which the notification was delivered to him.
    (b) After the Custodian has given notice as provided in subsection (a) - but not before then - he may participate in the management of the business of the partnership in the place of the absentee partner.
    (c) From the day of delivery to the Custodian of the notification under section 21(c) until the receipt of the notice of the Custodian under subsection (a), the partners who are not absentees may manage the business of the partnership in the usual way.
    (d) Where a notification under section 21(c) concerning an absentee partner has not been delivered, the Custodian may at any time, after giving notice to the other partners, participate in the management of the business of the partnership.
    (e) As soon as the Custodian has become authorized to participate in the management of the business of the partnership, he may - regardless of the terms of the partnership contract - leave the partnership and receive the share of the absentee partner from the partners who are not absentees or, failing their consent, dissolve the partnership by giving notice to those partners; the notice shall be treated like notice given under section 38(1)(c) of the Partnership Ordinance(17).

(f) The Custodian shall on no account be liable for debts and obligations of the partnership save to the extent of the value of the held property of the absentee partner.

25. Management of joint property

Where a part of any property of the category of immovable property has been vested in the Custodian, the Custodian is entitled to participate in the management of the whole of the property, together with the owners who are not absentees, with the same rights as the absentee had.

26. Where the property of the absentee is a bill-
(1) it shall be vested in the Custodian even if it has not been delivered to him and has also not come into his hands in any other manner;
(2) the Custodian is exempt from presenting the bill for acceptance or payment, from giving notice of dishonour and from protesting against non-acceptance or non-payment;
(3) non-presentation or non-notice or non-protest in pursuance of paragraph (2) shall not in itself release any party to the bill from the obligations thereunder.

27. Confirmation to non-absentee.
   (a) If the Custodian is of opinion that a particular person whom it is possible to define as an absentee under section 1(b)(1)(iii) left his place of residence -
(1) for fear that the enemies of Israel might cause him harm, or
(2) otherwise than by reason or for fear of military operations, the Custodian shall give that person, on his application, a written confirmation that he is not an absentee.
   (b) The Custodian may, in his sole discretion, but subject to the provisions of section 29, give a written confirmation that a particular person who is at the time lawfully in the area of Israel is not an absentee, even though it be possible to define him as an absentee, if the Custodian is of opinion that such person is capable of managing his property efficiently and that he will not in so doing be aiding the enemies of Israel.

(c) A confirmation under this section shall have effect from the day on which it is given, unless it is stated therein that it shall have effect from an earlier or a later date.

(d) From the day on which a confirmation under this section takes effect, the property of the person concerned ceases to be absentees' property, and if his property includes held property, the Custodian shall hand over the same to the person who in the opinion of the Custodian is entitled to possession thereof.

28. Release of vested property.

(a) The Custodian may, in his sole discretion, but subject to the provisions of section 29, release vested property by certificate under his hand; and as soon as he has done so, that property shall cease to be absentees' property and any right a person had in it immediately before it was vested in the Custodian shall revert to that person or to his successor.

(b) The Custodian may stipulate with a person who requests him to exercise his power under subsection (a) that at the time of the giving of a certificate as aforesaid some other property shall become held property. Where that person has agreed to the stipulation and the certificate has been given as aforesaid, the other property becomes held property.

(c) Where the Custodian has sold vested property, the property which has been sold becomes released property and passes into the ownership of the purchaser, and the consideration which the Custodian has received becomes held property; where the vested property is a voidable charge and the Custodian voids it for a consideration, or where it is a waivable right and the Custodian waives it for a consideration, the consideration becomes held property at the time of the voiding or waiving, as the case may be.

29. The Custodian shall not exercise his powers under section 27 (b) or section 28 unless such has been recommended, in respect of each case or a particular class of cases, by a special committee to be

appointed by the Government. Notice of the appointment of such a committee shall be published in Reshumot.

30. Rules of evidence.
    (a) Where the Custodian has certified in writing that a person or body of persons is an absentee, that person or body of persons shall, so long as the contrary has not been proved, be regarded as an absentee.
    (b) Where the Custodian has certified in writing that some property is absentees' property, that property shall, so long as the contrary has not been proved, be regarded as absentees' property.
    (c) A certificate of the Minister of Defence that a place in Palestine was at a particular time held by forces which sought to prevent the establishment of the State of Israel or which fought against it after its establishment shall be conclusive evidence of its contents.
    (d) A copy certified by the Custodian of an entry in his books or official files or of another document in his possession shall, in any action or other legal proceeding, be accepted as prima facie evidence of the correctness of its contents.
    (e) A written confirmation by the Custodian as to matters within the scope of his functions shall, unless the Court has otherwise directed, be accepted in any action or other legal proceeding as prima facie evidence of the facts stated in the confirmation.
    (f) The Custodian and his inspectors, agents and officials are not bound to produce in any action or other legal proceeding any book, file or other document the contents of which can be proved in accordance with this section, and are not bound to testify on matters which can be proved through a confirmation of the Custodian as specified in this section, unless the Court has otherwise directed.
    (g) A certificate, a confirmation, a permit or any other document which purports to have been signed, issued, given or delivered by the Minister of Defence, the Minister of Finance or the

Custodian shall, so long as the contrary has not been proved, be considered to have been so signed, issued, given or delivered.
(i) The plea that a particular person is not an absentee, within the meaning of section 1(b)(1)(iii), by reason only that he had no control over the causes for which he left his place of residence as specified in that section shall not be heard.

31. Plea that property is absentees' property reserved to Custodian.

A court shall not, in any civil proceeding, entertain the plea that some party, being the subject of litigation, is absentees' property, unless the Custodian is a party to the proceeding. If this plea is made where the Custodian is not a party, and the court finds that there is some substance in it, the court shall invite the Custodian to join the case as a party. If the Custodian does so, the court shall consider the plea; if he does not, the court shall regard the plea as invalid.

32. Custodian's remuneration and expenses.
   (a) At the time of the transfer of any property in accordance with this Law, at the time when any property ceases, under section 27, to be absentees' property, and at the time of the release of any property under section 28, there is due to the State from the absentee a remuneration equal to 4 per cent of the value of the property; but the Minister of Finance may, in respect of a particular case or class of cases, reduce or waive the remuneration.
   (b) For the purpose of determining the remuneration, there shall be regarded as the value of property of the category of immovable property the official value of that property within the meaning of section 19, and as the value of other property, the price which in the opinion of the Custodian it would have been possible to obtain for it if, at the time of determining the remuneration, it had been sold on the free market by a willing seller to a willing purchaser; and if the property (whether it be property of the category of immovable property or other property) has been sold by the Custodian, the price at which it was actually sold shall be regarded as its value.

(c) Besides the remuneration, there are due to the State from the absentee or the owner of the property, as the case may be, all expenses (including travelling expenses, costs of legal proceedings and the remuneration of advocates, agents or other persons employed by the Custodian in connection with the property) which have been incurred by the Custodian or with his consent, or which he has undertaken to incur, for the purpose of safeguarding, maintaining, repairing or developing absentees' property or property which the Custodian, considered to be absentees' property or for other similar purposes, plus interest at the rate of 6 per cent per annum from the day on which the expenses were incurred.

(d) The payments due under this section shall be a charge on all the property of the absentee or the owner of the property, as the case may be, which shall have priority over any other charge; and if that property includes moneys, the Custodian may deduct therefrom the amount of the payments.

(e) The Custodian may withhold the giving to any person of a confirmation or certificate under section 27 or section 28 until all payments due from that person under this section have been discharged.

33. Fees.

The Minister of Finance may, by order published in Reshumot, prescribe fees payable in respect of certificates, confirmations, permits or other documents, or other acts of the Custodian, under this Law.

34. Dealing with absentees' property before appointment of Custodian.

(a) If the Minister of Finance is of opinion that a person who dealt with Absentees' property, or with property which he had reason to believe to be absentees' property, during the period between the 16th Kislev, 5708 (29th November, 1947) and the day of publication of the Custodian's appointment did so to the best of his ability, in good faith and with the intention of handing over the property dealt with by him, and that such person handed over to the Custodian, at or about the time of the publication of his appointment, the property which was in his possession, the Minister of Finance may give a confirmation to such effect by notice published in Reshumot.

(b) The dealings of a person in relation to whom the Minister of Finance has published a notice under subsection (a) shall be regarded as lawful and justified in all respects; no act which formed part of those dealings and which was done by that person, or by another person upon his instructions, shall be a basis for a charge or a ground for a claim against that person or the other person, unless it is proved, beyond all reasonable doubt, that the accused or defendant did the act with malicious intent or through gross negligence.

35. Offences.

(a) A person who -
(1) contravenes any of the provisions of section 22 (a) ; or
(2) contravenes anything contained in order under section 11; or
(3) conceals absentees' property from the Custodian or does not hand over to him property which he is bound to hand over to him; or
(4) willfully delivers to the Custodian or to one of his inspectors, agents or officials a declaration or some information which is false in a material particular is liable to imprisonment for a term not exceeding two years or to a fine not exceeding five hundred pounds or to both such penalties.

(b) A person who
(1) does not deliver to the Custodian or to one of his inspectors, agents or officials a return, an account, a notice or another document, or some information, which he is bound to deliver under this Law; or
(2) through negligence delivers to the Custodian or to one of his inspectors, agents or officials a declaration or some information which is false in a material particular; or
(3) wilfully obstructs the Custodian or one of his inspectors, agents or officials in the exercise of any of his functions under this Law is

liable to imprisonment for a term not exceeding six months or to a fine not exceeding one hundred pounds or to both such penalties.

(c) Where a body of persons is guilty of an offence under this section, every person who at the time of the commission of the offence was the head, or a secretary, trustee, director or manager, or the chief or sole accountant, of that body shall be likewise guilty thereof unless he proves that it was committed without his knowledge or that he took all appropriate steps to prevent its commission.

(d) An action for an offence under this section shall be brought only by, or with the written consent of the Attorney- General.

36. Notices, etc.

(a) Any notice, requirement or direction which the Custodian is bound or authorised to give or make under this Law - except notices, requirements or directions requiring publication in Reshumot - may be sent by registered post to the person to whom it is addressed; and if it has been so sent, it shall be considered to have been delivered to that person at the expiration of ten days from the day on which it was delivered to the Post Office for despatch, unless it is proved that it came to his hands before then.

(b) Any notice, requirement or direction permitted to be delivered in the manner determined in subsection (a) may be delivered by the Custodian by publication in Reshumot, and he is not bound to indicate in the notice, requirement or direction the name of the person to whom it is addressed.

(c) Any notice, requirement or direction under this Law published in Reshumot shall be considered to have been delivered to everyone concerned on, the day of publication.

37. Replacement of Regulations.

The provisions of this Law shall replace the provisions of the Emergency Regulations (Absentees' Property), 5709-1948(18), from the 13th Nisan, 5710 (31st March 1950) onwards; but this Law shall be read as one with those Regulations, and for this purpose those Regulations shall be deemed to be a Law amended by this Law.

38. Validations of Acts.

An act which was done before the 13th Nisan, 5710 (31st March 1950) and which would have been validly done if, at the time it was done, the text of this Law as in existence on the 13th Nisan, 5710 (31st March 1950) had been in force shall be deemed to have been validly done.

39. Interpretation.

The Minister of Finance is charged with the implementation of this Law and may make regulations as to any matter relating to such implementation.

Signed by
DAVID BEN-GURION
Prime Minister
ELIEZER KAPLAN
Minister of Finance
CHAIM WEIZMANN
President of the State

Appendix 6

Some Twentieth-Century Wars and Coups in the Middle East

Below, I briefly outline some of the regional conflicts that affected the course of economic and political development in the Levant, Iraq, and Egypt.

Middle Eastern Theater of World War I

The Middle Eastern theater of World War I saw action between 29 October 1914 and 30 October 1918. The combatants were, on one side, the Ottoman Empire (including Kurds and some Arab tribes), with some assistance from the Central Powers; and on the other side, the British (with the help of Jews, Greeks, and Assyrians, and the majority of the Arabs), the Russians (with the help of Armenians and Assyrians), and the French, from among the Allied Powers. There were five main campaigns: the Sinai and Palestine Campaign, the Mesopotamian Campaign, the Caucasus Campaign, the Persian Campaign, and the Gallipoli Campaign. Several minor campaigns include the Arab Campaign (1916) and South Arabia Campaign. The crises mentioned below derive from decisions, treaties and promises taken by the victors in World War I.

1920, Franco-Syrian War الحرب السورية الفرنسية

This war took place during 1920 between the Hashemite rulers of the newly established Arab Kingdom of Syria, and France. During a series of battles which climaxed in the Battle of Maysalun, French forces defeated the forces of the Hashemite monarch King Faisal and his supporters, on July 24, 1920. A new pro-French government was declared in Syria on July 25, headed by 'Alaa al-Din al-Darubi and the region of Syria was eventually divided into several client states under the Mandate for Syria and Lebanon. The British government, concerned for their position in the new mandate in Iraq, agreed to declare the fugitive Faisal as the new king of Iraq.

1920, The Hananu Revolt ثورة الشمال السوري

This conflict, also known as the Aleppo Revolt, was an insurgency against French military forces in northern Syria, mainly concentrated in the western countryside of Aleppo. Support for the revolt was driven by opposition to the establishment of a French Mandate for Syria. Named after its leading commander, Ibrahim Hananu, the revolt consisted mainly of four allied insurgencies in the areas of Jabal Harim, Jabal Qusayr, Jabal Zawiya, and Jabal Sahyun. The rebels were led by rural leaders and mostly engaged in guerrilla attacks against French forces and the sabotage of key infrastructure.

1920, Jerusalem riots انتفاضة موسم النبي موسى

The intercommunal conflict in Mandatory Palestine was the civil, political, and armed struggle between Palestinian Arabs and Jewish Yishuv during British rule in Mandatory Palestine, beginning with the violent spillover of the Franco-Syrian War of 1920, and lasting until the onset of the Arab-Israeli War of 1948

1925, Great Syrian Revolt الثورة السورية الكبرى

A general uprising across Mandatory Syria and Lebanon aimed at getting rid of the French, who had been in control of the region since the end of World War I. The uprising was not centrally coordinated; rather, it was attempted by multiple factions, among them Sunni, Druze, Alawite, Christian, and Shia. The revolt was ultimately put down by French forces.

1936, Arab Revolt in Palestine ثورة فلسطين الكبرى

Also known as the Great Palestinian Revolt, this was a nationalist uprising by Palestinians in Mandatory Palestine against the British administration of the Mandate, demanding Arab independence and the end of the policy of open-ended Jewish immigration and land purchases with the stated goal of establishing a "Jewish National Home."

1948, Arab-Israeli War حرب ١٩٤٨

The war began following the end of the British Mandate for Palestine at midnight on 14 May 1948; the Israeli Declaration of Independence had been issued earlier that day, and a military coalition of Arab states entered the territory of British Palestine on the morning of 15 May. Eventually Egypt, Lebanon, Transjordan, and Syria agreed to formal armistice lines with Israel. For Palestine, it was the beginning of the Nakba.

1952, Egyptian Revolution ثورة ٢٣ يوليو

Also known as the 23 July Revolution, it began with the removal of King Farouk in a coup d'état by the Free Officers Movement, led by Mohammed Naguib and Gamal Abdel Nasser. The Revolution ushered in a wave of revolutionary politics in the Arab world and contributed to the escalation of decolonization and the development of Third World solidarity during the Cold War. In the first three years of the Revolution, the Free Officers moved to abolish the constitutional monarchy and aristocracy of Egypt and Sudan, end the British occupation of the country, and secure independence for Sudan.

1963, Iraqi coup d'état ثورة رمضان

The Ramadan Revolution, or the 8 February Revolution, was a military coup by the Iraqi Ba'ath Party that overthrew the prime minister, Abd al-Karim Qasim. Qasim's former deputy, Abdul Salam Arif, who was not a Ba'athist, was given the ceremonial title of president, while prominent Ba'athist general Ahmed Hassan al-Bakr was named prime minister. The most powerful leader of the new government was the secretary general of the Iraqi Ba'ath Party, Ali Salih al-Sa'di, who controlled the National Guard militia and organized a massacre of hundreds of suspected communists and other dissidents following the coup.

1963, Syrian coup d'état ثورة الثامن من آذار

The 1963 Syrian coup d'état, also known as the 8 March Revolution, was the successful seizure of power by the military committee of the Syrian Regional Branch of the Arab Socialist Ba'ath Party. The planning and the unfolding conspiracy were inspired by the Iraqi Regional Branch's successful military coup that same year.

1964, Syria Hama riot |1967, Arab-Israeli War |1970, Black September Hashemite-Palestinian clash |1972, Arab-Israeli War |1975, Lebanon Civil War |1980, Syria Hama uprising |1980, Iran–Iraq War |1987, Palestine First Intifada |1990, Iraq First Gulf War |1996, Israel Operation Grapes of Wrath on Lebanon | 2000, Palestine Second Intifada | 2003, US–Iraq War | 2005, Lebanon Cedar Revolution | 2006, Israel July war on Lebanon | 2011, Tunisia, Egypt, Yemen, Syria uprisings |…and many more to our present day.